TREATMENT APPROACHES
for
ALCOHOL
and
DRUG DEPENDENCE

TREATMENT APPROACHES
for
ALCOHOL
and
DRUG DEPENDENCE
An Introductory Guide

Tracey J. Jarvis
Jenny Tebbutt
Richard P. Mattick
National Drug and Alcohol Research Centre,
University of New South Wales, Australia

Foreword by
Nick Heather
Northern Regional Drug and Alcohol Service,
Newcastle upon Tyne, UK

JOHN WILEY & SONS
Chichester · New York · Brisbane · Toronto · Singapore

Reprinted August 1995, March and October 1996, September 1998, June 1999, April 2001
December 2002

This publication is designed to provide accurate and authoritative information in regard to
the subject matter covered. It is sold on the understanding that the Publisher is not engaged in
rendering professional services. If professional advice or other expert assistance is required,
the services of a competent professional should be sought.

Other Wiley Editorial Offices

John Wiley & Sons Inc., 111 River Street, Hoboken, NJ 07030, USA

Jossey-Bass, 989 Market Street, San Francisco, CA 94103-1741, USA

Wiley-VCH Verlag GmbH, Boschstr. 12, D-69469 Weinheim, Germany

John Wiley & Sons Australia Ltd, 33 Park Road, Milton, Queensland 4064, Australia

John Wiley & Sons (Asia) Pte Ltd, 2 Clementi Loop #02-01, Jin Xing Distripark, Singapore
129809

John Wiley & Sons Canada Ltd, 22 Worcester Road, Etobicoke, Ontario, Canada M9W 1L1

British Library Cataloguing in Publication Data

A catalogue record for this book is available from the British Library

ISBN 0 471 95373 3

Typeset in 10/12pt Palatino by Dorwyn Ltd, Rowlands Castle, Hants
Printed and bound in Great Britain by Antony Rowe Ltd, Chippenham, Wiltshire
This book is printed on acid-free paper responsibly manufactured from sustainable forestry
in which at least two trees are planted for each one used for paper production.

TJJ: For Greg, Elma, Greg S., Diana, June and Geof

JT: For PJ

RPM: For Susan and Anthony

CONTENTS

PART I   LAYING THE FOUNDATIONS

PART II   STRATEGIES FOR ACTION

PART III MAINTAINING CHANGE

PART IV DESIGNING AN INTERVENTION

PRACTICE SHEETS AND CLIENT HANDOUTS

ABOUT THE AUTHORS

Tracey J. Jarvis, Jenny Tebbutt and Dr Richard P. Mattick, National Drug and Alcohol Research Centre, University of New South Wales, PO Box 1, Kensington NSW2033, Australia.

Tracey Jarvis is a Senior Researcher within the Centre with extensive knowledge of the treatment of alcohol problems and alcohol dependence. She has published research articles in scholarly journals and been responsible for the review of treatment outcome research. She co-authored a major book on treatment, and is currently researching the relationships between sexual abuse and drug and alcohol use.

Jenny Tebbutt has worked with Nick Heather at the Centre for a number of years and has researched the nature and measurement of impaired control over alcohol problems. She has also contributed to several publications concerning the treatment of alcohol and other drug problems.

Richard Mattick is a Senior Lecturer in the Centre, and has been involved in treatment research and has written numerous articles and co-authored five books on the treatment of excessive drug use.

ACKNOWLEDGEMENTS

We acknowledge the assistance of Meredith Adams, Bob Cherry, Loretta Elkins, Nick Heather, John Howard, Gary Lake, Kaylene Noonan, Katy O'Neill, Justine O'Sullivan and Garth Popple, in reading and commenting on drafts of this book and providing feedback based on their clinical expertise. This was an important part of the method of developing the text so that it would be 'user friendly' to therapists in this field.

We also thank Alison Bell and Katy O'Neill for commenting on the motivational interviewing chapter; T. Sitharthan for his comments on the meditative relaxation procedures; Amanda Baker for providing examples of relapse prevention; and Eva Congreve for her expert assistance with retrieval of books and articles from libraries.

The work was partly supported by a grant from the Research into Drug Abuse Grants Scheme, National Drug Strategy of the Australian Department of Health and Human Services.

FOREWORD

This introductory guide arose from a Quality Assurance Project conducted at the National Drug and Alcohol Research Centre, University of New South Wales, Sydney, Australia, during the time that I had the honour to be Director of the Centre. 'Quality assurance' has come to possess a range of meanings, but in this instance it was an attempt to increase the effectiveness of the treatment available for drug and alcohol problems in Australia and, at the same time, to raise the level of communication between researchers, practitioners and policy-makers in the field.

The project was the brainchild of Dr Richard Mattick who had been involved in previous quality assurance exercises for a range of common psychiatric disorders and who suggested that a similar methodology could be applied to addictive disorders. Because of the controversies and fiercely held convictions typical of the drug and alcohol field, we recognised this might be a difficult task but one well worth pursuing. The gains, in terms of reaching some sort of consensus on what forms and contents of treatment were effective and in increasing the frequency with which these effective treatments were offered to people with drug and alcohol problems, were potentially significant. The three chosen areas were treatment of dependence on alcohol, opiates and nicotine.

The methodology of the project stemmed from the desire to avoid its being perceived as something prescribed by researchers for practitioners. The key to the project's success was that it should be seen to be 'owned' by the treatment and counselling community itself. For this reason, the project supplemented meta-analytic reviews of research literature with the views of practitioners experienced in the treatment of addictive disorders and the opinions of people recognised for their special expertise in the treatment of these disorders.

Having completed the project and produced three sets of treatment guidelines (Mattick & Baillie, 1992; Mattick, Baillie, Digiusto, Gourlay, Richmond & Stanton, 1994; Mattick & Hall, 1993, 1994; Mattick & Jarvis, 1993, 1994) we then perceived a need for some sort of manual which would assist therapists to implement the effective treatment methods that had been identified. Hence the present volume. We also recognised that, being based on the international literature and reflecting the practices of therapists who were strongly influenced by developments in treatment from all over the world, the guide had a far wider relevance than just to Australia. From the keen interest in the project elsewhere in the world and the encouraging comments of colleagues overseas, we were led to hope that the guide would be of practical use to those concerned with helping people with drug and alcohol problems wherever those problems arose.

The authors of this book are to be congratulated for producing a document that is at once accessible and highly informative. It is easy to read, very well structured and, to my mind, contains just the right level of detail. It will, of course, be important for the reader to make use of the suggestions for further study offered in the *Resources Lists* if full advantage is to be gained.

To say that something is 'state of the art' has become so hackneyed that one tries to avoid the phrase whenever possible. But in this case, it is hard to think of an alternative; the book includes information and guidance on how to use the very latest developments in responding to drug and alcohol problems and reflects the most up-to-date research evidence in the field. The gap between research findings and current practice is often lamented. If the book achieves its objectives, which I think highly likely, it will do much to reduce this gap.

The National Drug and Alcohol Research Centre is justly proud of the Quality Assurance Project and of this accompanying introductory guide to treatment procedures. I am confident the diligent reader will derive great benefit from it.

Nick Heather
Sydney
January 1994

RESOURCES LIST

Mattick, R. P. & Baillie, A. (1992). *An Outline for Approaches to Smoking Cessation: Quality Assurance in the Treatment of Drug Dependence Project*, National Campaign Against Drug Abuse monograph series No. 19. Canberra, Australia: Australian Government Publishing Service.

Mattick, R. P., Baillie, A. J., Digiusto, E., Gourlay, S., Richmond, R. & Stanton, H. J. (1994). A summary of the recommendations for smoking cessation interventions: The quality assurance in the treatment of drug dependence project. *Drug and Alcohol Review*, **13**, 171–177.

Mattick, R. P. & Hall, W. (1993). *An Outline for the Management of Opioid Dependence: Quality Assurance in the Treatment of Drug Dependence Project*, National Campaign Against Drug Abuse monograph series No. 21. Canberra, Australia: Australian Government Publishing Service.

Mattick, R. P. & Hall, W. (1994). A summary of the recommendations for the management of opioid dependence: The quality assurance in the treatment of drug dependence project. *Drug and Alcohol Review*, **13**, 319–326.

Mattick, R. P. & Jarvis, T. J. (1993). *An Outline for the Management of Alcohol Problems: Quality Assurance in the Treatment of Drug Dependence Project*, National Campaign Against Drug Abuse monograph series No. 20. Canberra, Australia: Australian Government Publishing Service.

Mattick, R. P. & Jarvis, T. J. (1994). A summary of recommendations for the management of alcohol problems: The quality assurance in the treatment of drug dependence project. *Drug and Alcohol Review*, **13**, 145–155.

The monographs cited above are available from the Drugs of Dependence Branch, Australian Department of Human Services and Health, GPO Box 9848, Canberra, ACT, 2601, Australia.

HOW TO READ THIS BOOK

WHO IS THIS BOOK FOR?

This book is written for people whose work involves assisting clients to change their use of alcohol and/or other drugs. In the text we refer to you as a 'therapist'. We trust that you will find this book equally useful whether you work in an inpatient unit, therapeutic community or outpatient setting. If you are a student you might also find this book a valuable introduction to a number of new methods or strategies that you might not have seen applied to the field of alcohol and other drugs. For established therapists this book provides guidelines to enable you to further refine your methods and to apply them in systematic ways that are designed to increase their effectiveness.

WHAT'S IN THIS BOOK?

This book provides brief, user-friendly descriptions of specific techniques that have been found to be effective in the treatment of substance abuse problems. We have chosen techniques that were recommended by clinical experts in the Quality Assurance Project (see *Foreword*). This book explains how to use these techniques to help your clients change their behaviour. In each chapter you will find:

- Information about the recommended use of the technique
- A description of key concepts underlying the technique
- An introductory guide to applying the technique and some trouble-shooting of any common problems you might encounter
- A list of detailed resource materials to follow up and, in some cases, some self-help material that you can recommend to your client
- Where appropriate, instruments for assessment
- Where appropriate, practice exercises and handout sheets for use with your clients

WHAT ISN'T IN THIS BOOK?

- This book does not provide session-by-session plans for therapy. Instead we provide a guide for using the basic building blocks of therapy.
- Various therapists and researchers have tended to teach the same skills in slightly different ways. We have not described all of these variations in this book and we strongly recommend that you refer to the *Resources List* at the end of each chapter for further information.
- Treatment research literature has not usually been included in the *Resources Lists* (except where it offers practical guidelines). We recommend the Quality Assurance Project monographs (see *Foreword*) for their comprehensive reviews of the treatment outcome research and further resource material.
- Tobacco use is not specifically addressed in this book because it is well covered elsewhere (e.g. Mattick *et al.*, 1994; see *Foreword*). However, many of the techniques described herein can be used to help clients to quit smoking.
- *This book is not designed to teach clinical skills*. To train clinical personnel, there is a need for specialist training courses. This book should not replace such courses although it may be a valuable resource tool for both trainers and students.

HOW DO YOU USE THIS BOOK?

The key to using this book is *flexibility*. For example, Chapter 2, *Assessment* outlines all the areas relevant to assessing clients who misuse alcohol or other drugs. You may choose to adopt this comprehensive assessment procedure or, if your treatment is intended to be brief, focus on one or two specific areas such as your client's drug use or drinking and the physical and personal negative consequences of that behaviour.

The choice of which combination of treatment techniques to use will emerge out of a process of negotiation with your client. The decision will depend both on the goal of treatment and on any other specific needs of your client that might be revealed during assessment or as therapy progresses. You might, for example, start off by working on problem-solving and relapse-prevention training and then later add sessions on assertiveness training because it has become clear that your client needs to develop assertiveness skills.

We do not provide any specific guidelines on the length of treatment. Some techniques require a minimum number of sessions to achieve results (such as relaxation training) while others should not be extended beyond a certain period of time without careful evaluation (e.g. Antabuse). The length of your treatment intervention will depend on a number of factors such as the time and resources you have available, your client's needs, and how long it takes for your client to learn to apply new skills to everyday life.

Chapter 18, at the end of the book, is entitled *Putting It All Together*. In this chapter we offer some practical examples of how various techniques can be combined to tailor a therapy programme to suit the needs of individual clients.

A NOTE ON GENDER

The techniques described in this book are appropriate for both male and female clients. We have therefore simply alternated the gender of the client referred to in each of the following chapters.

RESOURCES LIST

Two texts that we used as key resources for this book are:

Hester, R.K. & Miller, W.R. (1989). *Handbook of Alcoholism Treatment Approaches: Effective Alternatives*. New York: Pergamon Press.
Monti, P.M., Abrams, D.B., Kadden, R.M. & Cooney, N.L. (1989). *Treating Alcohol Dependence: A Coping Skills Training Guide*. New York: Guilford Press.

I

LAYING THE FOUNDATIONS

GENERAL COUNSELLING SKILLS

RECOMMENDED USE

When it comes to counselling, there is nothing unique about the field of alcohol and other drugs. The same skills that are effective for general counselling are also effective for counselling people with drug-related problems. Research has shown that treatment for alcohol and other drug problems is more likely to be successful if given by therapists with empathic counselling skills (Miller & Rollnick, 1991; Ward, Mattick & Hall, 1992). On the other hand, counselling alone is not usually sufficient to change the drug-taking behaviour of most clients. Rather, good counselling skills will enable you to develop a strong working relationship with your client that will support the implementation of specific strategies designed to combat the drinking or drug problem.

GOALS

The counselling process therefore aims:

- To build a trusting relationship where your client can communicate her concerns and describe her behaviours without fear of judgement.
- To encourage your client to see treatment as a mutual enterprise where she makes active decisions and where you value her ideas and support her endeavours. Your client is encouraged to develop a sense of responsibility and self-confidence.
- To reduce your client's fear and distrust of treatment programmes and thereby encourage her to continue attending treatment and follow-up appointments. Not all clients who are assessed will feel ready for treatment. If a client's initial experience of the treatment staff and environment is positive, this may encourage her to return for treatment at some future point in time.

METHOD

The counselling style described here combines the client-centred approach outlined by Egan (1994) with a motivational interviewing style developed by Miller and Rollnick (1991). It is an approach that encourages your client to explore her own concerns through open-ended questions and empathic feedback. It is client-centred because your client defines which issues are important. However, it is not a wholly 'non-directional' approach, because the motivational interviewing style (Chapter 3) selectively emphasises those issues that favour a change in your client's drug-using behaviour.

This approach is quite different from the style of counselling that involves confrontation. We do *not* recommend that you confront your client or argue with her in order to convince her of the need for change. Instead, we suggest that you foster your client's *self*-confrontation through open-ended questions and selective feedback.

The ideal counsellor is someone who:

- Is creative and imaginative
- Shows self-awareness by not imposing personal concerns on clients
- Has good common sense and social intelligence
- Shows respect for clients
- Is action-oriented

The microskills that will assist you in effective counselling are described below.

Empathy

Egan (1994) wrote that: 'Empathy as a form of human communication involves listening to clients, understanding them and their concerns to the degree that this is possible, and communicating this understanding to them, so that they might understand themselves more fully and act on their understanding' (p. 106). It is as if you are standing in the other person's shoes, looking at the world through their eyes and asking 'What is it like to be this person?' It involves fostering a therapeutic relationship that enables your client to correct inaccurate feedback, while studying herself through your reflection.

Empathy requires an attitude of respect towards your client. As an empathic therapist your role is to help your client to find her own solutions rather than to impose a solution on her. Show your client that you believe in her ability to make effective choices and that you value the time and effort you spend with her. Convey your empathy not only in what you say, but also in your intonation and body language. Be aware of any differences between you and your client in cultural background, age or sex and always check the accuracy of any assumptions you might make about your client's experiences.

Empathy is different from sympathy. If you feel sympathy, you tend to take sides with your client, and this can distort your ability to hear the whole story. For example, when feeling sorry for your client, you might overlook the way in which self-pity is preventing her from taking constructive action. Being empathic does not mean that you always agree with your client's opinion. Rather, it involves accepting her view and being interested in exploring its implications.

Things to Avoid

The key to an empathic approach is to avoid judgemental or evaluative responses. You are trying to understand how it *is* for the client, not how it *should be*. Some non-empathic approaches that can obstruct further understanding of your client's perspective include:

- Ordering or commanding
- Warning or threatening
- Giving advice or providing solutions
- Arguing or persuading
- Moralising
- Disagreeing, judging or criticising
- Ridiculing or labelling
- Interpreting or analysing
- Reassuring or sympathising
- Withdrawing, distracting or humouring

Open-ended Questions

Ask your client questions that encourage further elaboration. Closed questions that require a 'yes' or 'no' response or a one-word answer are useful for getting at specific information. They should be used sparingly, however, because they can turn the therapy session into a fact-finding mission. They discourage further exploration by your client. Try to transform them into open-ended questions. For example:

'Has your drinking changed over time?'

vs

'How has your drinking changed over time?'

Reflective Listening

Your client's answers to your open-ended questions should be followed by empathic feedback or 'reflective listening'. Listen carefully to what your client says and try to understand what she means. Try to identify the core message being expressed. What we *assume* people mean is not necessarily what they *really* mean. Reflective listening enables you to:

- Show your client that you are really listening to her
- Check whether your understanding of what your client has said is consistent with her intended meaning
- Feed back your client's stated concerns, thereby strengthening her awareness of her own reasons for change

Miller and Rollnick (1991) have also suggested that feedback in the form of a statement, rather than a question, is likely to be more effective in encouraging your client to explore. The following example taken from their book shows how exploring one of your client's concerns with reflective listening might encourage your client to identify other concerns:

CLIENT: 'I worry sometimes that I may be drinking too much for my own good.'
THERAPIST: 'You've been drinking quite a bit.'
CLIENT: 'I don't really feel like it's that much. I can drink a lot and not feel it.'
THERAPIST: 'More than most people.'
CLIENT: 'Yes. I can drink most people under the table.'
THERAPIST: 'And that's what worries you.'
CLIENT: 'Well, that and how I feel. The next morning I'm usually in bad shape. I feel . . .'
(Miller & Rollnick, 1991, p.75)

Resistance

Resistance is an observable behaviour (such as arguing, interrupting, denying and ignoring) that occurs during treatment. Resistant behaviours are often responses to the content and style of an interaction between a client and her therapist. It is important to *avoid* evoking or strengthening resistance because the more your client resists the less likely she is to change. That is, resistance allows clients to express well-practised reasons for not changing. There may be a number of reasons why clients 'resist'. For example, a client might have low self-esteem and little belief in her ability to change. Alternatively, she might have been coerced into treatment and therefore not yet be ready to consider change.

Miller and Rollnick (1991) have coined the term 'rolling with resistance' to describe non-confrontational methods for dealing with clients' resistance. Most of these involve reflective listening techniques. For example, suppose your client says:

'I don't see why my drinking is such a problem. All my friends drink as much as I do.'

By using some of the methods outlined by Miller and Rollnick (1991), you could respond to this statement in the following ways.

Simple Reflection

Acknowledge your client's resistance in your reflective response. For example:

'You can't see how *your* drinking can be a problem when your friends don't seem to have any problems.'

Amplified Reflection

Couch your feedback in an amplified or exaggerated form to elicit the other side of your client's ambivalence. This should be done in a way that avoids a sarcastic tone. For example:

'If your friends have no problem with their drinking then there's nothing for you to worry about.'

Double-sided Reflection

Acknowledge what your client has said and add the other side of your client's ambivalence. Try to draw on things that your client has said previously.

'I can see how this must be confusing for you. On the one hand you've come in because you're concerned about drinking and how it affects you, and on the other hand, it seems like you're not drinking any more than your friends do.'

Miller and Rollnick (1991) have provided further comprehensive examples and additional techniques in their chapter on *Dealing with Resistance*.

Reframing

Reframing is a way of acknowledging what your client has said and, at the same time, drawing her attention to a different meaning or interpretation that is likely to support change. For example, past experiences with treatment failure can be reframed as evidence that your client may not have found the

approach most suitable for her. Reframing your client's explanation of tolerance can also be important (see pp. 47–8).

Affirmation

Show support for your client's efforts during therapy through affirmations. For
example, you should acknowledge the courage involved in coming to therapy
and commend your client for taking that step. Highlight your client's strengths
in coping or refraining from drug use. Draw her attention to those positive
things that she might have trivialised.

Summarising

Summary statements help to draw together the material that you have discussed with your client and can be used for many purposes. Show your client
that you are actively listening by summarising the issues that she has raised.
Use summaries to:

- Highlight important discoveries
- Prompt a more thorough exploration
- Give the broader picture when your client seems blocked
- Provide an opportunity for your client to hear her own stated reasons for
  change
- Highlight your client's ambivalence by linking the negatives and positives
  together in the one statement (e.g. 'On the one hand, you have said that you
  like drinking because . . . while on the other hand, you are concerned about
  . . . So it sounds like you are torn two ways')
- Close a discussion

Confidence to Change

Raising your client's confidence in her ability to change is an intermediate step
towards changing her drug use. It is important to foster an optimistic view that
change is achievable. Try to ensure that the weekly goals of therapy are within
your client's capabilities so that she will experience a sense of mastery. Your
own belief that your client can succeed will also strongly influence her expectations. Be aware that there is a power relationship between you as the therapist,
and your client. The more you control the process, the less confidence you are
placing in your client's ability to make appropriate choices and to take respon-

sibility for changing. Empower your client by helping her to make her own choices and congratulating her when she makes progress.

WORKING IN A GROUP

All of the techniques described in this book can be applied in a group situation. In fact, the group setting provides some unique features that enhance some of these techniques. For example, a group of people can generate a greater variety of ideas in a brainstorming exercise (pp. 67–8) than you and your client can alone. In learning communication skills, your client can benefit from practising with, and receiving feedback from, people with different perspectives. Her plans for relapse prevention might also become more refined as she observes what works and what doesn't work for other people. Your client may also benefit from the opportunity for peer support. This is particularly the case if your clients continue their support for each other after treatment.

Some techniques require several sessions of ongoing group practice before the skills are acquired for example, relaxation therapy and assertiveness training. Other techniques could be used within an open group where members vary from week to week. For example, relapse-prevention and refusal skills could be applied in an open group. The following section mainly draws on the work of Vanicelli (1982) who has provided specific guidelines for running groups with alcohol-dependent people. Monti, Abrams, Kadden and Cooney (1989) have also provided guidelines about group rules.

Group Composition

Groups need to have a common goal. Therefore, a group that includes people working towards abstinence as well as those with a goal of moderation runs the risk of resentment, confusion and a loss of common purpose. It is better to run separate groups for clients with these different goals.

Keep your group down to a size big enough for group interaction but small enough for everyone to be able to participate. Rose (1977), for example, recommended that the ideal size for a group lies between 6 and 9 people. Such a number will also enable you to form subgroups, which give all group members the chance to try out newly acquired skills.

Finally, in planning your group, give some consideration to the ratio of men to women. Research suggests that women in therapy benefit more from all-female groups than from mixed-sex groups (Jarvis, 1992). This is particularly true if issues such as sexual abuse or domestic violence are likely to arise in the course of the group discussion.

Group Rules

Be quite clear and explicit in defining the group's primary goal and your clients' responsibility in working towards that goal. Tell your clients exactly what you expect of their participation in the group. Your ground rules might state:

- The minimum number of sessions that you wish clients to attend.
- That clients should attend regularly, be on time and give advance notice if they are unable to meet these requirements. Try to prevent early drop-outs from the group by contacting those clients who miss any of the first few sessions and encouraging them to attend the next one.
- That clients should not come to sessions under the influence of alcohol or other drugs. Explain that such behaviour would interfere with their ability to concentrate on the group tasks and might also distract other members of the group. If a client breaks this rule, she will be asked to leave the session and encouraged to come next time, when she is sober.
- That the identities of fellow group members and all the personal issues discussed during group sessions should remain confidential and not be discussed with family members or friends outside the group.

Group Communication

The group is a powerful setting for behavioural change. As noted above, members need to feel that the group is working towards a common goal and that they are supported by others in the group. Encourage this kind of 'togetherness' by reinforcing any comments by clients that show interest, concern or acceptance of other group members or positive statements about the group as a whole. For example, you might say:

'So you agree with X about . . .'.

Your group may go through a period where people challenge and disagree with you and each other. This is a natural process and, if handled correctly, the group will be able to move forward to a more stable and trusting level. It is important to make a distinction between disagreement that leads to constructive discussion within the group and disagreement that involves hostility. If group members become hostile to each other, they may undermine each other's progress and disrupt the group. Deflect hostile interaction between group members by getting them to tell you about their concerns rather than abusing each other. Emphasise empathy rather than confrontation as a model for the group.

Role-play

Role-play is a method of practising the use of a particular skill by rehearsing a situation that is likely to occur in real life. You can role-play situations with your client in individual therapy. However, the ideal setting for role-play is in a group that provides the opportunity for clients to learn from watching each other perform the same skills. When using role-plays, always begin by modelling the skills yourself, giving your clients an example to follow. At the end of each role-play ask the 'player' to say what she thought she did well and what she would have liked to have done differently. Then ask the group for some feedback, emphasising that comments must be constructive and specific, focusing on body language, tone or what was said. After the group have offered their feedback you can then offer your comments, restricting yourself to a couple of positive and critical points. Role-play can be used for groups learning problem-solving, drink- or drug-refusal skills, assertiveness, communication skills, couples therapy and relapse prevention.

Termination

Prepare your group in advance for breaks in the group routine (such as public holidays) and for the time when the group is going to finish. For example, you might want to encourage subgroups or pairs of clients to exchange phone numbers so that they can support each other's maintenance plans in the absence of the group sessions. Further suggestions that you might want to discuss with the group are in Chapter 17 on *Aftercare*.

RESOURCES LIST

Egan, G. (1994). *The Skilled Helper: A Systematic Approach for Effective Helping*. California: Brooks/Cole.
    —A comprehensive manual on the application of an empathic, client-centred style of counselling.
Egan, G. (1994). *Exercises in Helping Skills: A Training Manual to Accompany 'The Skilled Helper'*. California: Brooks/Cole.
    —A workbook for training empathic skills.

Jarvis, T.J. (1992). Implications of gender for alcohol treatment research: A quantitative and qualitative review. *British Journal of Addiction*, **87**, 1249–1261.
—A study that compared men and women in treatment and found that although their success rates are similar, they have different needs that should be addressed in treatment programmes.
Liberman, R. (1970). A behavioral approach to group dynamics. 1. Reinforcement and prompting of cohesiveness in group therapy. *Behavior Therapy*, **1**, 141–175.
—Gives evidence that therapists can modify group cohesiveness by selective reinforcement.
Miller, W.R. & Rollnick, S. (1991). *Motivational Interviewing: Preparing People to Change Addictive Behavior*. New York: Guilford Press.
—Strongly recommended as a guide to the motivational interviewing style of counselling.
Monti, P.M., Abrams, D.B., Kadden, R.M. & Cooney, N.L. (1989). *Treating Alcohol Dependence: A Coping Skills Training Guide*. New York: Guilford Press.
—Provides brief guidelines on building groups.
Nelson-Jones, R. (1992). *Lifeskills Helping: A Textbook of Practical Counselling and Helping Skills*. Sydney: Harcourt, Brace & Co.
—A comprehensive and well structured book, setting out guidelines for counselling and teaching clients new skills.
Rogers, C. (1973). *Client-centred Therapy*. London: Constable.
—Describes the application of the Rogerian style of client-centred counselling as well as the underlying theoretical principles.
Rose, S.D. (1977). *Group Therapy: A Behavioral Approach*. Englewood Cliffs, NJ: Prentice-Hall.
—Provides guidelines for running behaviour therapy groups, based on research findings.
Vanicelli, M. (1982). Group psychotherapy with alcoholics: Special techniques. *Journal of Studies on Alcohol*, **43**, 17–37.
—Outlines problems that are unique to running groups aimed at achieving abstinence from alcohol, and tips for resolving them.
Ward, J., Mattick, R.P. & Hall, W. (1992). *Key Issues in Methadone Maintenance Treatment*. Sydney: New South Wales University Press.
—Chapter 8 reviews research findings on the effectiveness of counselling for methadone maintenance clients.

2

ASSESSMENT

BASIC GUIDELINES

Assessment is a purposeful process with several functions. Some of these are outlined below.

- Assessment enables you to gather information that will help you to plan and modify treatment goals and strategies.
- The assessment process provides the chance for you and your client to build a rapport. As your client observes your empathy and courtesy, he will be less likely to take a defensive stance about his drinking or drug use.
- Assessment results enable you to give your client feedback that will help him to develop an alternative view of his situation. This is particularly true when you personalise the health effects of the drug use (pp. 46–8).
- Ongoing assessment helps you and your client to monitor his progress towards treatment goals.

Assessment is *not* about filling in endless forms! Acquiring a large amount of data that is unlikely to be useful in treatment is a waste of time. Therefore, you should focus on that information which is most likely to help you tailor treatment to meet your client's needs. Although information about past experiences can help to clarify the influences that have shaped your client's behaviour, feelings and beliefs, your focus should mainly be on the 'here and now', that is your client's present situation.

The assessment procedure, then, ideally takes the form of a semi-structured interview where you and your client together compile a narrative history. Standardised questionnaires are a useful addition, provided they are presented in the context of a relaxed interview. A well-chosen questionnaire (a) helps you to quickly obtain relevant information and (b) allows you to compare your client's results with those of other clients. *At all times, assure your client that what he tells you will remain confidential and will be used only for the purposes of planning his treatment.*

If you wish to use a standardised assessment interview, there are a number of excellent inventories available. In particular, we strongly recommend the *Comprehensive Drinker Profile (CDP)* (Miller & Marlatt, 1984a) or its brief form, the *Brief Drinker Profile (BDP)* (Miller & Marlatt, 1984b) for use with drinkers, and the *Opiate Treatment Index (OTI)* (Darke, Ward, Hall, Heather & Wodak, 1991) for use with users of other drugs, especially opiates and other injectable drugs. The following sections outline the basic areas that should be covered during assessment. *The extent to which you explore each of these areas will depend upon their relevance for your client.*

ASSESSMENT OF THE ALCOHOL OR DRUG PROBLEM

The Client's Reasons for Coming to See You

Explore whether your client's *current* reasons for seeking help are self-generated or stem from social or legal coercion. If your client does not see his substance use as being a problem (which may be the case with coerced clients), he may benefit from motivational interviewing (Chapter 3) in the first session. Also ask whether there were some specific events that influenced your client's decision to come and what he hopes to achieve by coming to see you.

Trouble-shooting

If your client is intoxicated, it is difficult to conduct a reliable assessment. In this case, focus only on developing rapport. Listen to what he wants to say but postpone formal assessment until the second session. Remind him of the importance of being unintoxicated for that next session.

Pattern and Context of Drinking or Drug Use

Past use

Exploring the history of your client's substance use will help you to determine the chronicity of his problem. It will also reveal the conditions under which he has been able to abstain or moderate his drinking or drug use, as well as the triggers to heavy substance use. This information will help to guide your selection of treatment goals and will also be particularly useful when planning relapse prevention (Chapter 16). A discussion about previous periods of abstinence—however short—can also help to build your client's confidence. As part of this history taking, also ask about your client's previous treatment experiences.

Current use

You will also need to collect a detailed description of his current substance use. To do this, you may need to look at three areas of drug use. These are discussed below.

Alcohol use: Ask your client how frequently he drinks. Does he drink daily or have periodic bouts of binge drinking? Find out how much alcohol your client drinks per week, on a typical drinking day and on a heavy drinking day. Your client may feel a little self-conscious about reporting exact amounts. It can be useful to overestimate your client's level of drinking, thereby allowing him to bring the estimate down to the correct level, without feeling embarrassed about admitting the large amount he drinks. An accurate estimate of your client's drinking levels provides a baseline for comparison to later stages in therapy, as well as being one index of his alcohol dependence. Drinking levels are usually measured in 'standard drinks'. These are defined on p. 121.

Ask your client to describe the sequence of events on a typical drinking day. Ask open-ended questions (p. 5) about the events and activities typically associated with drinking. For example, ask about the approximate time when he starts to drink; where and with whom he usually drinks; the period of time spent drinking; the amount and type of alcohol consumed; and when and how he stops drinking.

Injecting drug use: There are a range of illicit drugs that can be injected, including amphetamines, opiates and cocaine. Ask your client how often and how much he typically injects. Estimates of how much he usually spends on the drug each week can also help you to estimate the amount he uses if you know the current street value of the drug. This question has the added advantage of providing an opening to ask about your client's source of money, and therefore his social, vocational and criminal activities. When you are asking him about his pattern of injecting drug use, you might also ask about his needle-sharing behaviour (see p. 20).

Polydrug use: Obviously, most injecting drug users are polydrug users because access to their preferred drug is variable. For clients seeking help primarily for alcohol problems, other drug use should also be assessed, especially where drugs are used in conjunction with alcohol. In general, treatment should concentrate on the drug that is causing the most problems. When one drug is reinforcing the use of another, however, it may be more effective to focus on both drugs simultaneously.

Level of Dependence

An important factor in determining the goals of treatment is the level of your client's dependence on alcohol or drugs (see Chapter 4, *Goal-setting*). Physical dependence will also suggest the need for managed detoxification. Alcohol withdrawal can be life-threatening. Opiate and psychostimulant withdrawals are not life-threatening but may lead to relapse. Benzodiazepine withdrawal should be tapered because of the risk of seizures. You should liaise with medical personnel to determine the suitability of detoxification at home, inpatient detoxification and medical management of withdrawal. Withdrawal management procedures are set out elsewhere (Devenyi & Saunders, 1986).

The elements of the dependence syndrome first described by Edwards and Gross (1976) are outlined below.

(1) *Narrowing of the behavioural repertoire:* A person who is not dependent will vary the amount and type of substance use, depending upon the situation. With increasing dependence, the person will tend to consume or use the same amount each day.
(2) *Salience of drinking or drug use:* With increasing dependence, the substance use will be given greater priority in the person's life, to the detriment of dietary, health, financial and social factors.
(3) *Subjective awareness of compulsion:* The person's subjective experience of dependence is characterised by a loss of control over the substance use, an irresistible impulse to keep using the substance, an inability to stop using at certain times, or constant cravings when not using.
(4) *Increased tolerance:* Heavy use leads to an adaptation to higher amounts of the substance. This is known as tolerance and is evident when amounts that previously had mind-altering effects now produce fewer obvious effects. The dependent person responds to tolerance by using larger amounts in order to achieve the desired effect.
(5) *Repeated withdrawal symptoms:* As dependence increases, the frequency and severity of withdrawal symptoms also increases. For *alcohol* users these may include perspiration, tremor, anxiety, agitation, a rise in body temperature, hallucinations, disorientation and/or nausea; for *opiate* users they may include goosebumps (especially on the chest), perspiration, dilated pupils, runny nose or eyes, excessive yawning, vomiting, diarrhoea or nausea, reported loss of appetite, sneezing, aching or cramped muscles, heart pounding or high blood pressure, feelings of coldness, problems in sleeping, stomach cramps, restlessness, and muscle spasm or twitching. Withdrawal from *psychostimulants*, such as amphetamines and cocaine, can be associated with depression. *Benzodiazepine* withdrawal may lead to anxiety reactions and, infrequently, has been known to cause seizures. With-

drawal from *other drugs* is not typically associated with physical reactions but may be associated with agitation, mood swings or behavioural change.

(6) *Relief from or avoidance of withdrawal symptoms:* The person seeks relief from withdrawal symptoms through further substance use (e.g. morning drinking) or maintains a steady level of substance use in order to avoid withdrawal.

(7) *Post-abstinence reinstatement:* A return to substance use after a period of abstinence will be characterised by a rapid return to the pre-abstinence level of substance use and dependence symptomatology.

As well as asking questions about these signs of dependence, you may also wish to use standardised questionnaires to measure dependence. Three commonly used questionnaires are provided at the end of this chapter and described below.

- The *Severity of Alcohol Dependence Questionnaire* (*SADQ-C*; pp. 30–1) was developed by Stockwell, Sitharthan, McGrath and Lang (1994). The *SADQ-C* mainly measures the physical aspects of moderate–severe alcohol dependence. Answers to each question are rated on a four-point scale as follows: 0 = almost never, 1 = sometimes, 2 = often, 3 = nearly always. Scores lower than or equal to 20 indicate low dependence, scores between 21 and 30 indicate moderate dependence and scores higher than 30 indicate a high level of dependence.
- The *Short-form Alcohol Dependence Data Questionnaire* (*SADD*; p. 32) was developed by Raistrick, Dunbar and Davidson (1983). The *SADD* measures the more subjective aspects of early alcohol dependence. Raistrick *et al.* (1983) have recommended that scores of 1 to 9 be considered low dependence, 10 to 19 medium dependence, and 20 or more high dependence, on the basis of a four-point (0–3) rating scale similar to that used in the *SADQ-C*.
- The *Severity of Opiate Dependence Questionnaire* (*SODQ*; pp. 33–4) was developed by Sutherland, Edwards, Taylor, Phillips, Gossop and Brady (1986). It is scored in the same way as the *SADQ-C*.

PERSONAL BACKGROUND INFORMATION

Information about your client's background will serve three basic purposes. First, it will give you a more complete appreciation of his total life experience. Secondly, it is important to evaluate the resources available to your client as he tries to change the substance use. Finally, background information will highlight those problems and concerns which are either influencing or being influenced by your client's substance use.

Lifestyle and Social Stability

Both the *OTI* and the *BDP* are useful for assessing lifestyle problems that are associated with drug use or drinking. Areas that might be relevant for your client would include those listed below.

Vocational and financial background

Does your client's vocational background indicate a lack of stability or financial security? Does he have stable accommodation? Has he noticed any changes in work performance over the time he's been drinking or using drugs? Does your client's current occupation bring him in contact with drugs, other drug users or drinkers? Alternatively, are there features of his workplace that might help him during treatment? How much is his alcohol or other drug use costing him, financially?

Family background and social support

With whom does your client live? Who are the significant people in your client's life? Does he feel supported by his family, friends or partner? Is there any family history of substance use? Do significant others use drugs or drink excessively? Has your client been encouraged to or discouraged from entering treatment? The following areas may need further exploration if they are relevant for your client's family: dependent children, the need for child care while the client attends treatment, child abuse, domestic violence, marital distress, and unhappiness within the family home.

Interests and hobbies

It is helpful to find out what your client's current interests are as well as things that he used to enjoy in the past. You can build on these activities as substitutes for the drinking or drug use.

Involvement of significant others in treatment

If your client is accompanied by significant others when he comes to assessment, find out how they view his drug or alcohol problem. Are there any differences of opinion about the seriousness of the problem? Provide the opportunity for significant others to ask questions and voice their concerns and expectations about therapy. It is also a good time to help put the substance misuse into perspective. For instance, changing the substance misuse will not necessarily resolve all relationship or family problems.

Your client's progress will certainly be enhanced if he has the support of others. Consider the possibility that your client's family, friends or partner may wish to be directly involved in therapy. Formal family therapy is a specialist area and we would strongly suggest that such clients be referred to appropriately trained specialists. In this book, we have included two approaches that you could use to involve the client's partner in therapy. Chapter 13, *Antabuse*, shows how the partner can help the client to comply with treatment. Chapter 12, *Couples Therapy*, focuses on the couple's communication and shared experiences. Although the client's partner can be involved in therapy, you should also encourage her to look after herself rather than feel responsible for her partner's substance misuse.

Sexual problems or sexual abuse

Is your client having any problems with his fertility, sexual arousal or sexual responses? For some clients, such problems may be related to their substance use.

Is sexual abuse a relevant issue for your client? A high percentage of women in treatment for drug or alcohol problems have been sexually abused. Although the prevalence may be lower among men compared with women, it is still a possibility that you need to be aware of when counselling male clients. Questions about sexual abuse should be framed in a non-threatening way, allowing your client to discuss the experience without fear of rejection. It may help to ask about 'unwanted sexual contact' because your client might not know what you mean by 'sexual abuse'. Avoid probing further if rapport is still weak or if he does not seem ready to disclose. You may need to refer him to an agency specialising in sexual abuse issues. Raising traumatic material without the aid of specialist counselling adds to the risk of relapse, especially if your client has been misusing substances as a form of self-medication.

Perpetrators of child sexual abuse are also likely to misuse alcohol or other drugs. You may need to prepare your client for the possibility that official notification of his behaviour is necessary to prevent risk to others.

Legal problems

Is your client facing any current convictions? Has this resulted in legal coercion into treatment? How often during the last month has he been involved in crime? Has he ever been convicted for drink-driving or other crimes that were related to his drinking? Be careful how you record this information because your client's records could be subpoenaed at any time.

Risk-taking behaviour

It is important to assess the risk of HIV infection, particularly for those clients who use injectable drugs. This can be done in a standardised manner, using the *HIV Risk-Taking Behaviour Scale (HRBS)*, which is a subscale in the *OTI*. There are two main areas in which risk may occur:

(1) *Injecting drugs:* How often does your client inject drugs? How often does he share needles with other users? How often and how effectively does he clean the needles before reusing them?
(2) *Sexual behaviour:* How many sexual partners has your client had in the past month? Does he use condoms when having sexual intercourse? In what situations are condoms not used? How many times has your client had anal sex in the last month?

If your client is subjecting himself or others to a risk of HIV infection, intervention aimed at reducing this behaviour is appropriate. You may wish to assess your client's knowledge about which practices are safe and which are risky. Be aware that even if a client has this knowledge, he may continue to behave in an unsafe way. Further information about dealing with these clients is given in Chapters 4, *Goal-setting*, and 3, *Motivational Interviewing*.

PHYSICAL HEALTH PROBLEMS

Information from a medical check-up is useful for several purposes. First, it can add to your knowledge about your client's level of dependence. Second, you may need to use this information to determine whether your client is eligible for certain treatment techniques (such as methadone maintenance, Antabuse, covert sensitisation). It will also assist in the negotiation of appropriate treatment goals (Chapter 4). Finally, personalised feedback of the medical results can help to motivate your client towards change (pp. 46–8).

Alcohol-related Health Problems

People who misuse alcohol are vulnerable to liver dysfunction, pancreatitis and digestive disorders, problems with the heart and blood circulation, poor nutrition and alcohol-related brain damage. Frequent intoxication may lead to accidents and injuries. Excessive drinking during pregnancy may lead to foetal alcohol syndrome (retardation in development of the foetus). For the heavy-drinking client, a medical check-up should include some assessment of his blood pressure, cholesterol levels and liver function. Listed below are some of the enzymes that are important to liver function. A liver function test measures the levels of these enzymes in the blood. Any levels that are raised outside the normal range provide evidence that the person's liver is at risk of serious damage. The enzymes are:

- Aspartate aminotransferase (AST)
- Alanine aminotransferase (ALT)
- Gamma glutamyltransferase (GGT)
- Alkaline phosphate

Another test that is commonly included in the assessment of physical damage or risk related to heavy drinking is a measurement of the mean corpuscular volume (MCV). This measures the level of red blood cells and an abnormally low MCV can indicate bone marrow toxicity. For each of these tests, the pathologist's report will indicate whether or not your client's level falls within the normal, healthy range. Normal results do not necessarily imply that the person is drinking within safe limits. Special care should be taken to clarify this point when feeding back results (see pp. 47–8). A detailed summary of the detrimental physical effects of alcohol can be found in Appendix B of *An Outline for the Management of Alcohol Problems: Quality Assurance Project* (Mattick & Jarvis, 1993).

Drug-related Health Problems

Illicit drug users are vulnerable to poor nutrition, dental caries, respiratory illness, menstrual irregularities, skin disease, sexually transmitted diseases and chronic liver disease. Injecting drug users are particularly vulnerable to viral infections such as Hepatitis B and C, and HIV. Drug use during pregnancy may lead to withdrawal symptoms in the newly born child.

PSYCHIATRIC DISTURBANCES

Many people with drug or alcohol problems also suffer from psychiatric distress or disturbed moods. For some people, the substance use began with an attempt by the person to self-medicate depressed or anxious feelings. Alternatively, substance use can lead to depression or anxiety. The person's moods may considerably improve after a period of abstinence. You may need to assist him in developing strategies for dealing with stress without drugs or alcohol such as problem-solving and relaxation training (Chapters 5 and 10).

Given the effect of substances on moods, you might choose to assess your client's emotional and psychological state *both* at the first contact meeting and several weeks after abstinence or use reduction. Ask about moods, behaviours and beliefs. Symptoms of depression include a persistent sadness, lack of interest in his usual activities, lethargy, disturbances of sleep and/or appetite, feelings of worthlessness or suicidal thoughts. The degree of depression can be assessed by qualified personnel, using the *Beck Depression Inventory*. You should also assess your client's suicide risk and, if necessary, take action to ensure his safety.

An anxious client may have unrealistic, exaggerated or persistent worries about some life circumstances or a specific anxiety such as a phobia. Social phobia is common among people with alcohol or drug problems. Physical symptoms including restlessness, sleep difficulties, shortness of breath and heart pounding may accompany your client's anxiety. Anxiety can be screened by qualified personnel, using the *Beck Anxiety Inventory*. Either the *Symptom Check List (SCL-90)* or the *General Health Questionnaire (GHQ)* will provide a global assessment of mental health.

Your client may experience feelings of loss as a result of giving up his alcohol or drug use. He may feel grief, anger, sleeplessness, sadness, inadequacy, fear or anxiety. These normal reactions should be distinguished from serious psychiatric disturbance.

Psychotic disorders related to substance use may occur, such as 'alcoholic hallucinosis' and amphetamine psychosis, where abstinence will lead to improvement. In the case of other clients, the psychiatric problem may be an additional problem unrelated to substance use, which, if untreated, will complicate therapy.

The diagnosis of psychiatric disorders is a specialist activity but it is your responsibility to detect clients who may be suffering from a psychiatric disorder. Referral of clients with drug or alcohol problems to non-drug and alcohol agencies often results in the rejection of the client, the rationale being that the drug or alcohol problem needs attention first. This is frequently untrue.

Unfortunately, we can provide no guidance for determining which disorder should be treated first and believe that both disorders require attention and often concurrent specialist treatment. Although some psychiatric problems resolve when the drug and alcohol problem is treated, or vice versa, it is difficult to predict whether this will occur. Ongoing monitoring of psychiatric symptoms is therefore important. It is your responsibility to negotiate the treatment system for your client and this may be difficult. Building a good referral network will help.

ALCOHOL-RELATED BRAIN DAMAGE

There is a high prevalence of cognitive dysfunction among people with alcohol problems, particularly older clients with longer and heavier drinking histories (Lishman, 1987). Some signs of brain damage, such as the severe memory disturbances and confusion associated with Wernicke–Korsakoff's disease are easily detected. In other cases, the impairment is more subtle but might influence the person's capacity for learning new skills during treatment. Because any alcohol-related brain damage will be further aggravated by continued drinking, detection of impairment will favour the goal of abstinence.

Assess your client's ability to recall day-to-day information, such as telephone numbers, appointments, conversations and shopping lists, especially if heavy drinking is a part of the clinical picture. Be watchful for evidence of your client simply going blank in conversation, or forgetting why he had entered a room or rung a number. Open discussion with your client will assist in determining the extent of memory loss.

Because alcohol has an immediate effect on general cognitive functioning, assessment for alcohol-related brain damage should be carried out after two or three weeks of abstinence. The *Mini-Mental State Examination* is an assessment tool that is quick and easy to administer, although its sensitivity to more subtle deficits may be limited. Other more complex tests requiring qualified personnel are given in the Resources List at the end of this chapter. To maximise your client's test performance, ensure that he is sober and is not undergoing detoxification. Test-related anxiety can influence how he performs so try to encourage a relaxed approach.

Be aware that normal ageing brings about memory loss, and the distinction requires specialist assessment. If you think your client has some cognitive impairment, it is advisable to refer him to a clinical psychologist or neuro-psychologist for further testing. If he does have cognitive deficits, modify your therapy to accommodate his needs. Break therapy up into simple steps, present information repeatedly and use a variety of different materials that are both auditory and visual.

Alcohol (or benzodiazepines) can lead to a loss of memory for events that take place while a person is intoxicated. These 'blackouts' may be frequent for clients who are dependent on alcohol but can also be experienced by social drinkers after heavy drinking. Find out from your client if, when and how often blackouts are experienced and whether he views them as a problem. A blackout is a particularly salient example of how alcohol may interfere with your client's control over his life. By using motivational interviewing techniques to discuss your client's blackouts, you might heighten his ambivalence about continuing to drink.

Injecting drug use is unlikely to cause brain damage except where a person has overdosed. The possibility that this might have occurred is worth checking out with your client.

STAGES OF CHANGE

How a person fares in treatment may depend on how ready he is to change the drinking or drug-using behaviour. Prochaska and DiClemente (1986) have developed a model that you can use to assess your client according to his current 'stage of change'. Further research is still needed to test the applicability of this model. It is not recommended here as a rigid structure in which to pigeon-hole clients. Rather, we see it as a flexible framework that may be useful for assessing the client's willingness to participate in treatment. According to Prochaska and DiClemente (1986), there are five stages of change that will require different therapeutic responses. These are discussed below.

A pre-contemplative stage

During this stage, your client is not considering changing. He believes the positive aspects of drinking or drug use outweigh the costs. He might say: 'I enjoy drinking', or 'I am not interested in stopping drug use', or 'I've tried before and failed'.

People at this stage do not usually attend treatment centres unless they are coerced (for example, by the legal system or by a relative). They are most likely to be identified by general counsellors or health care workers. If your client is in the pre-contemplative stage, he will probably not respond to action-oriented intervention. It is therefore more appropriate to use careful motivational strategies (pp. 45–6) to provide him with information that will help him to move into contemplation.

A contemplative stage

During this stage, your client becomes more aware of the costs of drinking or using drugs and the benefits of changing, but is ambivalent about changing, may feel trapped and does not act. This ambivalence might be expressed as: 'I'd like to quit using drugs because of the bad things but I think I'd really miss the high.'

At this stage, motivational interviewing (Chapter 3) could be particularly effective. It encourages your client to thoroughly explore the pros and cons of drinking or using drugs and might culminate in a firm decision to take action.

A preparation stage

During this stage, your client is preparing to take action within the next month and may have already made a previous attempt at changing his behaviour. During this and the next stage, your client begins to believe that the negative consequences of drinking or using drugs outweigh the benefits. He may indicate a preparedness for action by saying: 'I'm ready to try now', or 'I'd like to find out more about how to give up'.

In addition to encouragement, your client will need assistance in setting goals (Chapter 4). This is also the time when you can introduce a menu of strategies for change.

An action stage

During this stage, your client is engaged in active attempts to reduce or stop drinking or using drugs. At this stage, your client will be involved in a treatment plan that may include a combination of those described in this manual (see Chapter 18, *Putting It All Together*).

A maintenance stage

This stage begins when your client changes his drinking or drug-using behaviour and continues as long as he needs to focus on sustaining that change. During this process, a large number of clients will relapse and return to an earlier stage of change. If your client has received training in relapse prevention (Chapter 16) and is supported by a well-planned aftercare programme (Chapter 17) he will be better equipped to prevent any slips from developing into full-blown relapses.

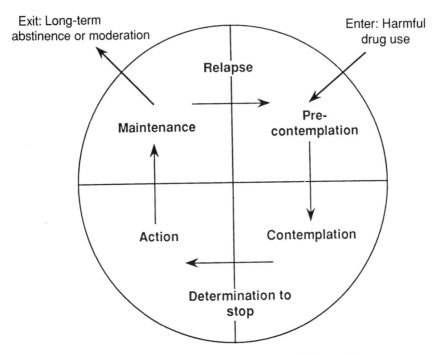

Figure 1:   A model of the change process in addictive behaviour
Source: *Adapted from Prochaska & DiClemente (1986)

Your client might progress in a linear fashion through these stages. However, this is the exception rather than the rule. Your client might relapse and return to an earlier stage several times before he achieves his goals. Each time this happens, he will gain new information about his behaviour and will be able to apply that information in the next attempt. This cyclical pattern of change is illustrated in Figure 1.

To assess your client's stage of change, simply discuss the issue with him. It might help to ask some specific questions about how much he wants to change. For example, you might ask: 'How interested are you in changing your drinking now?' and 'Do you feel that you *ought* to stop using drugs, or do you really *want* to?' To find out whether your client is prepared to take action for change, you might ask: 'What would you be prepared to do to solve this drinking problem?' and 'How confident are you that you can achieve this?'

If your client feels discouraged at previous unsuccessful attempts to stay abstinent or maintain moderation, you could use Figure 1 to put these attempts into perspective. Explain that each time he has gone around the circle, he has learnt something new that will help him next time. The discussion about preparedness for change can comfortably lead into motivational interviewing.

RESOURCES LIST

Assessment Instruments

Beck, A.T. & Steer, R.A. (1987). *Beck Depression Inventory: Manual.* USA: Harcourt, Brace, Jovanovich.
—Provides a validated measure of depression which is quick to administer. The inventory is available for purchase by qualified psychologists.

Beck, A.T. & Steer, R.A. (1990). *Beck Anxiety Inventory: Manual.* USA: Harcourt, Brace, Jovanovich.
—Provides a validated measure of anxiety which is quick to administer. The inventory is available for purchase by qualified psychologists.

Darke, S., Ward, J., Hall, W., Heather, N. & Wodak, A. (1991). *The Opiate Treatment Index (OTI) Manual,* Technical Report Number 11. Sydney: National Drug and Alcohol Research Centre.
—Although mainly designed for assessing opiate users, this scale assesses a whole range of different drugs as well as risk-taking and other lifestyle factors. For a copy of the Opiate Treatment Index and the accompanying manual, write to the National Drug and Alcohol Research Centre, University of New South Wales, Sydney, 2052, NSW, Australia.

Derogatis, L.R. (1983). *SCL-90-R: Administration, Scoring and Procedures Manual—II for the revised version.* Towson, MD, USA: Clinical Psychometric Research.
—This mental health screening device covers the areas of somatic, cognitive and phobic anxieties, obsessive-compulsive symptoms, interpersonal sensitivity, depression, hostility, paranoia and psychotic symptoms.

Folstein, M.F., Folstein, S.E. & McHugh, P.R. (1975). Mini-mental state. A practical method for grading the cognitive state of patients for the clinician. *Journal of Psychiatric Research,* **12,** 189–198.
—Designed as a simple, quick test of general cognitive functioning.

Goldberg, D. & Williams, P. (1988). *A User's Guide to the General Health Questionnaire.* Berkshire: NFER-NELSON.
—A mental health screening device that covers somatic symptoms, depression, anxiety and social functioning.

Kelly, J.A., St. Lawrence, J.S., Hood, H.V. & Brasfield, T.L. (1989). An objective test of AIDS risk behavior knowledge: Scale development, validation, and norms. *Journal of Behavior Therapy and Experimental Psychology,* **20** (3), 227–234.
—This 40-item scale can be used to identify misconceptions about how AIDS is transmitted. Unfortunately, there are only three items which directly mention injecting drug use.

Lezak, M.D. (1983). *Neuropsychological Assessment.* New York: Oxford University Press.
—This classic text describes some tests that can assist you in screening for alcohol-related brain damage, such as: *Rey–Osterrieth Complex Figure Test,* designed to test perceptual organisation and visual memory; *Rey Auditory-Verbal Learning Test (AVLT),* designed to measure memory recall and recognition; *Trail Making Test (TMT),* designed to test visual conceptual and visuomotor tracking.

Miller, W.R. & Marlatt, G.A. (1984a). *Comprehensive Drinker Profile*. Odessa, Florida: Psychological Assessment Resources.
—The original and more comprehensive version of the scale below.

Miller, W.R. & Marlatt, G.A. (1984b). *Brief Drinker Profile*. Odessa, Florida: Psychological Assessment Resources.
—An excellent measure of alcohol consumption and problems.

Raistrick, D., Dunbar, G. & Davidson, R. (1983). Development of a questionnaire to measure alcohol dependence. *British Journal of Addiction*, **78**, 89–95.
—This alternative to the SADQ-C includes items testing for psychological aspects of alcohol dependence such as subjective compulsion to drink, salience of drink-seeking behaviour and narrowing of the drinking repertoire.

Stockwell, T., Murphy, D. & Hodgson, R. (1983). The severity of alcohol dependence questionnaire: Its use, reliability and validity. *British Journal of Addiction*, **78**, 145–155.
—Presents results of test-retest reliability and validity for the SADQ, as well as normative data.

Stockwell, T., Sitharthan, T., McGrath, D. & Lang, E. (1994). The measurement of alcohol dependence and impaired control in community samples. *British Journal of Addiction*, **89**, 167–174.
—Describes the modification of the original SADQ so that it is applicable to drinkers in the community who have not sought treatment.

Sutherland, G., Edwards, G., Taylor, C., Phillips, G., Gossop, M. & Brady, R. (1986). The measurement of opiate dependence. *British Journal of Addiction*, **81**, 485–494.
—Designed to be comparable with the original SADQ, this scale measures physical and affective withdrawal symptoms, withdrawal relief drug-taking and rapidity of reinstatement of symptoms after abstinence.

Ward, J., Darke, S. & Hall, W. (1990). *The HIV Risk-taking Behaviour Scale (HRBS) Manual*, Technical Report Number 10. Sydney: National Drug and Alcohol Research Centre.
—This is a subscale of the *OTI*, described above.

Wechsler, D. (1981). *Wechsler Adult Intelligence Scale—Revised (WAIS-R)*. USA: Harcourt, Brace, Jovanovich.
—A comprehensive IQ test with both performance and verbal scales and 11 subscales which can be used by qualified psychologists.

Wechsler, D. (1987). *Wechsler Memory Scale—Revised Edition (WMS-R)*. USA: Harcourt, Brace, Jovanovich.
—A comprehensive test for both short- and long-term memory which is available to qualified psychologists.

Other Resources

Addiction Research Foundation. (1993). *Directory of Client Outcome Measures for Addictions Treatment Programs*. Canada: Addiction Research Foundation.
—An excellent resource book giving information about standardised measures that you can use in assessing substance use and dependence, situations that might lead to relapse, confidence in change, psychiatric symptoms, self-esteem, marital and family adjustment, cognitive functioning, and other lifestyle issues.

Bell, J., Batey, R.G., Farrell, G.C., Crewe, E.B., Cunningham, A.L. & Byth, K. (1990). Hepatitis C virus in intravenous drug users. *Medical Journal of Australia*, **153**, 274–276.
—This study found that Hepatitis C is very common among injecting drug users, particularly people who have been injecting in the long term.

Darke, S., Hall, W., Wodak, A., Heather, N. & Ward, J. (1992). Development and validation of a multi-dimensional instrument for assessing outcome of treatment among opiate users: The opiate treatment index. *British Journal of Addiction*, **87**, 733–742.
  —Provides data on the reliability and validity of the Opiate Treatment Index.
Devenyi, P. & Saunders, S.J. (1986). *Physician's Handbook for Medical Management of Alcohol- and Drug-related Problems*. Canada: Addiction Research Foundation.
  —An excellent handbook providing a summary of withdrawal management procedures.
Edwards, G. (1982). *The Treatment of Drinking Problems: A Guide for the Helping Professions*. London: Grant MacIntyre.
  —Chapter 10 gives structured assessment guidelines and a discussion about the interplay between assessment and therapy.
Edwards, G. & Gross, M.M. (1976). Alcohol dependence: Provisional description of a clinical syndrome. *British Medical Journal*, **1**, 1058–1061.
  —A detailed description of the symptoms of the alcohol-dependence syndrome and how they are likely to affect your client.
Lishman, W.A. (1987). *Organic Psychiatry: The Psychological Consequences of Cerebral Disorder* (2nd edn). Oxford: Blackwell Scientific Publications.
  —An excellent summary of cerebral dysfunction and clinical signs and symptoms thereof.
Mattick, R.P. & Jarvis, T. (1993). *An Outline for the Management of Alcohol Problems: Quality in the Treatment of Drug Dependence Project*, National Campaign Against Drug Abuse monograph series No. 20. Canberra, Australia: Australia Government Publishing Service..
  —A key resource providing guidelines for the assessment of clients with alcohol problems outlined in this monograph.
Miller, W.R. & Rollnick, S. (1991). *Motivational Interviewing: Preparing People to Change Addictive Behavior*. New York: Guilford Press.
  —Chapter 7 provides a brief discussion of the most important areas of assessment, including assessment of motivation.
Prochaska, J.O. & DiClemente C. C. (1986). Toward a comprehensive model of change. In W.R. Miller & N. Heather (Eds), *Treating Addictive Behaviors: Processes of Change* (pp. 3–27). New York: Plenum Press.
  —Describes the theoretical model of 'stages of change' and examines relevant research findings and implications for therapy.

Severity of Alcohol Dependence Questionnaire—Form C
SADQ-C

NAME _____ AGE _____ SEX _____

Have you drunk any alcohol in the past six months?   YES / NO

If YES, please answer all the following questions about your drinking by circling your most appropriate response.

DURING THE PAST *SIX MONTHS*

1. The day after drinking alcohol, I woke up feeling sweaty.
   ALMOST NEVER   SOMETIMES   OFTEN   NEARLY ALWAYS

2. The day after drinking alcohol, my hands shook first thing in the morning.
   ALMOST NEVER   SOMETIMES   OFTEN   NEARLY ALWAYS

3. The day after drinking alcohol, my whole body shook violently first thing in the morning if I didn't have a drink.
   ALMOST NEVER   SOMETIMES   OFTEN   NEARLY ALWAYS

4. The day after drinking alcohol, I woke up absolutely drenched in sweat.
   ALMOST NEVER   SOMETIMES   OFTEN   NEARLY ALWAYS

5. The day after drinking alcohol, I dreaded waking up in the morning.
   ALMOST NEVER   SOMETIMES   OFTEN   NEARLY ALWAYS

6. The day after drinking alcohol, I was frightened of meeting people first thing in the morning.
   ALMOST NEVER   SOMETIMES   OFTEN   NEARLY ALWAYS

7. The day after drinking alcohol, I felt at the edge of despair when I awoke.
   ALMOST NEVER   SOMETIMES   OFTEN   NEARLY ALWAYS

8. The day after drinking alcohol, I felt very frightened when I awoke.
   ALMOST NEVER   SOMETIMES   OFTEN   NEARLY ALWAYS

9. The day after drinking alcohol, I liked to have an alcoholic drink in the morning.
   ALMOST NEVER   SOMETIMES   OFTEN   NEARLY ALWAYS

10. The day after drinking alcohol, I always gulped my first few alcoholic drinks down as quickly as possible.
    ALMOST NEVER   SOMETIMES   OFTEN   NEARLY ALWAYS

SADQ-C continued

DURING THE PAST *SIX MONTHS*

11. The day after drinking alcohol, I drank more alcohol in the morning to get rid of the shakes.

    ALMOST NEVER   SOMETIMES   OFTEN   NEARLY ALWAYS

12. The day after drinking alcohol, I had a very strong craving for a drink when I awoke.

    ALMOST NEVER   SOMETIMES   OFTEN   NEARLY ALWAYS

13. I drank more than a quarter of a bottle of spirits in a day (OR 1 bottle of wine OR 7 middies[1] of beer).

    ALMOST NEVER   SOMETIMES   OFTEN   NEARLY ALWAYS

14. I drank more than half a bottle of spirits per day (OR 2 bottles of wine OR 15 middies of beer).

    ALMOST NEVER   SOMETIMES   OFTEN   NEARLY ALWAYS

15. I drank more than one bottle of spirits per day (OR 4 bottles of wine OR 30 middies of beer).

    ALMOST NEVER   SOMETIMES   OFTEN   NEARLY ALWAYS

16. I drank more than two bottles of spirits per day (OR 8 bottles of wine OR 60 middies of beer).

    ALMOST NEVER   SOMETIMES   OFTEN   NEARLY ALWAYS

IMAGINE THE FOLLOWING SITUATION:

   (1) You have HARDLY DRUNK ANY ALCOHOL FOR A FEW WEEKS
   (2) You then drink VERY HEAVILY for TWO DAYS

HOW WOULD YOU FEEL THE *MORNING AFTER* THOSE TWO DAYS OF HEAVY DRINKING?

17. I would start to sweat.

                    NOT AT ALL   SLIGHTLY   MODERATELY   QUITE A LOT

18. My hands would shake.

                    NOT AT ALL   SLIGHTLY   MODERATELY   QUITE A LOT

19. My body would shake.

                    NOT AT ALL   SLIGHTLY   MODERATELY   QUITE A LOT

20. I would be craving for a drink.

                    NOT AT ALL   SLIGHTLY   MODERATELY   QUITE A LOT

Source: From Stockwell *et al.* (1994). Reproduced by permission of Carfax Publishing Co., PO Box 25, Abingdon, Oxfordshire OX14 3UE, England.

[1]Middies are equal to one standard drink of beer (see definitions of standard drinks, p. 131).

The Severity of Alcohol Dependence Data Questionnaire (SADD)

The following questions cover a wide range of topics to do with drinking. Please read each question carefully but do not think too much about its exact meaning. Think about your MOST RECENT drinking habits and answer each question by placing a tick (✔) under the MOST APPROPRIATE heading. If you have any difficulties ASK FOR HELP.

	NEVER	SOME-TIMES	OFTEN	NEARLY ALWAYS
1. Do you find difficulty in getting the thought of drink out of your mind?	....	....	....	....
2. Is getting drunk more important than your next meal?	....	....	....	....
3. Do you plan your day around when and where you can drink?	....	....	....	....
4. Do you drink in the morning, afternoon and evening?	....	....	....	....
5. Do you drink for the effect of alcohol without caring what the drink is?	....	....	....	....
6. Do you drink as much as you want irrespective of what you are doing the next day?	....	....	....	....
7. Given that many problems might be caused by alcohol do you still drink too much?	....	....	....	....
8. Do you know that you won't be able to stop drinking once you start?	....	....	....	....
9. Do you try to control your drinking by giving it up completely for days or weeks at a time?	....	....	....	....
10. The morning after a heavy drinking session do you need your first drink to get yourself going?	....	....	....	....
11. The morning after a heavy drinking session do you wake up with a definite shakiness of your hands?	....	....	....	....
12. After a heavy drinking session do you wake up and retch or vomit?	....	....	....	....
13. The morning after a heavy drinking session do you go out of your way to avoid people?	....	....	....	....
14. After a heavy drinking session do you see frightening things that later you realise were imaginary?	....	....	....	....
15. Do you go drinking and the next day find you have forgotten what happened the night before?	....	....	....	....

Source: From Raistrick, Dunbar & Davidson (1983). Reproduced by permission of Carfax Publishing Co., PO Box 25, Abingdon, Oxfordshire OX14 3UE, England.

Severity of Opiate Dependence Questionnaire (SODQ)
SODQ

NAME _____ AGE _____ SEX _____

First of all, we would like you to recall a recent month when you were using opiates heavily in a way that, for you, was fairly typical of a heavy use period. Please fill in the month and the year.

MONTH _____ YEAR _____

ANSWER EVERY QUESTION BY CIRCLING ONE RESPONSE ONLY

1. ON WAKING, AND BEFORE MY FIRST DOSE OF OPIATES:

(a) My body aches or feels stiff:
NEVER OR   SOMETIMES   OFTEN   ALWAYS OR
ALMOST NEVER   NEARLY ALWAYS

(b) I get stomach cramps
NEVER OR   SOMETIMES   OFTEN   ALWAYS OR
ALMOST NEVER   NEARLY ALWAYS

(c) I feel sick
NEVER OR   SOMETIMES   OFTEN   ALWAYS OR
ALMOST NEVER   NEARLY ALWAYS

(d) I notice my heart pounding
NEVER OR   SOMETIMES   OFTEN   ALWAYS OR
ALMOST NEVER   NEARLY ALWAYS

(e) I have hot and cold flushes
NEVER OR   SOMETIMES   OFTEN   ALWAYS OR
ALMOST NEVER   NEARLY ALWAYS

(f) I feel miserable or depressed
NEVER OR   SOMETIMES   OFTEN   ALWAYS OR
ALMOST NEVER   NEARLY ALWAYS

(g) I feel tense or panicky
NEVER OR   SOMETIMES   OFTEN   ALWAYS OR
ALMOST NEVER   NEARLY ALWAYS

(h) I feel irritable or angry
NEVER OR   SOMETIMES   OFTEN   ALWAYS OR
ALMOST NEVER   NEARLY ALWAYS

(i) I feel restless and unable to relax
NEVER OR   SOMETIMES   OFTEN   ALWAYS OR
ALMOST NEVER   NEARLY ALWAYS

(j) I have a strong craving
NEVER OR   SOMETIMES   OFTEN   ALWAYS OR
ALMOST NEVER   NEARLY ALWAYS

SODQ continued

ANSWER EVERY QUESTION BY CIRCLING ONE RESPONSE ONLY

2. PLEASE COMPLETE ALL SECTIONS (a-f) OF THIS QUESTION.

(a) I try to save some opiates to use on waking
NEVER OR   SOMETIMES   OFTEN   ALWAYS OR
ALMOST NEVER   NEARLY ALWAYS

(b) I like to take my first dose of opiates within two hours of waking up
NEVER OR   SOMETIMES   OFTEN   ALWAYS OR
ALMOST NEVER   NEARLY ALWAYS

(c) In the morning, I use opiates to stop myself feeling sick
NEVER OR   SOMETIMES   OFTEN   ALWAYS OR
ALMOST NEVER   NEARLY ALWAYS

(d) The first thing I think of doing when I wake up is to take some opiates
NEVER OR   SOMETIMES   OFTEN   ALWAYS OR
ALMOST NEVER   NEARLY ALWAYS

(e) When I wake up I take opiates to stop myself aching or feeling stiff
NEVER OR   SOMETIMES   OFTEN   ALWAYS OR
ALMOST NEVER   NEARLY ALWAYS

(f) The first thing I do after I wake up is to take some opiates
NEVER OR   SOMETIMES   OFTEN   ALWAYS OR
ALMOST NEVER   NEARLY ALWAYS

3. PLEASE THINK OF YOUR OPIATE USE DURING A TYPICAL PERIOD OF DRUG
TAKING FOR THESE QUESTIONS:

(a) Did you think your opiate use was out of control?
NEVER OR   SOMETIMES   OFTEN   ALWAYS OR
ALMOST NEVER   NEARLY ALWAYS

(b) Did the prospect of missing a fix (or dose) make you very anxious or worried?
NEVER OR   SOMETIMES   OFTEN   ALWAYS OR
ALMOST NEVER   NEARLY ALWAYS

(c) Did you worry about your opiate use?
NEVER OR   SOMETIMES   OFTEN   ALWAYS OR
ALMOST NEVER   NEARLY ALWAYS

(d) Did you wish you could stop?
NEVER OR   SOMETIMES   OFTEN   ALWAYS OR
ALMOST NEVER   NEARLY ALWAYS

(e) How difficult would you find it to stop or go without?
IMPOSSIBLE   VERY DIFFICULT   QUITE DIFFICULT   NOT DIFFICULT

Source: From Sutherland *et al.* (1986). Reproduced by permission of Carfax Publishing Co., PO Box 25, Abingdon, Oxfordshire OX14 3UE, England.

3

MOTIVATIONAL INTERVIEWING

RECOMMENDED USE

Motivational interviewing is a style of counselling that can be used throughout the therapeutic process (see Chapter 1, *General Counselling Skills*). However, specific motivational interviewing strategies are thought to be particularly useful during initial sessions with substance users who are 'contemplators' experiencing ambivalence about changing drinking or drug use (see p. 24).

For other clients who are still 'pre-contemplators', motivational interviewing can be used to begin the process of thinking about change. Strategies suitable for use with these clients are discussed below although such people are unlikely to present to a treatment setting unless coerced by others. Pre-contemplators are more commonly encountered during screening for drug use in primary health care settings. With coerced clients it might be very useful to use a motivational interviewing style in your initial contact, setting a goal of having the client agree to a further assessment session.

If your client is already highly motivated and ready to change, the use of motivational interviewing strategies early in treatment will not be necessary. You may find it useful, however, to reinforce motivation with such clients by exploring and reaffirming what they hope to achieve by changing.

As motivational interviewing involves a highly individualised approach it is not generally undertaken in group settings. However, methods for enhancing motivation in a group setting are also discussed briefly below.

GOALS

In essence, the goal of motivational interviewing is to have your client talk herself into deciding to change drug-use behaviour. However, motivational interviewing emphasises the client's right to choose and to accept the responsibility for the results of her decision.

Motivational interviewing strategies avoid traditional confrontational methods because such 'offensive' tactics (e.g. *'you* have a major *problem'*) quite naturally bring out 'defensive' reactions (e.g. *'I don't* have a problem'). Such confrontation is both unhelpful and counter-productive when the aim is to get your client to take the position of being the one who presents the arguments for change!

KEY CONCEPTS

Empathy

Empathy is defined in detail in Chapter 1, *General Counselling Skills*. In motivational interviewing the concept is also used to describe the style of listening in which your client's comments are reflected back to her, often in a slightly modified or reframed fashion but always with an attitude of respect and acceptance.

This non-judgemental attitude does not imply that you need to agree with your client's perspective. Rather, your empathic acceptance builds a therapeutic rapport that supports your client's self-esteem and allows her the freedom to explore the possibility of change.

Ambivalence

Ambivalence is a common and natural experience of feeling torn between wanting and not wanting to do something. It is *not* a sign of unwillingness to change or one of denial. In the context of substance use it is the conflict between wanting to continue to drink or use drugs and the desire to cut down or stop. The closer your client is to deciding to change her drug use, the greater these feelings of conflict are likely to be. Ambivalence can be the greatest obstacle to commitment to change and the major reason for people being stuck in long periods of contemplation. The aim in motivational interviewing is to tip the balance of ambivalence in favour of action.

Self-motivational Statements

These are statements your client makes which: (a) express her willingness to accept input about her drinking or drug-using, (b) acknowledge her alcohol- or drug-related problems; and (c) indicate a need and/or desire to change her substance use. When these types of statements come from your client they are far more likely to persuade her to change than words spoken by you or any other person. Eliciting these 'self-motivational' statements from your client is one of the aims of motivational interviewing.

Counselling Microskills

Fundamental to the successful use of motivational interviewing strategies are a number of client-centred counselling microskills. These include the use of open-ended questions, reflective listening, affirmations and summarising. These are discussed in detail in Chapter 1, *General Counselling Skills*. In motivational interviewing (unlike many non-directive, client-centred approaches) all of these skills are used in a directive way to encourage your client to explore her ambivalence and to consider the possibility of change. For example, open-ended questions are used to evoke your client's concerns about drinking or drug use. Summary and reflective listening skills are also directive when you *selectively* reinforce those self-motivational statements made by your client which express concern about drinking or drug use and reasons for change.

Resistance

It is crucial to motivational interviewing that you avoid evoking or strengthening resistance in your client. We strongly recommend that you read the section on resistance in Chapter 1, *General Counselling Skills*.

METHOD

There are many and varied approaches to and interpretations of motivational interviewing. A number of these can be found in Miller and Rollnick (1991) and Rollnick, Heather and Bell (1992) listed in the Resources List. Common to many of these different applications of motivational interviewing, however, are a number of key strategies. Some of these strategies with examples are outlined below. These are drawn directly from the work of Baker, Rollnick, Saunders and their colleagues (see the Resources List).

There are several ways that these strategies can be used or combined. *Not all of these strategies will be appropriate or necessary to use with all clients.* Rollnick, Heather and Bell (1992) have suggested that when using any of the strategies you should try to begin with open-ended questions and use reflective listening skills to further explore your client's thoughts and feelings. Each strategy can take anywhere between 5 and 15 minutes. They further suggest that you summarise key points before moving on to another strategy. You might also find it useful to use a whiteboard or notebook to record important points. This will help you in summarising and can be a powerful visual tool to help your client weigh up the costs and benefits of her continued use.

Exploring the Good Things and the Less Good Things

The aim of this strategy is to let your client explore her thoughts and feelings about her drinking or drug use. It is also often the best way of assessing a client's stage of change. For this strategy to work well it is *essential* that you be non-judgemental and avoid expressing disapproval or surprise about your client's perceptions of what is either 'good' or 'less good' about her drinking or drug use. The four key aspects of this strategy are described below.

The good things

Focusing on the 'good things' first has the advantage of building rapport and of providing you with an understanding of the context of your client's drinking or drug use before you look at more negative aspects. Begin by asking an open-ended question such as:

'What are some of the good things about your use of . . .'

or

'What do you like about drinking/using . . .'

Acknowledge and summarise all the 'good things' about using without over-prolonging this aspect.

The less good things

The aim here is to allow your client (not you!) to identify the less good aspects of her drinking or drug use. A gentle approach will be more likely to encourage an open discussion, so avoid using phrases like 'bad things' or 'problems' unless your client does so. Often your client will raise the 'less good things' as you examine the 'good things'. This will allow you to move on easily to exploring this side of her substance use. Otherwise, after your summary of the 'good things', begin with an open-ended question such as:

'What are some of the less good things about . . .'
'What are the things you don't like so much about your use of . . .'

Try to find out why your client thinks these are 'less good things'. Remember, be non-judgemental. This exercise provides an opportunity for your client to explore less positive aspects of her drinking or drug use without the threat of having them labelled by others as problematic. Use follow-up questions such as:

'How does this affect you?'

or

'What don't you like about it?'

Prompt for specifics rather than vague reasons because the more that your client can hear herself describe issues in detail the more she will become convinced by them. For example, statements like 'I'm worried about my health' or 'I'm worried about the effect on my relationship' should lead you to ask:

'Can you give me a recent example of that?'
'Can you tell me a bit more about that?'

If your client has some difficulty in listing 'less good things' or if you feel that she has not explored some important areas (e.g. legal, social, financial, work, family, sexual relationships) you may choose to prompt gently for other reasons. However, you should use this tactic sparingly. For example:

'You mentioned feeling tense in social situations. Some people say they have hassles with their family, too. Is that something that happens with you?'

Exploring concerns

It is *critical* that you don't assume a 'less good thing' will be a problem or concern for your client. For example, your client's arguments with her partner may not be of major concern if she doesn't really care about the relationship. Clients will often be able to identify a number of 'less good' aspects of drinking or drug use that do not necessarily cause them any current concerns. It is therefore important to follow up your client's statements with further open-ended questions so that you can focus in on the less good aspects which *are* of concern, for example:

'How do you feel about that?'
'Is that a problem or concern for you in any way?'

This highlighting and further exploration of *concerns* is the central strategy of motivational interviewing. Less good aspects of drinking or drug use that are of little concern to your client are unlikely to motivate her to change. On the other hand, in recognising her own concerns about drinking or drug use, your client is more likely to feel a need to change. In exploring concerns with your client, your reflections and summaries are particularly important because you reinforce these concerns by repeating them to her.

At all costs, when using this strategy, avoid making comments like 'Don't you think that being in gaol twice is a problem?' It is your client who must define what is of concern to her. Confrontational statements are only likely to produce denial or defensive reactions.

Summarising

After you have talked about both the 'good' and 'less good' things summarise them in your client's words whenever possible. Such a summary might use statements like: 'It seems then, that on the one hand you like . . . *and* on the other hand . . .' Say 'and . . .' rather than 'but . . .' as the former better expresses empathy and understanding of the importance of both the positive and negative sides of drinking or drug use for your client.

Try to avoid simply listing all the 'less good' aspects your client may have mentioned. Instead, in summarising the 'less good' side, focus on the issues that your client has indicated are of some *concern* and which seem to make her most uncomfortable. That is, the aim is to help your client to feel that her concerns and worries outweigh the good things about continuing to use drugs. If appropriate, other strategies that can also help to tip the balance in favour of change are detailed below. Make sure that you allow your client time to react to your summary before moving on to another strategy.

Trouble-shooting

If your client is persistently showing resistant behaviours, it may be a sign that your method is either too confrontational or your strategies are inappropriate to your client's current stage of change. For example, if your client is not at all ready to consider change she may resist when the possibility of 'less good things' is being raised. Alternatively, she may be able to list a number of 'less good things' but be largely unconcerned by any of them. If you encounter such 'pre-contemplators', you should consider moving to the *Providing Information* strategy described below.

With other clients, the best response to resistance is to 'roll with it'. *Never* meet resistance head on by arguing, or by attempting to persuade, warn or confront your client. These responses will backfire severely because they will push your client into an oppositional position where she will vigorously defend her drinking or drug use!

There are a number of different ways to 'roll' with your client's resistance and these are discussed in detail in Chapter 1, *General Counselling Skills*. The underlying principle, however, is to avoid confrontation or argument. Instead, acknowledge and reframe your client's feelings or disagreements so as to allow the interview to continue exploring issues and concerns.

Saunders, Wilkinson and Allsop (1991; pp. 248–85) have also noted that sometimes clients might distance themselves from a 'less good thing'. For example, your client might say 'My doctor said I'd get AIDS if I shared needles'. Explore this response by asking 'But what do *you* think?' Sometimes an answer to that question might indicate that your client is either poorly informed or misinformed about some consequence of her drinking or drug use. Such misconceptions might need to be altered in an objective and non-confrontational way (see the section on *Providing Information*, below).

Life Satisfaction

To help raise issues and concerns, ask your client to think about how she saw herself in the past and what she would like to see for herself in the future. A contrast between her present and past hopes or future aspirations can often create an uncomfortable discrepancy for your client. This discomfort can be a powerful motivating force for change. Rollnick, Heather and Bell (1992) have suggested that this strategy should only be used with clients who are at least already somewhat concerned about their drug or alcohol use.

Looking back

Begin with the following types of question:

> 'When you were [eighteen] what sorts of things did you think that you'd be doing now?'

You can then explore with your client how her past expectations differ from the current situation by asking questions like:

'How does that differ from what is happening now?'
'How do you feel about that?'
'What effect did your use of . . . have on things?'

The aim of these questions is to guide your client to make links between substance use and her goals or aspirations.

Looking forward

Similarly, with regard to the future:

'How would you like things to be different in the future?'
'What's stopping you doing what you'd like to?'
'How does your use of . . . affect your life at the moment?'

Such questions often result in expressions of worry and concern about drug or alcohol use and lead your client into talking about a need for behaviour change. Some therapists alternatively ask more direct questions:

'If you choose to carry on drinking what do you think will happen?'

and

'How do you feel about that?'

When you have explored this area, summarise past/future aspirations in relation to the present and highlight the role of substance use. Use your client's own words wherever possible.

Trouble-shooting

This strategy can result in your client expressing strong feelings of hopelessness or despair. While acknowledging the distress, focus on the fact that while it *is* difficult, your client is able to make choices about changing her current behaviour. Also stress that changing substance use behaviour can lead to positive changes in her life and explore the benefits that your client might obtain from changing. Remember, belief in the possibility for change is an important motivator.

Self vs User

Similar to the strategy outlined above, this approach also aims to increase what Saunders, Wilkinson and Allsop (1991) have described as the 'psychological squirm' of your client. It allows her to consider the discrepancy between herself as a person versus herself as a substance user.

You might ask:

'What would your best friend say are your good qualities?'

(This wording of the question is useful with clients suffering low self-esteem.)

'Tell me . . . how would you describe the things you like about yourself?'

Explore these attributes using reflective listening statements and further questioning, summarise and then ask:

'And how would you describe you the heroin user/drinker?'

Again, explore these attributes in some detail, summarise, and then ask:

'How do these things fit together?'

Saunders, Wilkinson and Allsop (1991) noted that the trick with this exercise is to allow your client to focus on those aspects of herself as a substance user about which she might feel embarrassed or even ashamed. It is of course crucial that the setting for this examination is empathic and non-judgemental. Conclude the strategy with a summary, highlighting those discrepancies identified by your client.

Helping with Decision-making

If you have been successful in helping your client to express concerns about a need for change, the next step is to help her resolve to take action to alter the substance use behaviour. This step is crucial because clients can be concerned about their drinking or drug use but still not make a commitment to action. Miller and Rollnick (1991) have suggested that some signs that your client might be ready for this stage include: decreased resistance; fewer questions about the problem; more questions about change; and talking about how life might be after a change.

It is useful to begin this phase of motivational interviewing by summarising and drawing together the threads of the interview. This will involve reviewing your client's own perception of the problem and summing up her ambivalence—including what remains positive or attractive about the problem. You should also restate your client's comments about wanting or intending to change and offer your own assessment of the situation. Emphasise areas of concern you share with your client and include any objective evidence of the presence of risks or problems. The aim of the summary is to draw together as many reasons for change as possible, while at the same time acknowledging your client's mixed feelings about change.

Following the summary, move on to ask one of the following types of key questions:

> 'Where does this leave you now?'
> 'What's going to happen now . . . where do we go from here?'
> 'What does this mean about your drinking/drug use?'

If your client states that she wants to give up or reduce substance use it is extremely important that you do not 'take over' at this point and tell her what to do. This would undermine the whole process of motivational interviewing which has encouraged your client to express responsibility and concern for her behaviour. Remember also that her ambivalence has not 'disappeared', rather the balance has simply been tipped towards change. If you are over-eager or push too hard for action, this balance might well be reversed.

It is also important that you support your client in the belief that she is capable of change. One way that this can be done is by offering your client a range of possible treatment options such as those outlined in Chapter 4, *Goal-setting*. This allows your client to select strategies that meet specific personal needs and reinforces her perceived personal choice and control. Provide the information about the options in a neutral manner. You might also describe what other clients have done in similar situations. Emphasise that you will provide support and guidance to your client but that she is the best judge about what will be best for her.

When your client expresses a preference for a particular goal, spend some time examining that goal to see how achievable it is and what its likely consequences will be. Here are some questions (based on the work by Miller and Rollnick, 1991; p. 120) that will help to transform a vaguely expressed goal into a more complete picture that is relevant for your client's concerns:

> 'How would your life be different if you followed this idea and quit altogether?'
> 'You have said that you think you would like to cut down. How do you think this would work?'
> 'What can you think of that might go wrong with your plan?'
> 'What are some of the skills that you have now that might help you to achieve this goal?'

Providing Information for Pre-contemplators

Providing information can be a useful strategy in a number of contexts. It can be used to provoke thinking about change with some clients who are not currently concerned about their drug or alcohol use, or to correct misconceptions about risks associated with use. For example, in interventions aimed at reducing harm from injecting drug use, users may be at a contemplation stage for needle-sharing practices but be pre-contemplators with regard to using condoms. In this case, providing information and personalising the risk (see below) associated with unsafe sex can be crucial strategies (Baker & Dixon in Miller & Rollnick, 1991).

It is often useful to begin by asking clients what *they* know about the risks associated with their substance use. This serves to acknowledge your client's understanding of the hazards, and allows you to identify any misinformation that needs to be clarified. You can then ask your client if she would like to know more. It is often useful to ask permission to give information, in a very low-key fashion, for example:

'I wonder, would it be useful to spend a few minutes looking at this question of what is a safe level of use while you are pregnant . . .?'
'Would you be interested in knowing more about the effects of alcohol on the body?'

If your client agrees, refer to 'expert' opinions and provide the information in a neutral, non-judgemental and non-personal way, for example: 'What can happen to people who drink beyond the recommended limit is . . .' After providing the information ask your client:

'What do you make of this? How does it tie in with your use of . . .'

or

'I wonder, how is this relevant for you?'

These questions are the key motivational aspect of providing information and it is therefore important that you take time to explore the personal implications of the information for your client. However, you should ensure that you are not using the information as evidence to push the client into change; this is *not* the aim of providing information. Rather you are endeavouring to raise doubts and to increase your client's perception of the risks and problems associated with her drug use. If you are successful in doing so, you may wish to continue the interview by further exploring her concerns and their implications for change (see above).

However, remember that motivational interviewing emphasises the client's responsibility and for some clients this will mean the right to make an informed decision to continue her substance use for the present. With such clients it is nevertheless worthwhile recognising that information provided carefully in the present might well have an important impact some time later.

OTHER APPLICATIONS OF MOTIVATIONAL INTERVIEWING

Personalised Feedback of Assessment Results

The providing information strategy described above provides a model for feeding back results from assessment for all your clients. In personalised feedback, you provide your client with *both*: (a) objective measures of her situation (such as the severity of dependence, level of HIV risk-taking, cognitive performance or results from a liver function test); *and* (b) a simple explanation about what these results might mean and how they compare with population norms or the types of clients generally seen at your agency.

Personalised feedback helps to increase your client's motivation by providing selected information about health at a 'teachable' moment, such as a moment when her concern regarding her own health is heightened. This will be more effective than giving general education about the effects of alcohol and other drugs, because it is harder for your client to dismiss the personally relevant information that you are providing.

Present the feedback in a quiet, non-judgemental manner. Avoid 'scare' tactics. Your aim is to provide her with enough information for her to draw her own conclusions. If you are about to feed back the results of a standardised questionnaire such as the SADQ-C, begin by asking your client what things she noticed about her responses to the questionnaire.

Try to emphasise from the outset that your client will be free to form her own opinion. Miller and Rollnick (1991; p. 98) have suggested that you preface your feedback with a comment that clearly shows your interest in her opinion. For example:

'I don't know what you will make of this result, but . . .'

If you have carried out several standardised tests, present the results in a written format, perhaps even with diagrams. Use this written report as an aid to assist you in explaining the details to your client. Tell your client what her score was on a particular test and then explain how her score is compared with other people's. For instance, she might have scored 36 on the SADQ-C. Explain that people with high levels of dependence on alcohol tend to have scores above 30 on the SADQ-C. High levels of dependence are associated with a range of physical responses to alcohol. Describe these responses of tolerance, withdrawal, and drinking to avoid withdrawal.

Always follow up feedback of information by seeking your client's response. For example:

'What do you think about this?'
'How does this fit with your expectations?'
'How do you feel about this?'
'Does this surprise you?'

Be aware that information presented in this way may raise strong emotional issues for your client. Your empathy and reflective listening will help her to explore these feelings without becoming defensive.

If appropriate, provide your client with information explaining how a change in substance use can remedy abnormal findings. At the end of the feedback period, summarise the identified problems and risks and your client's reactions to that information. Emphasise any concerns your client expressed and any comments she might have made indicating her need or desire for change. Allow your client the opportunity to react to or modify your summary.

Trouble-shooting

Medical results within the normal range should be dealt with carefully. Your client, for example, might interpret a result in the normal range as indicating that her substance use is causing no problems. It is possible to counter this by suggesting that continued use will undermine your client's ability to maintain good health and that the results might have been even better if she were not drinking or using drugs.

For such clients, you might also choose to address in detail the issue of toler-ance. For example, a careful reframing of tolerance is particularly effective if your client has observed that she is less affected by alcohol than she used to be. Ask her what she sees as the advantages and disadvantages of this change. Having acknowledged these pros and cons, you might then ask whether she is aware of the physical implications of tolerance. Explain to her that the effects caused by alcohol are often warning signals that she has drunk too much. With increasing tolerance, however, she might not register these warning signals and will continue to drink even though she may have reached a physically harmful level. It might help to draw an analogy with the way in which pain is a kind of warning signal to prevent a person from further damaging their body.

Motivational Interventions in a Group Setting

Within the group setting, a number of motivational interviewing strategies can be used although it is unlikely that they will be as powerful as when used in the individual setting. For example, a consideration of the 'good' and 'less good' things might be brainstormed on a group level with home practice exercises involving each individual client writing down personally relevant issues in a decision matrix. An example of a matrix is found at the end of this chapter. It requires that clients examine the pros and cons of both change and continued drug use. Remember, when setting such a home practice exercise, you should instruct your clients to focus on those positive and negative issues that are really of concern to them. Otherwise they might simply tote up all the pros and cons while remaining emotionally unmoved.

SUMMARY

Miller and Rollnick (1991; pp. 56–62) have outlined and summarised the five broad clinical principles that underlie motivational interviewing. They are:

- Express empathy:
  Acceptance and respect for your client's position facilitates change.
  Skilful reflective listening is fundamental.
  Ambivalence is normal.
- Develop discrepancy:
  A discrepancy between present behaviour and important goals will motivate change.
  The client should present the arguments for change.
- Avoid argumentation:
  Arguments are counter-productive.
  Defending breeds defensiveness.
  Resistance is a signal to change strategies.
- Roll with client resistance:
  Statements that a client makes can be reframed slightly to create a new momentum towards change.
- Support the client's sense of ability to change:
  Belief in the possibility of change is an important motivator.
  The client is responsible for choosing and carrying out personal change.
  There is hope in the range of alternative approaches available.

RESOURCES LIST

Miller, W.R. (1983). Motivational interviewing with problem drinkers. *Behavioural Psychotherapy*, **11**, 147–172.
—This is the original and still one of the best descriptions of the principles of motivational interviewing.
Miller, W.R. (1985). Motivation for treatment: A review with special emphasis on alcoholism. *Psychological Bulletin*, **98**, 84–107.
—Also excellent background reading in this area.
Miller, W.R. (1989). Increasing motivation for change. In: R.K. Hester & W.R. Miller (Eds) *Handbook of Alcoholism Treatment Approaches: Effective Alternatives*, (pp. 67–80). New York: Pergamon.
—A brief summary of the approach.
Miller, W.R. & Rollnick, S. (1991). *Motivational Interviewing: Preparing People to Change Addictive Behavior*. New York: Guilford Press.
—This book provides an excellent and detailed account of the principles and practices of motivational interviewing. Chapters cover in detail the application of the approach to various types of clients and problems. We have drawn particularly on the following chapters: Baker, A. & Dixon, J., Motivational interviewing for HIV risk reduction (Chapter 22); Rollnick, S. & Bell, A., Brief motivational interviewing for use by the non-specialist (Chapter 14); Saunders, B., Wilkinson, C. & Allsop, S., Motivational intervention with heroin users attending a methadone clinic (Chapter 21). For further information concerning the personalised feedback of assessment information you can also refer to Using Assessment Results (Chapter 7).
Miller, W.R., Zweben, A., DiClemente, C.C. & Rychtarik, R.G. (1992). *Motivational Enhancement Therapy Manual: A Clinical Research Guide for Therapists Treating Individuals with Alcohol Abuse and Dependence*. Project MATCH Monograph Series, Volume 2. Rockville, MD: National Institute on Alcohol Abuse and Alcoholism.
—A session-by-session manual based largely on material from the book above.
Rollnick, S., Heather, N. & Bell, A. (1992). Negotiating behaviour change in medical settings: The development of brief motivational interviewing. *Journal of Mental Health*, **1**, 25–37.
—An extremely useful 'how to' article, particularly in the context of medical settings and brief interventions.
Saunders, B., Wilkinson, C. & Allsop, S. (1991). In Miller & Rollnick (1991) above.

Clinical Demonstration Videotapes

Mason, P. (1989). *Managing Drink*. UK: Aquarius.
—Available from the Centre for Education and Information on Drugs and Alcohol, PMB6, PO Rozelle 2039, NSW, Australia.
Miller, W.R. (1990).*Motivational Interviewing*. Albuquerque: University of New Mexico.
—Available from the Department of Psychology, University of New Mexico, Albuquerque, NM 87131, USA. European format available from the National Drug and Alcohol Research Centre, University of New South Wales, Sydney, 2052, NSW, Australia.
Rollnick, S. & Bell, A. (1991). *Motivational Interviewing: A Selection of Core Strategies*.
—Produced for training purposes only by the Centre for Education and Information on Drugs and Alcohol, PMB 6, PO Rozelle 2039, NSW, Australia.

A Decisional Balance Sheet

Here is an example . . .

Continuing to drink without change		Making a change to my drinking	
Pros	**Cons**	**Pros**	**Cons**
Helps me escape	Could lose my	Happier marriage	How to cope?
I like getting high	marriage	Helps money problems	Lose drinking mates
	Bad example for the	Time for kids	
	kids	Improve my health	
	Spend too much	Enjoy work more	
	Wrecking my health		
	Might lose my job		
	Feel awful		

Fill in your pros and cons below. Don't worry if they seem to contradict each other. The important thing is that they show how you see *your situation at the moment.*

Continuing to drink without change		Making a change to my drinking	
Pros	**Cons**	**Pros**	**Cons**

Source: Adapted from Miller & Rollnick (1991).

4

GOAL-SETTING

BASIC GUIDELINES

Goal-setting is an important process that applies the information that has been derived from assessment and lays down a mutually agreed plan for the direction of treatment. By explaining the various options in plain language, you can assist your client to make a responsible decision about his own welfare. The ideal style for negotiating treatment goals with your client is motivational interviewing, which was discussed in Chapter 3. It is also important to prepare your client for the possibility that the strategies and goals he has chosen might not work out as planned. He needs to understand that the treatment process can involve some trial and error in order to identify the plan that fits best with his personal needs.

Your goals should provide you and your client with *concrete* signposts to guide therapy and to measure progress over time. At the same time, your goals need to be flexible enough to allow adjustment to new information gained during the course of treatment. Ideally your goals should have the following characteristics:

- *Negotiated:* All goals should be negotiated between you and your client. This ensures that (a) your client is committed to the goals since he was instrumental in defining them and (b) the goals also reflect your professional judgement.
- *Specific and observable:* Each goal should be defined in concrete, behavioural terms so that both you and your client will be able to identify clearly whether that goal has been achieved. For example, 'cutting down gradually' is a vague term that cannot be clearly measured. 'Cutting down by 3 standard drinks a week' can be measured, leaving no doubt about treatment progress. You may find it useful to make a written summary of your client's goals and plans so that you can both measure his progress throughout therapy. An example of a 'Change plan sheet' designed by Miller, Zweben, DiClemente and Rychtarik (1992) is reproduced in the Practice Sheet at the end of this chapter.

- *Broken into short-term targets:* Working towards a large, major goal can be daunting for clients, particularly those who have experienced a sense of failure during past attempts at changing their drug use or drinking. If goals can be broken down into smaller targets, your client can develop a sense of mastery and encouragement as each target is reached. The experience of achievement will help to enhance your client's self-esteem and increase his motivation to continue in the treatment process.

While it is easy to see how the overall goals of moderation or reduced HIV risk-taking can be broken into smaller targets, the application of short-term targets to the goal of abstinence is less obvious since abstinence is usually achieved by immediate cessation of your client's drinking or drug using. Nevertheless, there may be a number of lifestyle changes that are required to help your client maintain abstinence and it will be easier for your client to manage these if they are broken down into prioritised targets.

- *Achievable:* Negotiation should focus on identifying goals that are achievable. Sometimes it may be necessary for you to compromise your expectations about the ideal goal if your client appears to be unable to achieve that goal at this stage. Success with less ambitious goals is preferable to your client experiencing a sense of total failure and dropping out of treatment as a result.

(Derived from West Australian Alcohol and Drug Authority, undated)

The later parts of this chapter describe goals concerning alcohol use and opiate/polydrug use. These *primary* goals should be the focus of your treatment. However, regardless of the type of substance that your client uses, he may also need help to improve his general lifestyle. Some lifestyle issues will need to be addressed before proceeding with treatment. For example, your client may need immediate assistance with detoxification, finding accommodation, stabilising financial income, or finding refuge from a violent family situation. Other issues might be less urgent but if left unaddressed throughout the course of treatment, they could undermine your client's progress towards a change in his drug or alcohol use.

GOALS TO IMPROVE LIFESTYLE

Clients who misuse alcohol and other drugs are also likely to have problems in other areas of their lives. These problems could have preceded and contributed to the drug dependence. For example, a client might be self-medicating to deal with psychological distress such as depression, post-traumatic stress or social phobia. Psychological discomfort or disturbances are very common among drug-using populations but it is not always clear whether the psychological disturbance preceded or resulted from the substance misuse. For many clients the substance use will have led to major disruptions in social, legal, psychological and/or financial stability. Your client may have structured his whole lifestyle around access to his favourite substance. These issues are therefore important to consider during the goal-setting process. Some issues can be dealt with in your treatment programme while others may best be addressed via referral to or liaison with specialist agencies, such as mental health, welfare and legal services. Potential areas for concern and suggested interventions are summarised in Table 1.

Table 1: Lifestyle treatment goals

AREA OF CLIENT'S LIFE	INTERVENTION
Family and relationships	Marital therapy, assistance for family members, specialist family therapy, parenting skills, childcare assistance, intervention for domestic violence or sexual abuse
Employment	Vocational assistance, skills-building, training in job interviews, financial aid, incentives to seek alternatives to drug-related crime
Legal	Legal advice, court liaison
Housing	Housing assistance, residential care
Psychological state	Therapy or treatment for psychological problems such as anxiety, depression, anti-social behaviour or trauma related to sexual abuse
Physical health	Medical treatment including detoxification, nutritional assistance, advice on dental health, respite care, exercise, assistance for pregnant women
Social functioning	Communication skills training, assertiveness training, drug-free social support networks (e.g. self-help groups)

GOALS CONCERNING ALCOHOL USE

There are three possible goals in the treatment of alcohol problems and these are described in Table 2.

As discussed above, these overall goals can be broken into smaller targets. For example, if the goal is moderation, you might want to begin by eliminating especially risky behaviours such as drinking while driving, heavy drinking binges or drinking in certain contexts. These issues are discussed at length in Chapter 11, *Behavioural Self-management*.

	Table 2: Alcohol-related treatment goals
GOAL	DESCRIPTION
Abstinence	Client quits drinking
Moderated drinking	Client moderates drinking to harm-free levels that reduce the risk of physical, personal or social problems that drinking may be causing. These levels are often guided by recommendations from health authorities. For more information, see Chapter 11, *Behavioural Self-management*
Attenuated/reduced drinking	For some clients, a reduction of drinking will help to reduce the harm to self or family. This is not an ideal goal but may be the only feasible goal for some clients

Choosing between Abstinence and Moderation

In addition to your client's personal preference, consider the following guidelines when choosing between abstinence and moderation:

- *Organic damage:* When physical damage has already occurred as a result of drinking, continued drinking is likely to further aggravate such damage. For example, a client who has liver or bone marrow dysfunction, pancreatitis or peptic ulceration should be directed towards abstinence.
- *Organic brain damage or cognitive dysfunction:* Abstinence is the preferred option for brain-damaged clients because continued drinking will aggravate existing cognitive dysfunction. Clients with brain dysfunction can also experience difficulty in learning the coping skills required for a moderated drinking goal.
- *Psychiatric comorbidity:* Abstinence may be the preferred treatment goal if your client has persistent psychiatric disorders such as anxiety, depression or personality disorder. These disorders should be addressed before deciding in favour of moderation.
- *Physical withdrawal:* If withdrawal has been frequent and/or severe (e.g. your client has had delirium tremens), then abstinence may be indicated.
- *Severity of alcohol dependence:* Abstinence is appropriate for clients with a high severity of dependence while less dependent clients may be able to moderate their drinking successfully.
- *History of drinking:* If your client has had repeated unsuccessful attempts at moderating his alcohol intake with professional assistance, then he may find the goal of abstinence more achievable. On the other hand, any evidence that your client has been able to control his drinking in some situations favours

the moderation goal. In circumstances where a drinker has repeatedly been unable to comply with abstinence, a moderation goal may be worth considering as an alternative, provided that there is no alcohol-related organic damage that would be aggravated by further drinking.

- *Social support:* If there are people within your client's social network whose usual level of drinking is light to moderate, this could provide a supportive setting for him to learn moderation. If, however, your client has based his social life around the pub scene and other heavy drinkers, the social support network may not be conducive to moderation. This client is more likely to benefit from a restructuring of his social network around support for abstinence such as is provided by Alcoholics Anonymous (see Chapter 15, *Self-help Groups*).
- *Partner's preference:* You might also need to consider the preferences of your client's partner and family members. For instance, your client's partner may have specific concerns about any repercussions from his continued drinking. The support provided by your client's partner, family members and friends for the treatment goal is also going to be an important contributor to outcome.

These factors are not hard and fast rules but are useful guidelines to discuss with your client during the decision-making process. *The guidelines will help you to arrive at a treatment goal that is attainable, safe and desirable.*

Trouble-shooting

Occasionally you and your client might disagree with the suitability of the goal that he has chosen. For instance, despite a high severity of problems associated with drinking, your client might want to aim for a goal of moderation whereas you might feel that abstinence is more appropriate. There are several ways that you could choose to deal with this difference of opinion. The following options have been derived from the work of Miller (1989). You might choose to:

(1) Decline to help your client toward his goal. You might select this option if you feel that it would be unethical for you to support your client's chosen goal. This decision might be best weighed up after considering the possibility of option 2.
(2) Accept your client's chosen goal on a provisional basis or make a compromise. For example, Miller and Page (in press; cited by Miller & Rollnick, 1991) have described three options that they called 'warm turkey' to contrast them with immediate abstinence or 'cold turkey'. These options are:

    (a) A negotiated period of trial abstinence. For example, if your client wants to try for moderation, suggest that a six-month period of abstinence would be an advantage before an attempt at moderation. The abstinent period provides time-out for your client to recover from the physical effects of the alcohol and to deal with any other problems related to his heavy drinking. Negotiate an agreement to review the treatment goals at the end of this time-out period.

(b) A gradual tapering of consumption down towards abstinence. To achieve this you will need to set realistic, intermediate goals and provide your client with a 'day diary' for self-monitoring his drinking, such as the one provided in Chapter 11, *Behavioural Self-management*.

(c) A period of trial moderation. For example, your client may want to test out whether or not he is able to learn how to drink in moderation. If, despite having appropriate skills training, he has found that moderation is too difficult to achieve, abstinence may then seem a more reasonable goal.

(3) Try to coerce your client to change his goal. You might choose this option if you feel that you are obliged or able to protect your client from an otherwise risky decision. This approach, however, may be counter-productive if your client becomes defensive and uncooperative. It is also likely to undermine the collaboration that you have so far achieved.

Even when you and your client agree from the outset about what the goal is to be, your negotiations should continue throughout the course of treatment as you regularly review your client's progress towards those goals.

A Menu of Strategies—Alcohol

Once you and your client have agreed upon a treatment goal, you will need to decide on the preferable strategies for achieving that goal. Provide your client with a menu of strategies from which to choose and discuss with him the relevance of each to his situation. A list of potential strategies is found in Table 3 and these are described in Parts II and III of this book.

GOALS CONCERNING OPIATE/POLYDRUG USE

From a harm-reduction perspective, the ideal goal is abstinence from drug use. However, where total abstinence is unrealistic, you and your client will need to consider methods for reducing drug use and associated drug-related harm (e.g. HIV risk-taking behaviours).

Table 3:   Alcohol-related treatment options

STRATEGIES FOR	
MODERATION OR ABSTINENCE	ABSTINENCE ONLY
Problem-solving skills training	Antabuse
Drink-refusal skills training	Covert sensitisation
Assertiveness training	AA and other self-help groups
Communication skills training	
Cognitive restructuring	
Relaxation training	
Behavioural self-management	
Couples therapy	
Relapse prevention	

Abstinence from Drug Use

The most common setting for treatment aimed at a drug-free lifestyle is the therapeutic community. Most clients will have strong preferences about whether or not they wish to pursue drug-free treatment. Empathic counselling and the skills-based approaches outlined in this book are extremely applicable to this setting. As many of these skills are most effectively taught in groups, the structure of therapeutic communities is ideally suited for this training.

As an alternative to drug-free treatment, methadone maintenance can provide a means of achieving abstinence or a reduction of illicit drug use. This intervention can stabilise your client's illicit opioid use, with associated reductions in criminal activity and risk of infection with HIV and Hepatitis B and C. Ward, Mattick and Hall (1992) have recommended that a client's suitability for methadone maintenance should be based not only on his level of dependence but also on the risks associated with his lifestyle and current health. For further information about methadone maintenance, the book by Ward and his colleagues (1992) provides a discussion of the key issues involved.

Reduction of Drug-related Harm

Harm reduction is especially concerned with reducing the risk of infection with the human immunodeficiency virus (HIV) and other infectious diseases related to drug use and lifestyle, such as hepatitis and other sexually transmitted diseases. The promotion of safer practices in drug use and sexual behaviour should be addressed in all types of settings. It could be a main goal of treatment if your client is likely to continue to use illicit drugs or be included as part of relapse-prevention training within drug-free programmes.

To teach your client effectively about harm reduction, you need to be clear about your own goal as a therapist. For instance, if part of your role is to 'police' your client's illicit drug use, your client may fear that talking honestly with you about his drug use is going to have an adverse effect on him within the programme. Ward, Mattick and Hall (1992) have suggested that policing and counselling should be carried out by two different workers, making it possible for you, as the therapist, to take a non-judgemental attitude when negotiating harm-reduction goals. It may also help to explain to your client that working towards harm reduction does not mean that you are condoning his continued illicit drug use.

Goals for reducing unsafe injecting practices

The following continuum of drug-using behaviours reads from the least to the most reduction in risk of HIV and hepatitis. You may wish to help your client identify attainable goals using this continuum:

(1) Sharing injection equipment but decontaminating effectively for HIV
(2) Only using new needles or sterile syringes for injection
(3) Taking illicit drugs without injecting
(4) Abstinence from illicit drug use

Goals for reducing unsafe sexual practices

Sexual practices can also be ranged in a hierarchy from those most likely to permit HIV transmission if one partner is infected (e.g. unprotected anal inter-course) to those that carry little risk (e.g. mutual masturbation). Safe sex is any sex where semen or pre-cum, blood or vaginal fluid cannot get into the blood-stream of the other person.

Safe sex means . . .

- Always using condoms and water-based lubricant for penises and sex toys, with vaginal or anal sex.
- Taking special care with condoms in anal sex.
- Cleaning sex toys before reusing (dildos, dolls etc.).
- Using gloves and lubricants in manual sex where there are cuts or sores on the hands.

- Avoiding menstrual blood when engaging in oral sex with women, if the mouth has cuts or sores (dental dams can be used).
- Engaging in self-masturbation, kissing and hugging, frottage (rubbing), or Spanish (between the breasts).
- Having sex with only one partner in an exclusively monogamous relationship after both people have had negative HIV test results and when they do not share fits or injecting equipment.
- Having no sex.

(Derived from CEIDA, 1991; Handout No. 9, p. 2)

A Menu of Strategies—Other Drugs

Most of the strategies used in the treatment of alcohol problems can also be used in the treatment of opiate/polydrug dependence. They can be used to assist clients to achieve a drug-free lifestyle, reduction in drug use, or reduction in risky needle-sharing and sexual practices. Techniques that are likely to have particular relevance are listed below:

- *Refusal skills and assertiveness training:* These will teach your client to refuse drugs and unsafe drug-use or sexual behaviour.
- *Other skills training:* This helps your client to enhance his communication skills and ability to solve problems.
- *Cognitive restructuring:* This challenges destructive thought processes and enhances self-esteem.
- *Relaxation training:* Will provide your client with an alternative way of dealing with anxiety, and a method for managing cravings.
- *Relapse prevention:* Will help your client to recognise and deal with situations in which he is likely to relapse to drug use or unsafe practices.
- *Self-help groups:* Groups such as Narcotics Anonymous provide support and assist your client in pursuing the goal of abstinence.

RESOURCES LIST

Australian I.V. League (1992). *Handy Hints.* Sydney: Social Change Media.
   —Produced by users for users, this booklet provides information about safe sexual and injecting practices. It also gives listings of services for Australian clients. For further information write to the Australian I.V. League via the Australian Federation of AIDS Organisations, Level 8, 33 Bligh St, Sydney 2000, NSW, Australia.
CEIDA (1991). *Educating Clients about HIV/AIDS.* Sydney: CEIDA.
   —A handbook for running educational programmes, including clear, informative handouts for clients. For copies write to the Centre for Education and Information on Drugs and Alcohol, PMB 6, PO Rozelle 2039, NSW, Australia.

Heather, N. & Robertson, I. (1983). *Controlled Drinking* (Rev. edn). New York: Methuen.
—Chapter 9 provides an extensive discussion of guidelines for deciding between abstinence and moderation goals.

Heather, N. & Robertson, I. (1989). *Problem Drinking* (2nd edn). Oxford: Oxford University Press.
—This classic text includes a discussion of the goals of abstinence and moderation and presents evidence supporting the use of skills-based approaches in treatment for alcohol problems.

Kelly, J.A., St. Lawrence, J.S., Betts, R., Brasfield, T.L. & Hood, H.V. (1990). A skills-training group intervention model to assist persons in reducing risk behaviors for HIV infection. *AIDS Education and Prevention*, **2** (1), 24–35.
—Practical guidelines for helping clients to reduce unsafe sexual practices.

Mattick, R.P. & Hall, W. (1993). *A Treatment Outline for Approaches to Opioid Dependence: Quality Assurance in the Treatment of Drug Dependence Project*, National Campaign Against Drug Abuse monograph series No. 21. Canberra, Australia: Australian Government Publishing Service.
—Reviews the research literature on the treatment of opioid dependence and makes recommendations regarding appropriate goals and intervention.

Mattick, R. P. & Jarvis, T. J. (1993). *An Outline for the Management of Alcohol Problems: Quality Assurance in the Treatment of Drug Dependence Project*. National Campaign Against Drug Abuse monograph series No. 20. Canberra, Australia: Australian Government Publishing Service.
—Provides both guidelines for setting goals and recommendations for the treatment of alcohol problems.

Miller, W.R. (1989). Matching individuals with interventions. In Hester, R.K. & Miller, W.R., *Handbook of Alcoholism Treatment Approaches: Effective Alternatives*. New York: Pergamon.
—Introduces the concept of 'matching'. This is where information from assessment is used to match different clients to different types of interventions.

Miller, W.R. & Rollnick, S. (1991). *Motivational Interviewing: Preparing People to Change Addictive Behavior*. New York: Guilford Press.
—Guidelines for negotiating goals and plans for action are discussed in Chapter 9: Phase II: Strengthening commitment to change.

Miller, W.R., Zweben, D.S.W., DiClemente, C.C. & Rychtarik, R.G. (1992). *Motivational Enhancement Therapy Manual: A Clinical Research Guide for Therapists Treating Individuals with Alcohol Abuse and Dependence, Project MATCH Monograph Series, Volume 2*. Rockville, MD: National Institute on Alcohol Abuse and Alcoholism.
—'Phase 2' of this session-by-session manual provides a motivational interviewing approach to strengthening commitment and setting goals.

Ward, J., Mattick, R. & Hall, W. (1992). *Key Issues in Methadone Maintenance Treatment*. Sydney: New South Wales University Press.
—A summary of methadone maintenance treatment research and clinical issues across a range of areas including dose, duration, ancillary services, methadone in pregnancy, reduction of infectious disease, and aftercare.

West Australian Alcohol and Drug Authority (Undated). *Short term goal setting*.
—A workshop paper about goal-setting.

PRACTICE SHEET

CHANGE PLAN SHEET

The changes I want to make are:

The most important reasons why I want to make these changes are:

The steps I plan to take in changing are:

The ways other people can help me are:

People   Possible ways to help

I will know that my plan is working if:

Some things that could interfere with my plan are:

Source: From Miller *et al.* (1992).

II

STRATEGIES FOR ACTION

5

PROBLEM-SOLVING SKILLS

RECOMMENDED USE

Problem-solving training provides your client with a general skill that will enable her to resolve life problems that might threaten her commitment to change her drinking or drug use. It is appropriate for all clients whether they have abstinence, moderation or harm-reduction goals, and for any type of drug problem. Problem-solving can be taught in either a group or an individual setting although learning is probably facilitated by working in a group of two or more clients.

You can probably teach the basics of problem-solving in one or two sessions. However, the skill requires practice to be effectively learnt. Therefore problem-solving strategies should be practised, refined and reinforced over the remaining course of treatment both in session time and with home practice exercises.

GOALS

The goals of problem-solving skills training are to enable your client to:

- Recognise when a problem exists
- Generate a variety of potential solutions to the problem
- Select the most appropriate option and generate a plan for enacting it
- Be able to evaluate the effectiveness of the selected approach

METHOD

Rationale for Your Client

Monti, Abrams, Kadden and Cooney (1989) suggested that you should offer the following rationale for your client. Discuss the way in which people are constantly faced with difficult situations as part of daily life. Difficult situations can either be drug- or alcohol-specific (e.g. being in a group where drugs are available) or more general (e.g. conflict at work). They can arise as a result of individual thoughts or feelings (e.g. depressing thoughts or strong desires to use drugs) or in the course of interactions with others (e.g. arguments). Point out that if a person is unable to deal effectively with such situations as they arise they can become problematic. Emphasise that too often we tend simply either to ignore a problem or to respond with the easiest or first impulsive reaction. However, pressure from an unsolved or poorly solved problem can build up and may well trigger a relapse to drug or alcohol use. You might like to get your client to generate some examples from her experience of when unresolved problems have triggered a relapse. You can then explain that effective problem-solving involves your client being able to recognise a problem situation and to take some time to work out an effective solution that will be in her own best interest.

Before Starting

It is probably useful to prepare a brief summary sheet of the strategy of problem-solving to give to your client. An example is provided in the first client handout at the end of this chapter. It is also useful, if possible, to have a whiteboard on which to record your client's brainstorming. In addition, your client should be encouraged to write down examples of the problem-solving process so that she can refer to them later.

The Process of Problem-solving

There are six stages to effective problem-solving.

(1) Defining *exactly* what the problem is
(2) Brainstorming options to deal with the problem
(3) Choosing the best option(s)
(4) Generating a detailed action plan
(5) Putting the plan into action
(6) Evaluating the results

Defining *exactly* what the problem is

If a problem is well defined, it almost solves itself! However, if the problem is understood only in vague terms, it remains almost impossible to solve. This is because it is unclear what *exactly* the problem is. Therefore, try to define the problem in terms of concrete behaviours that your client can modify. It also helps to break it down into specific parts.

For example, a global problem such as 'My life is out of control' is overwhelming. However, that problem might be broken down into the following more specific problems: (a) I'm lonely because I've lost contact with many of my friends; (b) I feel unattractive because I've gained a lot of weight recently; (c) My job is extremely stressful and unsatisfying; and (d) My boyfriend complains that I don't spend enough time with him. These problems can then be prioritised and the problem-solving technique applied to each. You can help your client clarify and/or break down global problems by careful listening and asking a series of questions such as 'What specific sorts of things happen that make you feel that way?' or 'When exactly do you feel that way?'

Have your client select a problem situation. A relatively easy 'high-risk situation' is a good place to start if these have been identified (see Chapter 16, *Relapse-Prevention Training*). Help her to frame that problem clearly in concrete behavioural terms. If necessary, get her to break it down into manageable subproblems and help her to decide the order in which these subproblems will be tackled.

Trouble shooting

For some clients, recognising when a problem exists may be the most difficult part of problem-solving! Monti *et al.* (1989) offer a number of clues for helping clients to identify situations where there may be a problem. These include occasions when your client is aware of: (a) unpleasant physical signs (e.g. craving); (b) negative feelings (e.g. depression, frustration, fear, annoyance); (c) negative reactions from other people (e.g. avoidance, criticism); (d) negative reactions to other people (e.g. anger, withdrawal); and (e) not meeting her own expectations of her behaviour (e.g. performance at work, at home or with friends).

You might also help your client to decide whether a problem area is worth focusing on by getting her to consider how comfortably she could continue to live with the problem and what the consequences would be if the problem were not resolved.

Brainstorming options to deal with the problem

Brainstorming is a technique for generating ideas. There are several rules that help this technique to work.

- *No criticism allowed.* Criticism stifles creativity. The options will be evaluated at a later stage.

- Be as wild, woolly and adventurous as possible—*any* idea is acceptable. The freer your client is the greater the chance that she might hit on a good novel solution.
- Quantity of ideas is important. The more alternatives there are the more likely a useful alternative will emerge. Often the best ideas come later in the brainstorming process.
- Think about solutions that have worked before. An old solution might have to be updated and changed but it can provide a good starting point. Ideas can also be combined or added to in the search for a solution. Your client could ask others for suggestions of what has worked for them in similar situations. She should also be encouraged to think about what she might suggest to a friend facing the same problem.

Brainstorming can work particularly well in a group setting and is often helped if you can start the process by suggesting several options among which are funny or outrageous solutions. Group exercises should involve working on at least one personally relevant problem for each of your clients in turn.

Trouble-shooting

Sometimes it can be difficult for a client to brainstorm effective options if she has not defined the problem in terms of a behaviour she can modify: e.g. 'My father bugs me' compared to 'I get annoyed by my father and I get sarcastic'.

Choosing the best option(s)

Begin by deleting any strategies that are obviously impractical. Work through the remaining options by considering the pros and cons of each. The pros and cons can include both the short- and long-term consequences of a choice. Also get your client to consider what factors might either hinder or help her in putting each option successfully into practice. After weighing up these factors get your client to choose the alternative(s) that she considers to be the most realistic and most likely to be effective.

If you are working with clients in pairs or in larger groups make sure that each client selects her own best solution to a problem. A solution selected by the group may not ultimately be the best or most relevant for the individual concerned.

Generating a detailed action plan

It is important to generate a detailed and concrete plan for putting the selected option into action. This may also involve breaking down the solution into achievable steps. For example, if a solution to a problem was to 'take up a new sport', then the action plan should include deciding what sport, then how to find out where and when to join up, and finally setting a date for the first game. In other words the plan should consider the timetable for action along with the 'when, where, how, and with whom', of the selected option.

Putting the plan into action

Your client should at least think through, that is mentally rehearse, her plan. In learning problem-solving skills it is also extremely useful, where appropriate, to practise carrying out the plan by using a role-play (as described on p. 11) in session. Home practice exercises can involve putting the plan into action as it was practised in the session.

Evaluating the results

Think carefully about whether the selected option resolved the problem totally or only in part. If it was partly or not at all successful, consider whether the action plan needed improving (go back to stage 4) or whether a new strategy is needed (go back to stage 3).

A worked example of problem-solving is shown in the second client handout at the end of this chapter, together with a home practice sheet.

RESOURCES LIST

D'Zurilla, T.J. & Goldfried, M.R. (1971). Problem solving and behavior modification. *Journal of Abnormal Psychology*, **78**, 107–126.
—This article provides the original and very useful description of the method of problem-solving.
Hawton, K. & Kirk, J. (1989). Problem solving. In K. Hawton, P.M. Salkovskis, J. Kirk & D.M. Clark (Eds), *Cognitive Behaviour for Psychiatric Problems: A Practical Guide* (pp. 406–426). Oxford: Oxford University Press.
—A general guide to problem-solving strategies.
Kadden, R., Carroll, K., Donovan, D., Cooney, N., Monti, P., Abrams, D., Litt, M. & Hester, R. (1992). *Cognitive Behavioral Coping Skills Therapy Manual: A Clinical Research Guide for Therapists Treating Individuals with Alcohol Abuse and Dependence. Project MATCH Monograph Series, Volume 3*. Rockville, MD: National Institute on Alcohol Abuse and Alcoholism.
—This session-by-session manual devotes one session to problem-solving, based on guidelines from the book by Monti *et al.*, below.
Monti, P.M., Abrams, D.B., Kadden, R.M. & Cooney, N.L (1989). *Treating Alcohol Dependence: A Coping Skills Training Guide* (pp. 83–87). New York: Guilford Press.
—A comprehensive section on problem-solving is provided.

SIX STEPS TO
SUCCESSFUL PROBLEM-SOLVING

(1) **Define *exactly* what the problem is.**
Make sure the problem is concrete and if necessary broken down into several subproblems.

(2) **Brainstorm options to deal with the problem.**
Remember—no criticism allowed—be adventurous!

(3) **Choose the best option(s) by examining the pros and cons of each potential solution.**
Which solution will work best?

(4) **Generate a detailed action plan.**
Plan the 'when, where, how and with whom' of the selected solution.

(5) **Put the plan into action.**
Role-play or mentally rehearse the plan and then actually carry it out.

(6) **Evaluate the results to see how well the selected solution worked.**
If the solution didn't work go back to stage 3 and try again!

PROBLEM-SOLVING EXAMPLE

Stage 1:   **My problem is:**

I have few friends and it's easy for me to start feeling lonely and depressed—especially in the evenings and on weekends. When I feel lonely, I usually try to drown my sorrows with beer.

Stage 2:   **Brainstorm possible solutions**

Join a club or a class in something that interests me.
Use personal ads or dating service to meet new people.
Join a gym or take up t'ai chi.
Get a dog!
Go out to discos to meet people.
Stop living alone and look for share accommodation.
Don't dwell on past missed opportunities.

Stage 3:   **Pros and cons of each solution.**

Possible solution	Pros	Cons
Go to discos	I like dancing	Risk of drinking
Move house	I'd have company at home I'd meet my flatmate's friends	It costs time and money to change accommodation
Join a club or attend a class	Would meet people who share my interests	I'm worried that I won't know what to say or I'll embarrass myself

. . . and the winner is: join a club or attend a class

Stage 4:   **What's my plan?**

How?	To find out what clubs or classes are available locally that might interest me. My interests: cooking, reading, dancing. I've always wanted to try painting.
When?	Find out the information before the next session.
Where?	Look in Saturday's paper. Ring up the local school or council. Get them to send me details about time, place and price.
With whom?	I'll go to the club or class alone but my therapist will help me practise some conversational skills before my first attendance.

PROBLEM-SOLVING

Stage 1:   **My problem is:**

Stage 2:   **Brainstorm possible solutions**

Stage 3:   **Pros and cons of each solution**

Possible solution   Pros   Cons

. . . and the winner(s) is/are _____

Stage 4:   **What's my plan?**
How?

When?

Where?

With whom?

Stage 5:   **Carrying out my plan.**

Stage 6:   **How well did it work?**

6

DRINK- AND DRUG-REFUSAL SKILLS

RECOMMENDED USE

All clients face situations where they experience social pressure to drink or use drugs. Drink- and drug-refusal training teaches clients how to refuse offers with confidence and without making limp excuses! It can be an invaluable tool for helping to prevent relapses for clients with abstinence goals (see Chapter 16, *Relapse-prevention Training*). Alternatively, it can be helpful in assisting clients with moderation goals to keep to predetermined limits in the face of temptation to over-drink (see Chapter 11, *Behavioural Self-management*). These refusal skills can also be easily adapted to help clients with harm-reduction goals avoid risk-taking behaviours such as needle-sharing and unsafe sexual practices.

In short, you should routinely offer this refusal training to clients who indicate a lack of confidence in dealing with social pressure to drink, use drugs and/or engage in risk-taking behaviours. You can teach the skills on an individual basis although a group setting can be particularly effective because clients learn from each other in role-play activities.

GOALS

To teach your client to refuse offers to drink or use drugs in an appropriately assertive way.

METHOD

Rationale for Your Client

Explain to your client that almost everyone, at some time, will be placed in a situation where he is offered drinks or drugs. If your client has chosen to abstain, point out that he will find it impossible to *permanently* avoid all the situations (e.g. restaurants or social functions) where he might be offered a drink or drugs. If your client has chosen moderation as his goal, explain that refusal skills can help him keep to his planned limits.

For all clients, acknowledge that saying 'no thanks' convincingly and confidently can often be difficult and explain that there are a number of strategies that can make saying 'no' easier. These include using appropriate body language, sounding confident and, of course, using direct statements to refuse the offer.

It is also important to stress to your client that there is absolutely no need for him to feel guilty about not drinking or using! In their work, Monti, Abrams, Kadden and Cooney (1989; p. 62) reminded clients that 'You have a right not to drink'. For clients with drinking problems it is also useful to point out that in many social situations people don't even notice who is or isn't drinking alcohol.

Having covered these important basics with your client you can then go on to teach the key elements of a successful refusal. These are drawn from the section on drink refusal by Monti *et al.* (1989) in their book referenced in the *Resources List*.

Body Language

Explain that feeling unsure or anxious about refusing offers of alcohol or drugs often leads people to slouch or hunch and avoid looking at the other person. Discuss with your client how such body language actually further decreases self-confidence and sends a timid and unconvincing message to the person offering the drink or drug(s). Therefore one of the first crucial hints for making refusals 'stick' is to *make direct eye contact* with the drink or drug 'pusher'. Standing or sitting straight also helps to create a confident air.

Tone of Voice

Again, a shy, uncertain tone will allow room for the other person to question the refusal. Therefore you should encourage your client to speak in a *firm and unhesitating* manner.

After covering these two 'rules', it might be very useful for you to model examples of 'wrong' and 'right' use of body language and tone of voice by having a client role-play offering you a drink or drug(s). By contrasting a timid with a confident approach you can provide a quite amusing but powerful demonstration of ineffective and effective ways of saying no!

What to Say

The following guidelines are based on Monti *et al.* (1989; p. 62):

(1) *Say 'no' first:* Explain to your client that when he hesitates to say 'no' people doubt that he means it. Therefore 'no thanks' are the best first words to come out of his mouth.

(2) *Suggest an alternative:* After saying 'no' then your client might:

   (a) suggest something else to do (e.g. going for a walk, to a coffee shop, or to the movies instead of going to a pub);
   (b) suggest something else to drink (e.g. coffee, orange juice) or to eat instead.

(3) *Request that the other person stop asking:* If the 'pusher' is being persistent your client should ask him to stop offering drinks or drugs. For example an offer like, 'Oh, go on, for old times sake, be a mate' might be met with 'If you want to be a mate, don't offer me a drink'.

(4) *Change the subject:* After refusing, your client should change the subject in order to avoid getting caught up in a long debate about drinking. For example: 'No, thanks, I'm not using. It's good to see you, I haven't seen you in ages. What are you doing these days?'

(5) *Avoid excuses and vague answers:* Explain to your client that in most cases it is better to try and avoid using excuses like 'I can't drink at the moment, I'm on antibiotics'. Such excuses can make it difficult to refuse in the future and are not really helpful for strengthening his new resolve to change. Being direct is generally the best course. Often just saying 'No thanks' in a firm fashion will be enough. At other times your client might find it useful to elaborate, for example 'I don't drink', 'My doctor advised me to quit', 'I am cutting down' or 'I decided to stop using, it wasn't doing me any good'.

After you have explained these principles get your client to describe a number of situations where, in the past, he had problems in refusing drinks or drugs. Choose one and begin by modelling an inappropriate way of responding. Have your client provide feedback about your performance in terms of your body language, tone and what you actually said. Get him to brainstorm more assertive and appropriate responses. Model the same situation again, this time with an effective response.

You should then ask your client to role-play (p. 11) a situation, either with you or with your other clients, if you are in a group setting. It will be important to have your client(s) practise being both a 'refuser' and a 'pusher'. Try to cover as wide a range of potential situations as possible but remember not to begin with the very difficult ones!

Trouble-shooting

As Monti *et al.* (1989) indicated, there will often be a temptation for clients who are the 'pushers' to get extremely enthusiastic in their task. This can sometimes be quite funny but it may be important to gently remind them that the point of the exercise is give each other a chance to learn how to respond effectively to realistically (not impossibly!) difficult situations.

RESOURCES LIST

Foy, D.W., Miller, P.M., Eisler, R.M. & O'Toole, D.H. (1976). Social-skills training to teach alcoholics to refuse drinks effectively. *Journal of Studies on Alcohol*, **37** (9), 1340–1345.
—An early description of drink-refusal training.
Kadden, R., Carroll, K., Donovan, D., Cooney, N., Monti, P., Abrams, D., Litt, M. & Hester, R. (1992). *Cognitive Behavioral Coping Skills Therapy Manual: A Clinical Research Guide for Therapists Treating Individuals with Alcohol Abuse and Dependence*. Project MATCH Monograph Series, Volume 3. Rockville, MD: National Institute on Alcohol Abuse and Alcoholism.
—This session-by-session manual devotes one session to drink-refusal skills, based on guidelines from the book by Monti et al., below.
Kelly, J. A., St. Lawrence, J. S., Betts, R., Brasfield, T. L. & Hood, H. V. (1990). A skills-training group intervention model to assist persons in reducing risk behaviors for HIV infection. *AIDS Education and Prevention*, **2**, 24–35.
—Applies refusal-skills training to the prevention of unsafe sexual practices.
Monti, P.M., Abrams, D.B., Kadden, R.M. & Cooney, N.L (1989). *Treating Alcohol Dependence: A Coping Skills Training Guide* (pp. 61–63). New York: Guilford Press.
—We have used their section on drink-refusal skills as our key resource for this chapter.

7

ASSERTIVENESS SKILLS

RECOMMENDED USE

Assertiveness training is recommended for clients who have particular difficulty in expressing their needs and emotions to others. For many clients, this inability to communicate openly and directly results in feelings of frustration, anger and distress which may contribute to a return to excessive drinking or drug use.

Assertiveness training is equally useful for clients who wish to cut down or abstain from alcohol, other drugs, or risk-taking behaviours. It may be helpful to teach assertiveness in conjunction with drink- or drug-refusal and/or communication-skills training (Chapters 6 and 8). Assertion skills need to be taught over four or more sessions depending on the pre-existing level of asser-tiveness of your client(s). Role-play is an essential part of learning assertiveness skills, making group settings ideal for teaching this technique.

GOALS

Assertiveness training does *not* aim to ensure that your client will always 'get what she wants'. Rather, the goals are to enable your client to:

- Recognise when she is being unassertive
- Develop a variety of ways of dealing appropriately with situations where the usual response is either under-assertive or aggressive
- Express personal needs, feelings and opinions in a way that she finds satis-factory and which can be clearly understood by others

KEY CONCEPTS

Assertiveness

Assertiveness is a method of expressing feelings, needs, wants and opinions, directly and honestly without hostility or rudeness. Being assertive means that, when she chooses to, your client can effectively communicate her view in a way which respects the rights of others.

Non-assertiveness

There are several types of non-assertive behaviour of which the two most common are under-assertion and aggression.

Passive under-assertion

Passive under-assertion is self-denying, inhibited behaviour which allows other people to make decisions or otherwise infringe on your client's rights. Passive clients tend not to let others know what they think or feel. This form of non-assertiveness often leads to feelings of frustration and resentment. For some clients, being under-assertive may result in their bottling up their feelings until they reach a point when they explode aggressively.

Aggression

Aggression is standing up for one's views, but with a disregard for the views or rights of others. Aggression often leads to an escalation of feelings of anger and hostility in your client. Alternately, after an aggressive outburst your client may feel guilty and ashamed of her behaviour. In both cases these strong negative emotions may increase the risk of a relapse to drug use or drinking.

Human Rights

It is important that your client becomes aware that she and others have basic human rights which should be respected in interpersonal situations. These rights, which define the framework for assertiveness, are listed at the end of this chapter.

METHOD

Rationale for Your Client

Begin by introducing the notion of assertiveness to your client. Assertiveness is often referred to as the ability to effectively express positive and negative emotions, thoughts and opinions in everyday situations. It is not a simple skill to master for those who have not practised it. Using the descriptions in *Key Concepts* (above), outline the advantages of being assertive and the disadvantages of being aggressive or under-assertive. In particular, stress that the non-assertive behaviours can lead to strong negative emotions and that such emotions tend to increase the likelihood of relapse to drinking or using drugs.

Explain to your client that assertiveness training involves learning how not to be 'put down' or taken advantage of by others and so will teach her how to acquire more choice and control over her life. This may in turn help to improve her self-esteem and self-respect. The areas focused on by assertiveness training include giving criticism, handling criticism, making requests and dealing with requests from other people, and giving and receiving compliments.

Before Starting

There are a number of self-help manuals and books which may provide both you and your client with helpful reading and practical exercises for learning assertiveness skills. Several of these are listed in the *Resources List* at the end of this chapter. No doubt a perusal of your local bookshop's self-help and psychology sections will yield further titles.

The Process of Assertiveness Training

There are a number of stages to teaching appropriate assertiveness. They are:

(1) Defining *exactly* what the problem is
(2) Discussing non-assertiveness
(3) Dispelling myths
(4) Deciding to change non-assertiveness
(5) Introducing the 'Bill of Rights'
(6) Putting assertiveness skills into practice
(7) Handling tricky situations

Defining *exactly* what the problem is

In defining what assertiveness is and is not, it is most useful to employ examples from your client's own experiences. Most clients can relatively easily generate situations in which they have been unable to express their feelings clearly and effectively. Have your client identify a number of situations where she was either aggressive or under-assertive. Write these examples down to use for practice exercises in later sessions.

Discussing non-assertiveness

Get your client to consider how her family members have handled difficult situations and conflict. It is often the case that we learn our way of relating to others from the people we have grown up with. Additionally, through her past relationships your client may have learnt that being assertive brings disapproval or punishment. Openly explore the reasons why your client may have become non-assertive with a view to highlighting the areas where she has the most difficulty, so that you can address these in therapy.

Dispelling myths

It is also common for those who are non-assertive to hold a number of faulty beliefs or myths about being assertive with others. These myths are important for you to address because they may be supporting your client's non-assertiveness.

Individuals will often believe that it is a virtue to be humble 'at all costs' and never to accept compliments. They may also believe that to be a good friend or family member, one has to constantly meet the needs of others and never be prepared to criticise anyone. For these individuals, the notion of expressing unhappiness about something to a friend is seen as a challenge to the friendship rather than as an appropriate way of expressing feelings.

Another common myth believed by non-assertive clients is that others should be able to know how they feel (without being told). Comments like 'He should have understood why I said that' are examples of this myth in action. Your client may often fail to get her needs met because of this mistaken assumption that other people are mind-readers.

Clients may also take on roles or responsibilities, and hold the belief that it is difficult or inappropriate for them to step outside these roles. Such beliefs may prevent your client from challenging a person or situation even though there may be personal costs in not doing so. This frequently happens in the workplace, for example, where your client may feel uncomfortable about asserting herself in a situation with the boss for fear that this would be construed as rudeness or disrespect. Similarly in family relationships, beliefs about 'the woman's role' might lead your client to feel frustrated and often exhausted, especially if she is attempting to cope with the pressures of her job as well as domestic and childcare responsibilities.

Identifying the beliefs that your client holds about behaviour will further assist you in targeting areas for intervention, and is indeed a part of the intervention. Ask your client whether or not she takes on responsibility or obligations for areas which are not strictly hers. If she does, get her to list situations where she has felt that she is doing things for others which they should take responsibility for.

Deciding to change non-assertiveness

It is of course important to establish whether or not your client wishes to become more assertive. Explore with her the pros and cons of changing. For example, the benefits of under-assertiveness may include avoiding conflict and responsibility, maintaining familiar patterns of interacting, and an acceptance by others. On the other hand, being under-assertive may decrease your client's satisfaction with social interactions, reduce her influence over decisions made by others and curb her independence. This may in turn reduce her self-respect and the respect that others have for her rights and needs.

Introducing the 'Bill of Rights'

If your client decides that she wants to become more assertive it is time to help her generate a list of her rights in interpersonal situations. This type of list has often been called a 'Bill of Assertive Rights' and typically includes the right to:

- Make mistakes
- Change one's mind
- Offer no reasons or excuses for one's behaviour
- Make one's own decisions
- Not have to work out solutions for other people's problems
- Criticise in a constructive and helpful fashion
- Say 'no' without feeling guilty
- Tell someone that you do not understand their position or else 'do not care'
- Not have to depend on others for approval
- Express feelings and opinions
- Be listened to by others

- Disagree with others
- Have different needs, wants and wishes from other people

Such a list is included in the client handout at the end of this chapter. It should be tailored to your client's particular situation, and other rights specific to her may be added. Some clients may feel uneasy about a 'Bill of Rights' and it may be worth explaining that these rights also entail some responsibilities. In particular, she will need to respect the same rights for others.

Putting assertiveness skills into practice

To use these assertive rights in a healthy and non-aggressive way requires lots of practice. As a starting point, a number of useful exercises are set out below. It is valuable to work through these (or similar) structured exercises with your client even if they do not directly apply to her. These exercises are equally useful for groups because they cover a wide range of assertiveness skills and situations.

Each of the examples lists an under-assertive, an aggressive and an appropriately assertive response. In some examples the responses are left blank to allow your client to generate possible responses. It is *essential* that your client uses role-play to practise providing appropriately assertive responses. You can help her feel more comfortable with the use of role-play by initially modelling examples of under-assertive, aggressive and assertive responses for her. Your examples can then be discussed and used to guide your client's attempts. For further information about offering your client feedback on her role-play performance, see p. 11.

In learning how to be assertive, your client may need to be trained in some basic communication skills. For example, you may need to teach her how to use I-statements when communicating her feelings and opinions. These skills are discussed in detail in Chapter 8, *Communication Skills*. Your client will also be more effective in her assertiveness if she is direct in her tone of voice, eye contact and body language (see Chapter 6, *Drink- and Drug-refusal Skills*), avoids anger and unnecessary 'snipes', keeps responses succinct, and respects the rights of the other person.

In Example 1 below, the assertive speaker begins by 'fogging' (p. 87) to diffuse her mother's criticism. She then goes on to present her own opinion regarding the children. She finishes by using 'I-statements' to say specifically what she finds hurtful and to request a change in her mother's behaviour.

Example 1:   Dealing with criticism

In this example your mother harshly criticises the way that you deal with your children when they come home from school because you allow them to eat food before dinner. You find this annoying and hurtful and believe you're correct in allowing them to have a snack. What do you say to her?

UNDER-ASSERTIVE: 'Yes, you're probably right. I guess it isn't good for them.'

AGGRESSIVE: 'You should mind your own business! They are not your children.'

ASSERTIVE: 'You may be right Mum, but I find that if I don't give them a snack they become very tired. Besides, they eat their dinner without a problem. If you don't like how I am dealing with the children, I'd prefer if you would say so without sounding so critical. I find your tone is often hurtful.'

Example 2:   Dealing with criticism

Your boss criticises you inappropriately in a meeting over something which you have said which he has misunderstood. It was clear that he took you to mean something which you had not intended, but you did not have an opportunity to clarify the situation within the meeting. What do you say later?

UNDER-ASSERTIVE: You say either nothing or 'I apologise' and then try to explain what you had intended.

AGGRESSIVE: You accuse your boss of not understanding what you were talking about, but do not explain what you had been attempting to say in the meeting.

ASSERTIVE: You explain to your boss that you had been attempting to inform the meeting of your views on the situation at hand and you are concerned that he has misunderstood what you were saying. You ask him not to be abrupt with you in a meeting again as you find it offensive.

In Example 2 above, pay special attention to body language, eye contact, and again, the use of 'I-statements'.

Example 3:   Dealing with requests from other people

A friend of yours whom you think is a very bad driver asks to borrow your new car to go out to an important meeting. You do not wish to lend the car because you do not feel confident in your friend's driving abilities. What do you say?

UNDER-ASSERTIVE: 'OK! You can borrow the car, but be careful with it.'
AGGRESSIVE: 'You have no right to borrow my car. I wouldn't be so silly as to lend it to you—you're a terrible driver!'
ASSERTIVE: 'Sorry John, I'm not prepared to lend the car to you. However, I'm willing to give you a hand by dropping you to your meeting if I can.'

In Example 3 above, emphasise that an assertive response does not obligate the speaker to apologise or offer an excuse when turning down a request. However, this example illustrates that assertiveness can involve offering a constructive alternative suggestion. This may help reinforce the message that it is the request, not the person, that is being rejected.

Example 4:   Making requests of other people

You have been extremely busy at work. You are having guests to dinner and the house is in a complete mess. Your partner gets home and collapses in front of the television. You need help to clean up the house. What do you do?

UNDER-ASSERTIVE: Say nothing, do it yourself and end up too exhausted to enjoy the company of your friends.
AGGRESSIVE: Say nothing but be angry and hostile all evening and eventually lose your temper over something unrelated to your reason for being angry.
ASSERTIVE: Ask your partner for some help.

In Example 4 above, the request for help would be framed in a direct and non-accusatory way. If the partner persistently ignores this request for help, the 'broken record technique' (p. 86) might be one way for the assertive speaker to ensure that her needs are understood.

Example 5: Making complaints

You have purchased an electric appliance from a department store. Upon using the appliance for the first time you discover that it is faulty and return it to the store. You expect to be given a replacement, but instead you are told that because the box has been opened the appliance will have to be returned to the manufacturer for repair and that will take four weeks. What do you say?

UNDER-ASSERTIVE:

AGGRESSIVE:

ASSERTIVE:

Example 6: Giving criticism

Some workmen at your home have failed to repair a crack in the wall of your house before painting over it. What do you say?

UNDER-ASSERTIVE:

AGGRESSIVE:

ASSERTIVE:

Very often clients who are non-assertive are too ready to accept criticism and are unable to accept praise. Explain to your client that by acknowledging compliments appropriately she lets others know that what they have said is important. By rejecting or ignoring compliments she will discourage others from offering future compliments—and thereby only reinforce her own low self-esteem and confidence. Being able to both give and accept compliments is therefore an important part of effective assertive communication.

Example 7: Receiving compliments

You have impressed co-workers with your abilities in a difficult project. They praise you for your abilities. What do you say?

NON-ASSERTIVE:

ASSERTIVE:

Example 8:   Giving compliments

You wish to praise a friend for help that she gave you in a time of crisis.

Non-assertive:

Assertive: .

When you have finished these exercises review the key areas where a lack of healthy assertiveness causes difficulties for your client. Work with your client's personal examples using the same method as you used in the exercises above. Again, make sure that your client practises her assertive responses in the session using role-play. You should also negotiate weekly home practice exercises with your client to encourage her to apply the skills in situations that arise at home or work. Review her progress with these home exercises at the beginning of each session.

Handling tricky situations

There are a number of situations where being straightforward and direct with people does not bring about the desired result. Despite your client's attempts to explain herself in a reasoned and straightforward way, other people may still behave irrationally. Offer your client the following strategies and role-play them to assist her in handling problem situations.

Strategy 1—the broken record technique: The Broken Record technique could help your client in situations where somebody is making persistent demands on her or refusing to hear what she is saying. It involves simply repeating the same message over and over, hence the name, 'broken record technique'. By using this method, your client can stick with what she wants to say and avoid being drawn into an argument. This may seem unnatural at first but it can be done in a respectful, non-monotonous way. Some examples from Dickson (1982) show how your client could precede her repeated message with an acknowledgment of the other person's perspective:

'I know that you're tired as well *but I'd still like you to do your share of the work.'*
'I know you're disappointed, *but I still have to say 'no'.*

Strategy 2—disarming anger: This strategy is best used when someone is inappropriately aggressive or so angry with your client that reasoned conversation is impossible. Your client may need to actually get the other person's attention if that person is caught up in an angry outburst. She might do this by saying the person's name and making eye contact. She would then say that she can see the other person is angry and that she feels it would be more constructive to talk about the situation once they have calmed down. Of course your client must be prepared to listen to the other person if and when they do calm down!

Strategy 3—dealing with requests: People are often put on the spot by a request and make a hasty, non-assertive decision which they later regret. If your client is often put into this kind of situation instruct her to initially react to requests by saying 'I'm not sure'. This answer allows her to reserve her right to say 'no' or 'yes'. It also gives her more time to decide and, if necessary, a chance to ask for more information. You may need to assist her in role-play to ask assertively for more information. An alternative response to requests that put your client on the spot is 'I will think about it and get back to you'. Your client then has the opportunity to think through the request and perhaps to talk to others about it. If she later decides to agree to the request, she should be direct in saying so and add in conditions if there are any. Assertive responses should not always involve saying 'no'!

Strategy 4—selectively ignoring requests or comments: If another person continues to harp on a subject despite clear messages from your client that she no longer wishes to discuss it, then 'selective ignoring' can be useful. This strategy requires that your client totally ignore the unwelcomed comments while responding to other aspects of the conversation. If your client always fails to respond to a particular topic the other person will eventually give it up. It can be quite difficult to continually ignore comments, especially if they are perceived as unfair or critical. It may be useful to tell your client to say to the individual:

> 'I've heard what you have to say. I do not agree with it. I'm not willing to discuss it with you further. If you raise it again I will ignore it but I will talk to you about other things.'

Strategy 5—'fogging': Sometimes when faced with unfair criticism it may be useful to be able to 'turn it off' with minimum effort. Your client can do this by simply agreeing with the critic in a vague fashion. She could use phrases such as 'You may be right', or 'I understand that's your point of view', or 'Really!?' It will be helpful to role-play conversations to ensure that your client is comfortable with this method.

Strategy 6—sorting out the issues: Interpersonal conflict often clouds reason and causes issues to become confused. When this happens it may be difficult for your client to be clear about what is a reasonable response on her part. For example, a refusal by your client to do something might lead to a (sometimes wilful or manipulative!) misinterpretation like: 'because you won't do my ironing anymore, it's obvious you no longer care about me . . .' It is important that your client is able to sort out facts from interpretations. For example, in response to the above situation she might learn to say something like: 'I do care about you . . . its just that I don't want to do your ironing.'

This problem of misinterpretation commonly occurs when a client begins to be assertive. At that time those around her will be surprised or threatened and may feel that the assertiveness is equivalent to rejection. If appropriate, help her to practise and role-play different situations where others might confuse appropriate assertion with rejection.

RESOURCES LIST

Kadden, R., Carroll, K., Donovan, D., Cooney, N., Monti, P., Abrams, D., Litt, M. & Hester, R. (1992). *Cognitive Behavioral Coping Skills Therapy Manual: A Clinical Research Guide for Therapists Treating Individuals with Alcohol Abuse and Dependence*. Project *MATCH Monograph Series, Volume 3*. Rockville, MD: National Institute on Alcohol Abuse and Alcoholism.
—This session-by-session manual describes sessions for assertiveness training and receiving criticism, based on guidelines from the book by Monti et al., below.
Monti, P.M., Abrams, D.B., Kadden, R.M. & Cooney, N.L (1989). *Treating Alcohol Dependence: A Coping Skills Training Guide* (pp. 31–35; 46–61; 63–67). New York: Guilford Press.
—Provides sessions addressing giving and receiving compliments, assertiveness, giving and receiving criticism, and refusing requests. A specific session for responding to criticisms about drinking is also included.

Self-help Books

The following is a list of self-help books on assertiveness skills (by no means exhaustive). Your client will benefit from having one practical book on the subject and working through its exercises.

Alberti, R. E. & Emmons, M. D. (1974). *Your Perfect Right* (2nd edn). San Luis Obispo, CA: Impact Publishers.
Baer, J. (1976). *How to be an Assertive (Not Aggressive) Woman: In Life, in Love, and on the Job*. Middlesex, UK: Signet.
Dickson, A. (1982). *A Woman in Your Own Right*. London: Quartet.
Fensterheim, H. & Baer, J. (1975). *Don't Say 'Yes' When You Want to Say 'No'*. London: Warner.
Galassi, M. D. & Galassi, J. P. (1977). *Assert Yourself: How to be Your Own Person*. New York: Human Sciences Press.

Kotzman, A. (1989). *Listen to Me, Listen to You: A Practical Guide to Improving Self-esteem, Listening Skills and Assertiveness*. Ringwood, Vic., Australia: Penguin.
Linderfield, G. (1992). *Assert Yourself: A Self-help Assertiveness Program for Men and Women*. London: Thorsons.
Lloyd, S.R. (1988). *Developing Positive Assertiveness*. California: Crisp.
Phelps, S. & Austin, N. (1975). *The Assertive Woman*. San Luis Obispo, CA: Impact Publishers.

BILL OF ASSERTIVE RIGHTS

- The right to make mistakes
- The right to change your mind
- The right to offer no reasons or excuses for your behaviour
- The right to make your own decisions
- The right to not have to work out solutions for other people's problems
- The right to criticise in a constructive and helpful fashion
- The right to say 'no' without feeling guilty
- The right to tell someone that you do not understand their position or else 'do not care'
- The right to not have to depend on others for approval
- The right to express feelings and opinions
- The right to be listened to by others
- The right to disagree with others
- The right to have different needs, wants and wishes from other people

Add in your other rights below:

-

-

-

-

8

COMMUNICATION SKILLS

RECOMMENDED USE

Communication-skills training overlaps with assertiveness training, and the two can be profitably taught together. Communication-skills training aims to teach your client how to start and continue conversations, cope with silences, interpret social cues, actively listen to others and comfortably communicate personal feelings, thoughts and opinions. The importance of appropriate communication skills is that they help to reduce your client's feelings of embarrassment and social tension which can lead to a relapse to excessive drinking or drug use.

Communication-skills training can be used with those clients who wish either to cut down or to abstain from drinking alcohol or other drug use. It is especially well suited to group settings because different individuals can provide examples to others of good and poor communication patterns. Being able to role-play and model situations is an extremely important aspect of training when using this technique. Communication-skills training is also an important aspect of couples therapy (Chapter 12).

GOALS

The major goals of communication-skills training are to enable your client to:

- Initiate conversations and continue these in a comfortable fashion
- Be sensitive to social cues that provide information about how others are perceiving what he is saying
- Be able to express important feelings to others
- Understand the feelings of other people

KEY CONCEPTS

I-statements

An 'I-statement' is a statement that begins with the first person. For example, statements starting with the words 'I feel . . .', 'I think . . .' or 'I need . . .' are all I-statements. By starting speech with an I-statement, your client conveys a direct message about his intentions. He also takes responsibility for his feelings and opinions, without blaming or placing that responsibility on others. This approach therefore allows the listener to respond without defensiveness.

Positive Specific Requests

O'Farrell and Cowles (1989) describe positive specific requests as a form of communication in which your client expresses what he wants rather than what he does not want in specific terms and in the form of a request rather than a demand. This kind of communication is clear, non-threatening and leaves matters open to negotiation.

METHOD

Rationale for Your Client

Discuss with your client the way in which people sometimes use alcohol or other drugs to help them feel comfortable or to numb their embarrassment when in conversation or social situations. Ask your client to think of some examples from his own experience where he might have used alcohol or drugs in this way. Explain to your client that the communication-skills training will focus on both giving and receiving communication without relying on the effects of substances, and will therefore help to prevent relapse. At first, the skills may not be easy to use but with practice (initially as often as three times a week for 10–15 minutes) they will become more automatic.

Assess your client's current communication skills. You may need to begin by working on methods for initiating and maintaining general conversations. He may also need assistance in expressing personal opinions, feelings and requests. Some techniques concerning giving and receiving compliments or criticism have already been outlined in Chapter 7, *Assertiveness Skills*. You should also focus on developing your client's listening skills and his ability to validate the point of view of others. You might also wish to explore how your client's cognition or self-talk may impede the communication process (see below).

Starting or Entering a Conversation

To start or enter a conversation your client has to have something to say! Have your client write a list of his areas of interest. Then help him to recognise those topics which may be interesting to others and those which will probably be of limited conversational value.

It may be that your client has few areas in his life that are of general interest. For instance, if his leisure time has completely revolved around drinking at the hotel, he may have few hobbies and might lack general knowledge so that he finds it difficult to contribute to conversations. Encourage him to take the time to learn about events by reading newspapers or books and to develop new hobbies and interests. These new activities will also have the advantage of distracting him from drinking or using drugs!

Before attempting to enter a conversation, your client should listen to what the other people are interested in talking about. Stress the importance of staying with topics that are of mutual interest and contrast this with taking over or 'hijacking' a conversation, which is likely to quickly end it, especially if those involved were enjoying the existing topic.

So that your client does not try to 'burst' into conversations, introduce him to the skill of asking others open-ended questions (see Chapter 1, *General Counselling Skills*). Use role-play (p. 11) to show how these types of questions encourage discussion. As another useful way of starting or entering conversations, also get him to practise offering small 'titbits' of information. Contrast these strategies with sudden intrusive comments which tend to disrupt the flow of discussion.

Tell your client that many good conversationalists do not talk about significant matters. Enjoyable casual conversation often focuses on the day-to-day aspects of existence, such as the weather, sporting results or what happened at the weekend. As Monti, Abrams, Kadden and Cooney (1989; p. 29) said, *Small talk is okay*! The idea that conversation can occur on a number of levels may be new to your client if he feels pressured to talk only about things that are important. Emphasise the need to practise conversing on different levels.

Keeping the Conversation Going

Dealing with silences

Your client may feel that it is his responsibility to keep the conversation going. This sense of obligation might lead him to feel uncomfortable with silences and he might try to cope by talking in monologues. The danger of long monologues is that they tend to dominate the discussion and lose other people's interest. Explain that short silences are natural within conversation when people are thinking about what has been said and what to say next. Use role-play to develop your client's skills and flexibility in altering the topic and direction of conversation and picking up a conversation that has stopped.

Non-verbal communication

Discuss with your client the importance of non-verbal language in maintaining conversations. Appropriate eye contact, facial expressions and an interesting tone of voice are very important aspects of good communication. Get your client to consider how non-verbal language can sometimes undermine an intended verbal message. For example, a person might *say* that he is interested in what his friend is talking about *but* his lack of eye contact and mumbling voice convey the opposite. Use role-play to enhance your client's awareness of these subtleties of non-verbal communication. Further details on improving non-verbal communication are provided in the Chapter 6, *Drink- and Drug-refusal Skills.*

Communicating Personal Information

Using I-statements

Discuss how I-statements can make it easier to express personal messages directly and clearly in conversation. For example, you might get your client to compare these two statements:

'Why can't *you* stop criticising me?'
'*I* feel angry when you find fault with me in front of other people.'

Ask your client how he would feel if he was at the receiving end of either of these statements. Explain that the first statement is likely to generate a defensive answer and lead to further conflict. The second statement conveys a more direct and specific message and leaves room for negotiation.

Montgomery and Evans (1983) have called the second type of statement an X-Y-Z statement because it takes the form: 'When you do X in situation Y, I feel Z.' This kind of specific statement focuses the speaker's comment on a particular behaviour rather than on the entire person. It avoids sidetracks, generalisations and personal insults which can cause conflict to escalate. Some other examples of X-Y-Z statements (which are also I-statements) include:

'When you borrow my things and don't bring them back, I feel annoyed.'
'I enjoy your company when we go out to the movies.'
'I find it very helpful when you get the kids off to school.'

Notice that the last two examples express positive feelings. Use these examples to demonstrate that I-statements make it easier to express both critical and complimentary feelings towards others. Emphasise the importance of being specific and genuine about what is liked or disliked.

Positive specific requests

Introduce the concept of positive specific requests as a way to assist your client to ask for what he needs. They are 'positive' because they state what your client wants rather than what he doesn't want. They are 'specific' because they state what, when and where. They are 'requests' rather than demands because they allow for negotiation. For example, you might get your client to compare these statements:

'If you keep on ignoring me, I won't be around much longer.'
'I would like you to listen to what I say when we talk at dinner time.'

Get your client to write down at least five positive specific requests. If necessary, help him to make them more specific or positive.

Active Listening

Ask your client to listen to something said by you or another client and then repeat that message as accurately as possible. Instruct the listener to repeat both the words and the feelings that were expressed. He should try to do this in a way that is paraphrasing rather than parroting what the other person said. Model this reflective listening approach with specific examples such as: 'What I heard you say was . . . Is that right?' The power of these examples will be enhanced if you have incorporated reflective listening as part of your overall counselling style (see p. 6). Explain to your client that reflecting back what has been said in this way will enable him to verify that he has heard the message accurately as well as showing the speaker that he is actively listening. This approach helps to avoid the misunderstandings that happen when one person tries to read another person's mind.

Active listening also involves observing the other person's non-verbal language. As mentioned above, cues such as facial expression, intonation, voice quality and body posture can provide valuable information about how the speaker is feeling.

Validating the Other Person

Validating is perhaps the most difficult communication skill. By validating, the listener not only indicates that the information has been received but also acknowledges or accepts the feelings expressed. This does not mean that the listener has to agree with the speaker's opinion. It means that the listener respects what the other person has said about how he feels rather than insisting that he feel some other way. For example:

'Yes, I can understand how you would feel angry about me being late.'

This validation of the speaker's feelings does not invalidate the listener's perspective. It rests on the underlying assumption that people have the right to think differently, and are prepared to acknowledge that right for each other.

Self-talk

If your client is having difficulty in communicating, get him to check what he is saying to himself. He may be thinking negatively about how the other person views him or what his or her intentions are. It may often be the cause of his difficulty, and the answer is to change this 'negative self-talk'. For example, your client's attempt to compliment somebody might be impeded by his negative self-talk about being rejected:

'There's not much point. She's probably not interested in me anyway.'

Encourage your client to think of examples of self-talk that would help him, rather than hinder him, in his communication, such as:

'I feel a bit nervous about this but unless I say something, she won't know that I like her.'

Self-talk is also discussed in Chapter 12, *Couples Therapy*, and Chapter 9, *Cognitive Restructuring*. Chapter 9 describes how self-talk that leads to drinking or drug using can be effectively challenged.

RESOURCES LIST

Kadden, R., Carroll, K., Donovan, D., Cooney, N., Monti, P., Abrams, D., Litt, M. & Hester, R. (1992). *Cognitive Behavioral Coping Skills Therapy Manual: A Clinical Research Guide for Therapists Treating Individuals with Alcohol Abuse and Dependence. Project MATCH Monograph Series, Volume 3.* Rockville, MD: National Institute on Alcohol Abuse and Alcoholism.
—This session-by-session manual describes sessions that deal with starting conversations and non-verbal communication, based on guidelines from the book by Monti *et al.*, below.

Montgomery, B. & Evans, L. (1983). *Living and Loving Together.* Ringwood, Australia: Penguin.
—Chapter 3 of this self-help book about relationships provides a practical guide on communication skills, including I-statements, X-Y-Z statements, validation and self-talk.

Monti, P.M., Abrams, D.B., Kadden, R.M. & Cooney, N.L (1989). *Treating Alcohol Dependence: A Coping Skills Training Guide* (pp. 28–32; 35–45; 67–72). New York: Guilford Press.
—An excellent resource for communication-skills training which covers skills in handling conversations, non-verbal communication, listening and intimacy.

O'Farrell, T. J. & Cowles, K. S. (1989). Marital and family therapy. In R.K. Hester & W.R. Miller (Eds), *Handbook of Alcoholism Treatment Approaches: Effective Alternatives* (pp. 183–205). New York: Pergamon Press.
—Provides detailed information on methods of communications therapy with special focus on couples.

Tannen, D. (1988). *That's Not What I Meant!* London: Virago.
—This self-help book explores how misunderstandings occur in communication and the cultural factors that influence conversational style.

COGNITIVE RESTRUCTURING

RECOMMENDED USE

Cognitive restructuring involves teaching your client to identify and challenge thoughts or feelings that may lead to drinking or drug use. This cognitive skill has been shown to be particularly effective when it is taught in combination with other more behavioural coping skills (such as drink-refusal and assertiveness training). Cognitive restructuring can be taught in either an individual or a group setting although, because of its abstract nature, this strategy may not be suitable for clients who suffer from alcohol-related brain damage (see p. 23).

In addition to their usefulness for coping with urges to use drugs or alcohol, cognitive restructuring techniques can also help your clients with other life problems such as low self-esteem, anxiety or depression. More detail on these applications of cognitive restructuring are found in the materials listed in the *Resources List*.

The basic principles of cognitive restructuring can probably be communicated in a minimum of two or three hour-long sessions. However, like other skills, cognitive restructuring needs to be practised across the *entire* course of treatment in order for your client to be able to use the skill effectively after treatment ends.

GOALS

The goals of cognitive restructuring are for your client to be able to:

- Recognise when she is thinking negatively or in a way that could lead to drinking or drug use

- Interrupt that train of thought
- Challenge the negative or unproductive thoughts and replace them with more positive or reasonable ones

KEY CONCEPTS

Automatic Thoughts

The thoughts that lead to bad feelings or urges to drink or use drugs often happen so quickly that your client may be unaware of them occurring. These thoughts are therefore commonly referred to as negative 'automatic' thoughts.

Self-talk or Self-statements

These are other useful terms for describing the thoughts preceding feelings and behaviours. Negative self-talk is the series of thoughts that result in negative feelings or urges and cravings. Positive self-talk or self-statements are those that help to decrease urges, increase self-confidence or change negative feelings.

METHOD

Rationale for Your Client

Explain to your client that thinking influences the way she both feels and behaves. That is, emotions aren't usually caused as a direct result of something happening in the outside world. Rather, the way she feels depends on her *interpretation* of an event or what she 'says to herself' about a particular situation.

You can use a simple example like the effects of dropping a plate to illustrate this point. Some people might respond to this event by thinking things like 'I'm such a useless idiot' or 'I'm totally stupid'. If unchecked, these kinds of thoughts can lead to feelings of anger, frustration or depression. Such feelings often lead to urges to drink or use drugs.

You could also point out that often, as in the example of the broken plate, negative thoughts like 'I'm totally stupid' are unnecessary overreactions to a situation. Because of their undesirable consequences, Monti, Abrams, Kadden and Cooney (1989) noted that such thoughts are colourfully referred to in Alcoholics Anonymous as 'stinking thinking'!

Explain to your client that the aim of the following sessions will be to help her learn how to catch herself thinking negative or unhelpful thoughts. Having learnt to identify such thoughts she can then learn how to challenge and replace them with more constructive self-talk.

Becoming Aware of Negative Thinking

The first step is to help your clients learn to identify bad thinking habits. Monti *et al.* (1989) introduced Ellis's A-B-C model as a way of emphasising and clarifying the relationship between thoughts, feelings and behaviours. That is:

(A)ntecedent event	⇒ **(B)**eliefs	⇒ **(C)**onsequences
For example:		
Losing my keys	⇒ 'I'm a bloody idiot'	⇒ Angry, irritable
Late for child's concert	⇒ 'I'm a lousy mother'	⇒ Depressed, anxious

Use this model to generate some exercises for your client. Get her to identify several situations from the recent past where she either experienced strong negative emotions or ended up drinking or using other drugs. Ask her to begin by describing the anteceding events (A) that 'caused' her feelings. Then spend some time considering what she was telling herself, that is, what her beliefs (B) were about the situation. Finally, explore the consequences (C) of this self-talk in terms of how it led her to feel bad and/or to drink or use drugs.

Having generated a number of different examples of negative or unproductive self-talk, it can often be useful to introduce your client to the different types of thinking errors that have been identified by Ellis (1975). Some of these types of thinking errors are described in the first client handout at the end of this chapter. Use this list to classify some of the negative thoughts your client identified in the exercise above. Categorising thoughts using such a list can help clarify what it is about the thoughts that is unproductive or unhelpful.

You should also explain that often such negative thoughts happen so quickly that they almost seem not to have happened at all. For this reason it is often useful to describe them as being 'automatic' thoughts. Often the first sign of trouble your client will detect is a sense that she is beginning to feel bad or is experiencing an urge or craving. These feelings are crucial signals for her to stop and to identify the 'automatic' thoughts that caused her to feel that way. Sometimes anxious clients might find it particularly difficult to recognise when an automatic thought has occurred. In such cases it is useful to suggest that these thoughts commonly precede very strong and prolonged emotional reactions or cravings.

It is essential that your client practises catching her negative automatic thoughts. This is best achieved by using home practice exercises. A thought-monitoring practice sheet is provided at the end of this chapter. At this stage of therapy your client should only be concerned with filling in the first three columns of the sheet. During the week, whenever she starts to feel bad or crave, she should immediately say 'STOP, SLOW DOWN' to herself and then fill in the sheet. Get her to describe the situation leading to the unpleasant feelings and specify what the feelings are. She can rate her feelings on a scale of 0–100 where 1 would indicate a slight feeling and 100 would indicate the most intense feeling possible. Ask her to write down the automatic thoughts or self-statements that are causing her to feel that way. She can also rate the strength of her belief in those thoughts from 0% (don't believe at all) to 100% (completely believe).

Challenging Negative Thinking

Get your client to choose a situation from her home practice or an earlier session where an unhelpful or 'automatic' thought was identified. Teach your client to review the automatic thought using four key questions (from Fennell, 1989):

(1) *What is the evidence to support this thought?* You must be quite strict about what you accept as 'evidence'. Very commonly clients mistake their feelings or beliefs for facts. Evidence must be objective, fit the facts and be accepted as true by other people. In answering this question, your client might actually find that there is evidence to contradict her automatic thought!

(2) *What are the advantages/disadvantages of thinking this way?* Many automatic thoughts have *some* advantages for your client—that's why they keep recurring! For example, your client may have an automatic thought that helps her to avoid a difficult situation. However, she should consider whether this advantage is outweighed by disadvantages (e.g. prolonged anxiety, drug use). If the disadvantages outweigh the advantages, it will be worthwhile for your client to try to work out some new ways of thinking.

(3) *Is there a thinking error?* Is the automatic thought an example of one of the categories of thinking errors listed in the client handout?

(4) *What alternative ways of thinking about the situation are there?* Have your client brainstorm as many alternative positive thoughts as possible (see Chapter 5, *Problem-solving Skills*). It might be useful to have your client think about how another person would see things or what she might say to a friend in the same situation. Some other examples of tips for challenging negative thoughts are presented in the second client handout at the end of this chapter.

Get your client to write down the positive thoughts that helped her to feel even a little bit better. Stress to her that she should not expect huge changes at first. Rather it will take time and practice before she becomes good at being able to successfully challenge her negative self-talk.

Encourage your client to practise challenging negative thoughts during the following weeks. Ask her to use the thought-monitoring sheets again, this time also completing the last three columns. Get her to write positive challenges to her automatic thoughts and rate her belief in these challenges (0–100%). After identifying the positive challenges, she can then re-rate her belief in the original automatic thoughts and feelings. The third client handout at the end of this chapter presents a completed example for your client. This home practice exercise will help you and your client to identify the kinds of positive challenges that she finds most useful.

RESOURCES LIST

Beck, A., Rush, J., Shaw, B. & Emery, G. (1979). *Cognitive Therapy of Depression*. New York: Guilford Press.
   —A classic guide to the use of cognitive restructuring principles in the treatment of depression.
Burns, D.D. (1980). *Feeling Good: The New Mood Therapy*. New York: New American Library.
   —Another very useful text in this area.
Ellis, A. (1975). *The New Guide to Rational Living*. New York: Harper & Row.
   —This is the original description of the use of rational emotive therapy, on which elements of the above approach are based.
Fennell, M.J.V. (1989). Depression. In K. Hawton, P.M Salkovskis, J. Kirk & D.M. Clark (Eds), *Cognitive Behaviour Therapy for Psychiatric Problems: A Practical Guide* (pp. 169–234). Oxford: Oxford University Press.
   —An excellent, detailed chapter for therapists on the application of cognitive restructuring techniques.
Goldfried, M.R. & Goldfried, A.P. (1975). Cognitive change methods. In F.H. Kanfer & A.P. Goldstein, *Helping People Change* (pp. 89–104). New York: Pergamon Press.
   —A more theoretical and broad-based approach to the use of cognitive change methods for a variety of psychological problems.
Kadden, R., Carroll, K., Donovan, D., Cooney, N., Monti, P., Abrams, D., Litt, M. & Hester, R. (1992). *Cognitive Behavioral Coping Skills Therapy Manual: A Clinical Research Guide for Therapists Treating Individuals with Alcohol Abuse and Dependence. Project MATCH Monograph Series, Volume 3*. Rockville, MD: National Institute on Alcohol Abuse and Alcoholism.
   —This session-by-session manual includes a detailed session on dealing with negative moods and depression.
Monti, P.M., Abrams, D.B., Kadden, R.M. & Cooney, N.L (1989). *Treating Alcohol Dependence: A Coping Skills Training Guide* (pp. 103–116). New York: Guilford Press.
   —Two excellent sections on awareness of, and dealing with, negative thinking as well

as a practical guide for teaching clients how to manage anger. The major resource for this chapter.

Tanner, S. & Ball, J. (1989). *Beating the Blues: A Self-help Approach to Overcoming Depression*. Sydney: Doubleday.

—A terrific book for both clients and therapists dealing with depression. Also a great resource book for teaching cognitive restructuring procedures.

COMMON THINKING ERRORS

(1) <u>All or nothing thinking</u>

Seeing things in black or white categories. For example:

'If I can't be the best it's pointless trying at all.'
'If I don't succeed in this job I'm a total failure.'

(2) <u>Overgeneralisation</u>

Expecting that because something has gone wrong, it will always do so. For example:

'I relapsed after I stopped five years ago, I'll never be able to stop drinking/using.'

(3) <u>Mental filter</u>

You see only the negative things and dwell only on them so that it distorts your view of a person or situation.

'I'll never forget the way they let me down that time.'

(4) <u>Converting positives into negatives</u>

You reject your achievements and other positive experiences by insisting that they 'don't count' for some reason. In this way you can maintain a negative belief that is contradicted by your everyday experience. For example:

'He only gave me that compliment because he knows how bad I feel.'
'I only stayed sober because there wasn't a lot of pressure to drink.'

(5) <u>Jumping to negative conclusions</u>

Drawing a negative conclusion when there is little or no evidence to support it.

(a) *Mind reading.* You conclude that someone is reacting negatively to you, and you don't bother to check this out. For example:

'My friend has interrupted me twice. I must be really boring to listen to.'

(b) *The 'Fortune Teller' error.* You anticipate that things will turn out badly, and are convinced that your prediction is an already established fact. These negative expectations can be self-fulfilling. For example:

'They won't like me, so why even try to participate?'
'This relationship is sure to fail.'
'I'll never be able to change my drinking.'

CLIENT HANDOUT

Common Thinking Errors (*page 2*)

(6) Catastrophising

Exaggerating the impact of events and convincing yourself that if something goes wrong it will be totally unbearable and intolerable. For example:

'If I get a craving, it'll be unbearable.'

(7) Mistaking feelings for facts

Confusing facts with feelings or beliefs. No matter how strong a feeling is—it is not a fact! For example:

'I feel like a failure—therefore I am a failure.'

(8) Personalising

Blaming yourself for anything unpleasant. You take too much responsibility for other people's feelings and behaviour.

'My husband has come home in a bad mood—it must be something that I have done.'

(9) Self put-downs

This involves undervaluing yourself and putting yourself down. It can often be the result of an extreme over-reaction to a situation, such as making a mistake. For example:

'I don't deserve any better.'
'I'm weak/stupid/ugly.'
'I'm an idiot.'

(10) Should statements

Using 'shoulds', 'oughts' and 'musts' leads to guilt and sets you up to be disappointed. Directing should statements towards others will make you feel frustrated, angry and resentful. For example:

'I must not get angry.'
'He should always be on time.'

Source: Adapted from Burns (1980), Monti *et al.* (1989) and Tanner & Ball (1989).

STRATEGIES FOR CHALLENGING NEGATIVE THOUGHTS

Decatastrophising

Are you over-reacting? Often events are much less catastrophic than you automatically think. What is really the worst that can happen? How likely is it that the worst could happen? What could you do to manage even if the worst were to happen?

Hopefulness statements

Be kind and encouraging to yourself! Pessimism can be a self-fulfilling prophecy. Try self-statements like 'Even though it's tough, I can handle this situation'. 'I can change nothing is written in stone.'

Blame the event, not yourself

Everyone makes mistakes sometimes. Mistakes you make in a particular situation are not permanent reflections on you as a person.

Reminding yourself to stay 'on task'

Try to focus on what you need to do. Taking action will make you feel better.

Avoid the 'shoulds' and 'musts'

If you find that your automatic thoughts are full of these types of words then it probably means that you are setting unreasonable demands on yourself or others. Removing these words from your thoughts can allow you (and others) more freedom to be yourself.

Recall good things

Focus on the positive! For example: What other things have gone well recently? What things do you like about yourself? What personal skills do you have that have helped you cope with challenging situations in the past?

Relabelling the distress

Remember, negative thoughts and feelings don't mean you are going to end up drinking. Think of them rather as signals or signposts to use your coping skills to help yourself to feel better.

Encourage yourself

Pat yourself on the back for making positive changes.

Source: Adapted from Monti *et al.* (1989).

EXAMPLE OF A THOUGHT-MONITORING SHEET

Describe SITUATION leading to unpleasant feelings e.g. 1. Event 2. Daydreams, thoughts, or memories	FEELINGS 1. Specify angry, sad, craving, etc. 2. Rate intensity of feelings 1–100	AUTOMATIC THOUGHTS 1. Write automatic thought(s) that preceded feelings. 2. Rate belief in automatic thought(s), 0–100% 3. Type of thinking error? e.g. catastrophising	POSITIVE CHALLENGE 1. Write positive challenge to automatic thought(s) 2. Rate belief in positive challenge, 0–100%	OUTCOME– THOUGHTS Re-rate belief in automatic thought(s), 0–100%	OUTCOME– FEELINGS 1. Specify feelings 2. Rate intensity of feelings 0–100
Had a fight with my partner after I got home late from work	Angry (85) Hopeless (95) Craving (90)	My partner hates me and doesn't trust me and things will never change (100%). There's no point in trying any more—I want a drink (95%). Catastrophising, overgeneralising	! We both had lousy days. As I forgot to phone, my partner was worried about me (40%). S This was our first argument since I started treatment and otherwise my partner has been supportive and pleased with how I'm doing (70%). O An occasional fight isn't the end of the world—people do get angry from time to time (60%). !	Partner hates me? (10%) No point in trying? (30%)	Angry (40) Hopeless (20) Craving (15) Pleasantly surprised by these changes (80)

Source: Adapted from Fennell, (1989).

THOUGHT-MONITORING SHEET

PRACTICE SHEET

Describe SITUATION leading to unpleasant feelings e.g. 1. Event 2. Daydreams, thoughts, or memories	FEELINGS 1. Specify angry, sad, craving, etc. 2. Rate intensity of feelings 1–100	AUTOMATIC THOUGHTS 1. Write automatic thought(s) that preceded feelings. 2. Rate belief in automatic thought(s), 0–100% 3. Type of thinking error? e.g. catastrophising	! S T O P !	POSITIVE CHALLENGE 1. Write positive challenge to automatic thought(s) 2. Rate belief in positive challenge, 0–100%	OUTCOME– THOUGHTS Re-rate belief in automatic thought(s), 0–100%	OUTCOME– FEELINGS 1. Specify feelings 2. Rate intensity of feelings 0–100

Remember, ask the questions: (1) What is the evidence for this thought? (2) What are the advantages/disadvantages of thinking this way? (3) Is there a thinking error? (4) What alternatives are there?

RELAXATION TRAINING

RECOMMENDED USE

Relaxation training involves a range of procedures designed to teach your client how to voluntarily release tension. The tension can be either physical tension in the muscles or psychological or mental tension. Relaxation training will allow your client to recognise tension and achieve deep relaxation during practice. It will also teach him how to relax in everyday situations when stress arises.

Relaxation training is appropriate when your client has reported or displayed some level of tension. It is suitable for clients aiming for either abstinence or moderation and as part of the treatment for any type of drug problem. You can teach the procedures in either group or individual settings. Economies can be achieved in group settings, provided that any of your clients' individual difficulties in learning the procedures are recognised and addressed.

GOALS

The goals of relaxation training are to enable your client:

- To recognise tension when it exists, either physical or psychological
- To learn to relax his body in a general, total sense
- To learn to actively release tension in day-to-day situations in specific muscle groups
- To use mental imagery or meditative procedures to reduce psychological tension
- Through this process to learn to cope with high levels of tension that might otherwise increase his risk of relapse to excessive drug or alcohol use

KEY CONCEPTS

Tension

Tension is an unpleasant feeling of being on edge, being apprehensive or 'stressed'. If the tension is physical your client might report to you trembling, muscle twitching, shakiness, muscular tension, muscular aches or soreness, restlessness or easy fatigue. Alternatively, it might be psychological tension where your client experiences worry or anxiety.

Relaxation Response

According to Benson (1975), each person has a natural response which protects against 'overstress'. This response, which Benson calls the 'relaxation response', decreases the heart rate, lowers metabolism and slows breathing. The elements required to achieve a relaxation response are: (a) a quiet environment; (b) a comfortable position; (c) a passive attitude; and (d) a mental or physical device that promotes tension reduction.

METHOD

Rationale for Your Client

Explain to your client that people have an innate, genetically determined response to threat or stress, known as the flight or fight response. As part of this flight or fight response, the muscles become tense, breathing becomes more rapid and shallow, and the person becomes alert and vigilant for danger. These reactions enable people to deal with threatening situations in an adaptive manner. Normally, the muscles will not remain tense constantly, but will activate and relax according to the situation's needs. Most people will therefore have fluctuating patterns of tension and relaxation over time. However, when a person experiences stress for long periods of time, muscle tension levels can remain high. If this goes on, it can become hard even to recognise the tension, let alone get rid of it.

Inform your client that constant tension might cause him to feel anxious even in ordinary or trivial daily situations. Should his tension get out of hand, it could trigger a relapse to drug or alcohol use. No doubt your client will be able to generate examples from his own experience of psychological or physical tension leading to drug or alcohol use as a way of coping or relaxing. Try to incorporate your client's examples into your rationale. Explain to him that relaxation procedures can be used in tension-provoking situations as a healthier and more effective way of reducing tension than drug or alcohol use.

It is important to point out to your client that effective relaxation training is more than simply thinking of a pleasant scene or relaxing in a non-stressful situation. Although he will begin by learning to relax in relatively unchallenging situations, he will ultimately learn to relax in an efficient manner in the face of real stressors which create a high level of tension. Many people continue relaxation procedures for years after learning the skill. Those who gain the most from these procedures either practise regularly or use the procedures as soon as they notice any increases in tension or anxiety.

Before Starting

It is important for you as the therapist to understand the nature of relaxation training, so learning the procedures yourself is important (and may provide you with a fringe benefit!).

Conditions for Training

It is possible for you to teach basic relaxation procedures to your client in one to three sessions. However, to develop the ability to recognise tension and the skill to release this tension, he will need to practise regularly for up to eight weeks, with your encouragement and supervision. You will need to negotiate an agreement about practice before commencing the exercises. Explain to your client that this practice will help him to achieve really long-lasting effects and will allow him to be able to react to tension with a relaxation response in an easy and reliable fashion. The more he practises, the more he will benefit from the exercises. Try to have some relaxation-training tapes available to assist your client when he practises at home. Play the relaxation tape once with your client and then advise him to practise relaxing to the tape at least once a day, especially in the beginning.

Recommend that your client practises relaxation in a quiet environment which is free of distractions. He may need to find a private room, take the phone off the hook or explain to other household members that he is going to be unavailable for about half an hour. He should also choose a time when he is not mentally preoccupied with other concerns.

Warn your client against practising relaxation in bed because he will probably go to sleep. Explain that sleep is not the same as relaxation because people can be quite tense while they are asleep. One aim of the practice is to learn how to relax while awake. Ideally, your client should practise in a comfortable armchair with good support for his body including his head and shoulders. Practising relaxation in bed is appropriate if your client has had sleeping difficulties and relaxation training is being used to assist him to sleep. Even then, however, it is important that he practises while sitting in a chair as well.

Recognising Tension

In order to be able to relax, your client needs to learn to identify both the triggers that increase tension and the areas of his body where tension occurs. Have your client consider which day-to-day events cause increased tension. Possible candidates are difficulties in relationships, loud noise, or negative feelings such as boredom, sadness, impatience and anger.

After identifying the triggers that increase tension, ask your client to identify where the tension occurs in his body. In particular, you might ask your client to tell you whether he notices tension in his neck, face, jaw, forehead, arms or legs. The 'tension monitoring sheet' at the end of this chapter will assist you and your client to record these points of tension.

Emphasise that tension can be not only physical but also psychological. Ask your client whether he feels worried and apprehensive. Depending on whether your client experiences physical or psychological tension, you might choose to teach him progressive muscle relaxation or a meditative approach involving mental imagery. You could also combine aspects of both.

Types of Relaxation

Progressive muscle relaxation procedures

Progressive muscle relaxation involves the active tensing and then relaxing of muscle groups in the body in an orderly and progressive sequence (hence the name). Typically, the individual is required to tense his foot muscles and relax these, then his leg muscles, working upwards through the body and each of the major muscle groups. The aim is to teach your client both to recognise excessive tension by having him produce it deliberately, and to recognise the release of tension and feelings of relaxation.

Meditative relaxation procedures

Meditative relaxation procedures involve mental or psychological relaxation techniques. Suggestions of relaxation are combined with focused attention which can have a meditative effect. For example, your client might focus on pleasant imagery. Alternatively, he could focus on silently repeating a word. The word 'relax' is a good one to use for obvious reasons.

Isometric relaxation procedures

Isometric relaxation procedures involve one muscle working against another or exerting pressure against an immobile object. While your client might be able to sit quietly in a chair and reduce his tension, this skill may not transfer adequately to everyday situations. For this reason, it is important that your client learns a technique which he can use to help him relax in these everyday situations without others being aware that that is what he is doing. Most of the isometric relaxation exercises do not involve any apparent movement or change in posture and therefore your client can practise them without embarrassment. Other isometric exercises involve some degree of movement and they can be practised when activities such as stretching are not likely to draw attention or be inappropriate.

If using the isometric procedures, encourage your client to practise several times each day so that he becomes skilled in their use. It is especially important that he practises using them when he is in stressful situations. The aim is gradually to train your client to relax in a way that is semi-automatic or without conscious thought.

Important points to remember

When practising any of the different types of relaxation procedures, your client should:

(1) carry out relaxation exercises whenever tension is noticed;
(2) recognise that relaxation is a skilled activity that will improve only with practice; and
(3) avoid tensing his muscles to the point of discomfort or holding the tension for long periods of time.

Training Procedures

Scripts are provided below for the first two types of relaxation procedures. These scripts are for guidance only and the specific details should be changed and expanded to accommodate the personal needs of your client. The whole procedure should take 20 to 30 minutes to complete. Once you have developed a script for your client, you can read it to him in a session and/or make a relaxation tape for him. It is also important to use your client's practice tape in therapy sessions so that there is continuity between therapy and home practice.

Begin with a brief overview of the ideal conditions for the technique. For example you might say:

'I want you to listen to my voice, and to focus on what I am going to say and what I ask you to do. Be sure that you are seated comfortably and that your legs, arms and head are supported. Try to sit in a position where you are able to rest for 30 minutes without pressure points or discomfort developing. If necessary disconnect the telephone, turn off the stove, and ask other household members not to interrupt you for 30 minutes. At first, you may find the procedure difficult to master, but with practice it will become easier. Eventually, with daily practice, your natural response to tension will be relaxation. Also be aware that you are in control and if you feel unpleasant sensations, you may stop the exercise.'

Progressive muscle relaxation

First, begin by preparing your client for the overall process. For example, you could say:

'I am going to guide you through a series of simple exercises which will involve tensing and relaxing groups of muscles in your body in an orderly sequence. Remember, when tensing your muscles it is important not to strain or cause pain but to use only a moderate amount of tension. Your aim is to learn to identify and contrast the feelings of tension and relaxation, so that you can reduce tension later. At the end of the exercises, you will feel more relaxed and this restful feeling should last for some time afterwards.'

Second, guide your client through tensing and relaxing phases for each of the muscle groups you have chosen to work on. For example, you might begin with the feet, then the legs, stomach, arms, hands, neck and head muscles. Get your client to tense and relax each muscle group twice. Notice that the tensing phase is short and sharp, while the relaxing phase allows for a gradual unwinding and time to enjoy the sensations. During the tensing phase, allow your voice to speed up a little and, in contrast, slow your voice down for the relaxation phase. Here are some examples of the phases for the feet and legs which can be modified to apply to any muscle group:

Tensing phase: feet
'We will start with your feet in a moment. I will ask you to tense the muscles in your feet by curling the toes either downwards or upwards, and while you are doing this please notice where the tension occurs and how it feels. I will ask you to hold the tension for five seconds. Now, put the tension into your feet and hold that tension for five seconds—one, two, three, four, five.'

Relaxing phase: feet
'Now, let that physical tension go and as you do, feel yourself starting to relax in those muscles and more generally. Notice the tension slipping away and the changes in the sensations which you experience. Let all of the tension go. Actively let the tension flow out of your muscles, and notice how they relax, loosen, become slack and unwind. Really focus on those sensations of relaxation in your feet. As you do, feel yourself dropping down in your chair. Your whole body is benefiting from the relaxed sensations. Enjoy these sensations for a few seconds now . . . Let any remaining tension go from your feet. You will notice that your feet might be feeling warm. Focus on these pleasant feelings. Allow yourself to focus on the feelings and let other thoughts drift away. When distracting thoughts come to mind, let them go again by bringing your attention back to the feelings in your feet.'

Repeat tensing and relaxing phases.

Tensing phase: legs
'Now, tense the muscles in your legs, and notice where the tension occurs and how it feels. Hold the tension for five seconds—one, two, three, four, five.'

Relaxing phase: legs
'Now, let all the physical tension drain out of your legs. Feel yourself relaxing in those muscles and more generally. Let all of the tension go. Check that your feet are relaxed as well. Feel your legs and feet becoming warm and heavy. Enjoy these sensations for a few seconds now . . . Let any remaining tension go from your legs. Allow yourself to focus on the feelings and let other thoughts drift away.'

Repeat tensing and relaxing phases. Then go on to tense and relax other muscle groups.

Meditative relaxation

In the following example, meditative relaxation combines deep breathing with a focus on the word 'relax'. This meditative approach can be used alone or in combination with any of the other relaxation methods outlined in this chapter:

Speak slowly and calmly. . .

'I am going to guide you through a series of simple exercises which will involve thinking of a word over and over again and letting other thoughts slide by. Your aim is to develop a sense of mental calm, and thereby reduce worrying thoughts and physical tension. Close your eyes and begin by focusing on your breathing. Take a deep breath. Hold it for a couple of seconds. And breathe out. Think of the word 'relax'. Visualise it and see it floating in your mind. Now as you breathe in, count 'one'. As you breathe out say the word 'relax' in your mind. As you breathe in, count 'two'. Then say 'relax' as you slowly breathe out and really feel the tension and worries leaving you. Again breathe in and count 'three'. Breathe out and say 'relax'. And with that word 'relax', let all the tension in your body drop away. Feel yourself becoming more calm and relaxed. Continue to focus on your breathing and each time you breathe out, say that word 'relax' and allow all distracting thoughts to just pass by. Continue to do that now.'

Another approach to meditative relaxation is to combine a simple imaginary scene with deep breathing. The scene described below could be combined with some of the other methods outlined in this chapter, including the meditative approach described above. Alternatively, you could expand the scene to a 30-minute script, using specific details based on what your client sees as a pleasant, relaxing environment. Designing the imaginary scene around your client's preferences is important because a script which is relaxing to one person might provoke anxiety for another person. Here is a short script of an imaginary scene designed to induce relaxed feelings:

'Close your eyes and focus on your breathing. Take a deep breath. Hold it for a couple of seconds. And breathe out. Just notice your breathing for a few moments. Imagine that you are somewhere outdoors, in a very pleasant place. A place that feels safe and quiet. Notice your surroundings. The weather is pleasant and warm. The sky is clear and blue. Imagine yourself resting in this place. Notice your breathing. Take slow deep breaths. Hold for a moment and let go. As you let go, feel yourself become more and more relaxed. Imagine yourself looking up at the sky. You see a feather gently floating down. A slight breeze blows it along and it flutters and turns. You can feel the breeze caressing your skin as you watch the feather. Slowly the feather falls. As you watch it coming down, feel yourself sinking deeper and deeper into a relaxed state. Notice your breathing is becoming slower and deeper. Continue to relax as you watch the feather gently floating towards the ground.'

Isometric relaxation

Training in progressive muscle relaxation will greatly enhance your client's ability to practise isometric relaxation exercises. Before commencing isometric exercises, reassure your client that the length of time he holds his breath is not critical and that some people find it difficult to hold their breath for very long without feeling distressed. Remind him that he is in control of the exercise and should make adjustments to suit his own needs. Demonstrate the exercises for each muscle group before commencing the procedure and then get your client to try them out. The following is an example of isometric relaxation procedures, using one muscle group and incorporating some aspects of meditative relaxation:

'Take a small breath and hold it for a short time—say, to a count of seven. At the same time, pull yourself down into the chair with your hands and hold that tension. At the count of seven, breathe out slowly and silently say the word 'relax'. As you do this, let go of all the tension in your arms. Just let your hands rest by the side of the chair. Now, for a minute or so, notice your breathing and say 'relax' to yourself each time you breathe out. Allow all the tension to leave your body.'

This procedure should be followed for approximately one minute and may be repeated as necessary until your client feels relaxed. You and your client may wish to choose one or more of the following isometric exercises:

(1) Tense all the muscles in the thighs and calves.
(2) Push one muscle group against another. This might involve crossing the legs and pushing down with the upper leg while trying to lift the lower leg.
(3) Place hands under each side of a chair and pull down into the chair.
(4) Place hands behind the head with interlocked fingers. Push forward while pushing the head backwards into the hands (the net effect of which would be no obvious movement).
(5) When standing, straighten legs to tense all the muscles, bending the knees back as far as possible and then releasing the tension.
(6) If travelling on public transport or in a public venue, push against a solid rail or a wall, placing tension in the arms or legs.

Encourage your client to identify muscle groups where tension will typically occur for him and focus on these in the isometric relaxation exercises. For example, if he tends to tense his neck muscles, then exercise (4), where he pushes his head backwards against his interlocked hands can help to dissipate the tension in his neck.

Trouble-shooting

There are a number of difficulties which your client can encounter with relaxation training. Your client for example may initially complain that he cannot relax and that the procedure is not working. Emphasise from the outset that the techniques take time to learn and that the benefits will gradually come with regular practice.

People who have been chronically tense for long periods can also sometimes experience the relaxation sensations as a loss of control and this can be frightening. Warn your client that he may experience unusual sensations at first. Explain that with time these new feelings of relaxation will become familiar and therefore more comfortable to him. Explore your client's reactions immediately after the relaxation exercise. If he indicates that he finds these sensations disturbing, allow some time to discuss his experience. It is also important for you to emphasise and demonstrate that he is in control of the exercise at all times.

Your client may encounter obstacles to practising relaxation, such as insufficient time or a lack of privacy. While helping him to plan a solution to these problems, also remind him of the value of investing time now for greater returns later. Motivational interviewing techniques (Chapter 3) will be useful if your client seems to be making excuses to avoid practising. You can also use problem-solving techniques (Chapter 5) to help him incorporate the exercises into a daily routine. One strategy might be to schedule the exercises into his old drinking or drug-using time-slot so that he is learning to use time more constructively. If he continues to have problems with home practice, ask him to make notes about them at the time of practice and bring them along for discussion.

RESOURCES LIST

Benson, H. (1975). *The Relaxation Response*. New York: Morrow.
  —An excellent overview of the effects of relaxation procedures on physiological and psychological parameters.
Clarke, J. C. & Saunders, J. B. (1988). *Alcoholism and Problem Drinking: Theories and Treatments*. Sydney: Pergamon Press.
  —Provides an excellent summary of the rationale and method of various relaxation procedures. It is especially useful for trouble-shooting information.
Monti, P.M., Abrams, D.B., Kadden, R.M. & Cooney, N.L (1989). *Treating Alcohol Dependence: A Coping Skills Training Guide* (pp. 89–103). New York: Guilford Press.
  —Presents detailed guidelines for progressive muscle relaxation and meditative relaxation.

PRACTICE SHEET

MONITORING YOUR MUSCLE TENSION

Name: _____   Date __/__/__

Over the coming weeks, while you are practising relaxation procedures, use this form to monitor the tension in your body. You will need to do this each day, so make sure that you have enough copies of the form. Before you do your relaxation exercise, indicate the location and intensity of your muscle tension by ticking the appropriate box. After you have finished your relaxation exercise, re-rate your muscle tension by putting a cross in the appropriate box. You can then compare ticks and crosses to monitor the changes you are experiencing as a result of the relaxation procedures. For instance, you might be feeling a medium amount of tension in your neck prior to doing the exercise, so you would tick the box for 'medium'. After the exercise, you might find that your neck tension has reduced and you can put a cross in the 'low' tension box, to reflect this change.

Location of tension	Muscle tension rating			
	High	Medium	Low	Nil
Hands				
Forearms				
Upper arms				
Shoulders				
Neck				
Forehead				
Jaw				
Back				
Upper legs and calves				
Feet				

11

BEHAVIOURAL SELF-MANAGEMENT

RECOMMENDED USE

Behavioural self-management training involves a series of strategies such as self-monitoring, setting drinking limits, controlling rates of drinking, drink refusal, identifying problem drinking situations, learning alternative coping skills and self-reward.
127

Behavioural self-management is intended for those clients who wish to cut down rather than abstain from drinking and who do not have severe problems with or dependence on alcohol. Details of guidelines for helping to assess when a moderation goal is appropriate are discussed in Chapter 4, *Goal-setting*. In brief, however, it is stressed that clients choosing moderation should be free from any drinking-related physical problems or brain damage which would indicate a need to abstain for health reasons. Clients are also more likely to succeed with moderation if they have a drinking history suggesting that they can keep to drinking limits, have no diagnosed psychiatric problems (e.g. depression or personality disorder), and they have not shown frequent and/or severe signs of physical withdrawal (e.g. the DTs) when they stopped drinking.

Elements of the self-management training approach overlap with many therapeutic techniques dealt with in other sections of this book. This section will cover in most detail those techniques which are useful for moderating drinking and will cross-reference other sections of the manual where necessary.

You can provide behavioural self-management training in either individual or group settings. Researchers using this approach have varied treatment from 6 weeks of 90-minute sessions with individual clients to 8–10 weekly group sessions, each again of approximately 90 minutes.

GOALS

The goal of behavioural self-management is to teach your client specific skills so that she can reduce drinking to stable levels that minimise both the risk of physical ill-health and any other personal or social problems which her drinking might currently cause. These limits are often based on guidelines for 'responsible' or 'low-risk' drinking produced by health authorities. These guidelines are outlined in Table 4.

KEY CONCEPTS
Standard Drinks/Units

As different drinks contain different amounts of alcohol a standard drink provides a useful way of recording drinking. While the absolute amount of alcohol in a standard drink varies slightly from country to country (Australia = 10 g, UK = 8 g and US = ½ US fl. oz) a standard drink generally approximates the size of a typical serve of beer, wine or spirits. Pub measures equal to a standard drink are shown in Figure 2, at the end of this chapter.

Self-monitoring

Self-monitoring is one of the most useful and important aspects of self-management training. It involves daily recording of the amount drunk and the circumstances surrounding drinking. The aim of self-monitoring is to help your client become aware of how much, when, where and why she is drinking. It also provides an important and concrete way to record progress. In the early stages of treatment this information can be extremely useful in helping you and your client to identify those situations that are causing her problems, as well as those drinking situations that are troublefree. This information can then be used to create drinking rules and to develop strategies for coping with situations in which she is likely to drink more than her set limits. An example of a daily drinking diary is included for your use in the practice sheet at the end of this chapter.

METHOD
Rationale for Your Client

In introducing the self-management approach, emphasise that the aim is to teach your client skills to help her cut down drinking to a harm-free level. The

Table 4:   Guidelines for 'responsible' or 'low-risk' drinking

LEVEL OF RISK	AUSTRALIA[a]	UNITED KINGDOM[b]	USA
Responsible or low risk: Level at which drinking is unlikely to cause health problems	*For men*: 4 standard drinks per day, with a maximum of 28 drinks per week *For women*: 2 standard drinks per day, with a maximum of 14 drinks per week	*For men*: A maximum of 21 drinks per week *For women*: A maximum of 14 drinks per week	There are no official limits set in the USA However, a consensus of clinical opinion recommends that a limit of 3 drinks per day is responsible drinking
	Australian authorities recommend that your client have *at least two alcohol-free days* per week		
Hazardous or increasing risk: Level at which there is an increasing risk of problems such as raised blood pressure, stroke, CHD, various cancers and liver cirrhosis	*For men*: 4–6 standard drinks per day, or from 28–42 drinks per week *For women*: 2–4 standard drinks per day, or from 14–28 drinks per week	*For men*: From 21–50 drinks per week *For women*: From 14–35 drinks per week	
Harmful or definitely dangerous: Sustained drinking at this level is likely to cause physical, mental and social problems	*For men*: More than 6 standard drinks per day or 42 drinks per week *For women*: More than 4 standard drinks per day or 28 drinks per week	*For men*: More than 50 drinks per week *For women*: More than 35 drinks per week	

[a]*Source:* Pols & Hawks (1992).
[b]*Source:* Secretary of State for Health (1993).

target level of drinking will be decided by your client with your help. Emphasise that learning new drinking habits is difficult and requires considerable patience and effort. Practising the skills and completing any agreed upon homework tasks will therefore be extremely important to making progress. It is also important to be confident in your approach, so tell your client that if she follows the programme there is a very good chance of success. You might, however, also wish to say that moderation is not the best solution for all who try it and that if desired you will also be able to help your client work towards a goal of abstinence.

Before Starting

It is recommended that before beginning with the specific self-management aspects of this approach, some time should be spent with your client in focusing on and strengthening her resolution to change. On an individual basis this might involve motivational interviewing strategies (Chapter 3). In a group context clients could discuss the pros and cons of drinking, with home practice involving writing down personal reasons for cutting down. Basic educational information, including personalising the health effects of alcohol (pp. 46–8) could also be addressed in early sessions. You might also like to recommend a self-help manual to your client (see *Resources List*).

Elements of Behavioural Self-management

Behavioural self-management training involves the following steps:

(1) Daily self-monitoring.
(2) Setting limits on drinking.
(3) Keeping to set limits.
(4) Identifying troublesome (high-risk) and troublefree drinking situations and devising strategies to cope with the former.
(5) Maintaining new drinking habits.

Daily self-monitoring

You will first need to ensure that your client understands what a standard drink is. Explain that as different drinks contain different amounts of alcohol a standard drink provides a useful way of recording drinking. Describe how much alcohol a standard drink contains, as explained in *Key Concepts* above, and show your client Figure 2 at the end of this chapter which illustrates the standard units of alcohol. In discussing this figure you might also point out that large beer glasses (such as schooners or pints) are 1½, not 1 standard drink. It is also important to warn your client that home-poured drinks are often bigger and therefore contain more alcohol. For this reason you might suggest that your client practises pouring standard drinks at home, using a measuring glass.

You can then introduce the notion of 'self-monitoring'. Explain that filling in a 'day diary' will help your client to keep track of her drinking and will be a good reminder that she is trying to limit drinking. It will also be a good way of learning more about when, where and why she drinks and will be a concrete way for both of you to see how she is progressing over the following weeks. Show your client how to complete a day diary such as the one provided at the end of this chapter. We suggest that your client record the day and date, hours over which she drank, where she was and with whom, what she was doing, how she felt before drinking and what happened (if anything) as a result of drinking. 'What happened' might include either good consequences such as 'met some nice people', or less desirable outcomes such as 'got drunk and angry'. The last columns involve writing down the type of beverage and the amount drunk and then converting that information into standard drinks.

As it might not always be realistic to expect that your client will fill in such details while she is drinking in a public setting, encourage her to complete the diary *as soon as possible* after drinking. It might, however, be very useful to suggest that your client jots down on a small piece of paper, even in tally form, each drink as she consumes it. You should also discuss with her any potential problems or obstacles that might prevent her from filling in the forms. Day diaries should then be reviewed at the beginning of each session throughout treatment, highlighting successes and briefly discussing problems.

Setting limits on drinking

It is crucial to the success of behavioural self-management that your client sets realistic and concrete limits to her drinking. These limits should be set at levels that minimise both the risk of physical ill-health and any other social problems which your client's drinking might currently produce. Of course, your client must also be confident that the limits are achievable for her.

You could use the guidelines for responsible drinking provided by the various national health authorities as a basis for setting these limits. These guidelines are set out in Table 4 and can be used to set either weekly or daily limits. While you might choose to focus on weekly limits, with flexibility in daily levels of drinking, you should stress that, on the basis of definitions of binge drinking provided by health authorities, men should *never* drink more than 8 drinks and women *never* more than 6 drinks in a row on any day. Health authorities in Australia also recommend that your client should have *at least two alcohol-free days* each week.

There are two ways of helping your client to reduce her overall drinking to within responsible limits. The first involves a 'tapering off' approach. Using this method, you would negotiate limits with your client each week, that would be gradually reduced until she reached her final, low-risk goal.

The second, quite different approach (from Sanchez-Craig, 1984) involves negotiating with your client for an initial period of abstinence (say, over the first two weeks of treatment) after which she would recommence drinking within set limits. This approach has the advantage of providing a 'time-out' period from all drinking habits. During this period you and your client can focus on monitoring situations in which she is tempted to drink, identify the strategies she has already mastered to cope with urges and temptations, and develop further skills to cope with any situations in which she was not able to successfully abstain (see *Troublesome and Troublefree Drinking Situations*, below). A period of abstinence will also ensure that your client has recovered from any minor dulling of mental functioning which regular heavy consumption might have caused. After the period of abstinence has been completed, strategies to slow down and limit drinking can be introduced while you continue to identify and solve any new troublesome drinking situations that occur.

Trouble-shooting

If your client has not been able to show strong signs of being able to reduce her drinking within six weeks then discuss a goal of abstinence with her and reassess whether other treatment strategies might be of assistance.

Keeping to set limits

Provided at the end of this chapter is a list of strategies that your client can use to help her to keep within her drinking limits. Discuss these strategies with your client and encourage her to try them out over the following weeks. Ask her to note on her day diary when a certain strategy has been useful so that she learns to recognise which techniques are most effective for her. Two further strategies are also discussed in more detail below.

Tracking blood alcohol concentrations: A simple rule to help pace drinking is that of never drinking more than one drink per hour. While this is probably the easiest and most efficient rule to recommend to your client, you might also wish to introduce the notion of blood alcohol concentrations (BACs) using the charts provided at the end of this chapter. These charts show roughly how many standard drinks can be consumed across different lengths of drinking sessions in order to maintain a level of alcohol in the blood of 0.05% or 0.08%. For example, a woman who is less than 60 kg should not drink more than 3 drinks in 4 hours if she wishes to remain under 0.05%.

Of course, clients should be discouraged from drinking *at all* if they intend to drive or operate any other complex machinery. Drinking before swimming, engaging in water sports or in any other potentially hazardous environment should also be strongly discouraged.

For any prospective drinking session encourage your client to plan both how long she intends to drink for and the maximum BAC she will allow. The charts can then be used as a rough guide to how long each drink should last.

Stress that the charts provide only rough guides because people's bodies deal in different ways with alcohol. For example, the same amount of alcohol has a greater effect: (a) on a light rather than a heavy drinker; (b) on women rather than men (due to lower amounts of water in women's bodies to dilute the alcohol); (c) if drunk quickly (as the rate of drinking exceeds the rate the liver can remove the alcohol); and (d) if drunk on an empty stomach or in a 'bubbly' mixer (as the alcohol gets into the bloodstream more quickly).

Drink refusal: Drink-refusal skills are also important for occasions when your client has reached her set limit or is trying to space out her drinks. These skills are essential if your client has difficulty in resisting social and/or peer pressures to drink. Teaching drink refusal involves demonstrating both appropriately assertive and inappropriate ways of refusing offers of drinks. Your client should also have the opportunity to role-play refusing drinks in a variety of situations. Details of drink-refusal training are found in Chapter 6.

Troublesome and troublefree drinking situations

These strategies overlap with aspects of relapse-prevention training and are discussed only briefly here. For more detail refer to Chapter 16.

After a few weeks of self-monitoring, examine your client's day diaries with her and identify troublesome or 'high-risk' drinking occasions. These situations where drinking to a set limit was difficult to achieve or where drinking resulted in problems. Your client might also generate further examples of these situations from her past experiences. Look for common themes in the troublesome drinking occasions, such as particular drinking friends or places; times of day or certain days of the week; whether your client was hungry or thirsty; how long the drinking sessions lasted; or the way she was feeling before starting to drink. For example, your client might find that she always over-drank in the company of certain friends, when she had lots of money with her or when she was angry or upset.

It is important that your client attempts to avoid drinking in these troublesome situations. You may wish, therefore, to use the characteristics of the trouble-some occasions to create some drinking rules. In the example above, your client might decide that she: (a) will avoid drinking with the problem friends; (b) limit the amount of money she carries to any drinking session; and (c) not drink when she is angry or upset. The characteristics of the troublefree drinking situations can also be included in the rules. For example, if your client never has trouble keeping to limits when she has another activity planned for later, one of her drinking rules might state that she will drink only when she has planned something to do afterwards. Encourage your client to write down her drinking rules and keep them in a readily accessible place!

In addition to creating these rules, it will be important to work with your client in generating a range of thoughts and/or behaviours that provide an alternative to drinking in the troublesome situations. For example, if she drinks when angry or upset, work on listing other ways of dealing with those feelings. These might include going for a walk, visiting another friend or applying assertiveness skills (Chapter 7).

You should also stress to your client the importance of *planning ahead*, that is of considering strategies to help her cope *before* entering a situation where alcohol will be available and where the temptation or pressures to overdrink are strong.

Trouble-shooting

In some instances you might find that your client has difficulty in generating alternative thoughts or actions to help her cope with high-risk situations. Under these circumstances you might wish to spend some time teaching problem-solving skills. Details of this procedure are found in Chapter 5. You might also discover that other common themes emerge. For example, your client could be drinking to cope with pressure or anxiety, or drinking as a result of conflict with her spouse. Such themes might indicate that your client would benefit from training in other specific skills such as relaxation, assertiveness or communication skills, or couples therapy. Details of these skills training procedures are given in the relevant chapters in this book.

Maintaining new drinking habits

Important aspects of maintaining change involve establishing self-rewards for achieving goals and exploring alternatives to drinking. Encourage your client to reward herself for cutting down her drinking and sticking to her drinking rules. In doing so emphasise that her rewards should be meaningful, planned in advance and given only when a well-defined goal has been met, not given for 'near' successes, and given as soon as possible after they have been earned.

Work with your client in generating the list of rewards that will help her stay on track. Her list could include fun activities or special rewards from her partner. However, it is strongly recommended that your client should avoid using a partner to police her behaviour—especially if goals aren't being met. Another simple self-reward might involve charting weekly progress. This would involve drawing a simple graph on which the total amount drunk each week was plotted.

It is also extremely important that you encourage your client to take up pleasurable activities to replace hours that were once spent drinking. Examples of activities might include taking up a new hobby, family outings, volunteer work, joining a club or a gym, and so on. Help your client to set in place specific and detailed action plans to ensure that she initiates these new activities.

Terminate treatment when your client has reached her goal and is relatively confident that she can cope with potentially high-risk situations. Encourage your client to continue self-monitoring. Make sure that you have discussed ways of coping if she experiences a slip or relapse to heavy drinking. This important aspect of relapse-prevention training is discussed on p. 184. Finally, it is also essential to negotiate arrangements with your client for adequate aftercare (see Chapter 17). Clients who are unable to maintain moderated drinking should be offered assistance towards achieving an abstinence goal.

AN IMPORTANT NOTE ON BRIEF INTERVENTIONS FOR PROBLEM DRINKERS

For some clients who want to moderate their drinking, particularly those who present with low dependence and few alcohol-related problems, it is likely that a brief intervention over a few sessions (e.g. one to five sessions) will be all that is required, and often all that is wanted. These clients should find that a self-help manual, with brief support and guidance from you, provides them with enough assistance to produce their desired behaviour change. You should of course ensure that you offer such clients adequate access to follow-up and aftercare.

RESOURCES LIST

Self-help Manuals

Heather, N., Richmond, R., Webster, I., Wodak, A., Hardie, M. & Polkinghorne, H. (1989). *A Guide to Healthier Drinking: A Self-help Manual*. Sydney: Clarendon Printing.
—This brief and colourful manual is available from the Brief Intervention Unit at the University of New South Wales, Sydney, NSW 2052, Australia.
Miller, W.R. & Munoz, R.F. (1982). *How to Control Your Drinking* (rev. edn). Albuquerque, NM: University of New Mexico Press.
—An extremely comprehensive and detailed manual. It is particularly useful as a reference for therapists.
Robertson, I. & Heather, N. (1985). *So, You Want to Cut Down Your Drinking?* Edinburgh: Scottish Health Education Group.
—Adapted for local readers, this attractive publication is free for those in Scotland but sample copies are available from Scottish Health Education Group, Woodburn House, Canaan Lane, Edinburgh EH10 4SG, UK.
Robertson, I. & Heather, N. (1986). *Let's Drink to Your Health! A Self-help Guide to Safe and Sensible Drinking*. The British Psychological Society, St Andrews House, 48 Princess Road East, Leicester, LEI 7DR.
—An extremely useful and comprehensive self-help manual, written for UK readers.
Robertson, I. & Heather, N. (1987). *Let's Drink to Your Health! A Guide to Safe and Sensible Drinking*. Sydney: Angus & Robertson.
—An adaptation of the above manual for readers from Australia or New Zealand.

Other Resources

Heather, N. & Robertson, I. (1989). *Problem Drinking* (2nd edn). Oxford: Oxford University Press.
—This is a classic text on the practical applications of social learning theory to problem drinking. It includes a discussion of the goals of abstinence and moderation and presents evidence supporting the use of skills-based approaches in treatment for alcohol problems.
Hester, R.K. & Miller, W.R. (1989). Self-control training. In R.K. Hester & W.R. Miller (Eds), *Handbook of Alcoholism Treatment Approaches: Effective Alternatives* (pp. 141–149). New York: Pergamon.
—Provides practical guidelines for behavioural self-management as well as research findings regarding its effectiveness.
Miller, W.R., Heather, N. & Hall, W. (1991). Calculating standard drink units: International comparisons. *British Journal of Addictions*, **86**, 43–47.
—As the title suggests, this article provides detailed international comparisons of the measurement of standard units. It is also useful for those who are interested in the effects of differing strengths of beer, wine and spirits in calculating alcohol consumption.

Pols, D. & Hawks, D. (1992). *Is There a Safe Level of Daily Consumption of Alcohol for Men and Women?* Canberra: AGPS.
—Describes and explains guidelines for sensible drinking recommended by the Australian National Health and Medical Research Council.
Sanchez-Craig, M. (1984). *Therapist's Manual for Secondary Prevention of Alcohol Problems: Procedures for Teaching Moderate Drinking and Abstinence.* Toronto: Addiction Research Foundation.
—This therapist's manual also details treatment guidelines for clients with abstinence goals and can be obtained from the Addiction Research Foundation Bookstore, 33 Russell St, Toronto, Ontario, M58 2S1, Canada.
Secretary of State for Health. (1993). *The Health of the Nation: A Strategy for Health in England.* London: HMSO.
—Describes goals and targets for improving the health of people in England, including the most recent guidelines regarding sensible drinking.
Sitharthan, T. & Kavanagh, D.J. (1990). Role of self-efficacy in predicting outcomes from a programme for controlled drinking. *Drug and Alcohol Dependence,* **27,** 87–94.
—Describes the development of a scale to assess your client's confidence in maintaining moderation across a range of situations.

Different alcoholic drinks vary a lot in strength. A standard drink is **CLIENT HANDOUT**
one which contains about 10 grams of alcohol. The servings
shown below are all equal to one standard drink.

LOW ALCOHOL BEER

2 x 285ml (middies)
(2 x 10oz)
10gm alcohol

ORDINARY BEER

285ml (middie)
(10oz)
10gm alcohol

TABLE WINE

PORT OR SHERRY

SPIRITS/LIQUEURS

120ml	60ml	30ml (nip)
(4oz)	(2oz)	(1oz)
10gm alcohol	**10gm alcohol**	**10gm alcohol**

Most people at home pour larger than standard drinks.
Especially when socialising, the habit of topping up drinks can
make it difficult to work out how much is actually being consumed.
From this table you can measure how much you drink.
For example, if you drink two double scotches and a middie
of ordinary beer, that's equivalent to five standard drinks.

Figure 2:   Measuring standard drinks

Source: Reprinted with permission of CEIDA (NSW, Australia), The Centre for Education and Information
on Drugs and Alcohol   PMB 6, PO Rozelle 2039 NSW, Australia

TIPS FOR DRINKING IN MODERATION

- PLAN AHEAD! Decide on the time period over which you will drink and what your limit will be. Then work out how long each drink must last and pace your drinking accordingly. Limit the amount of money you take with you to spend

- AVOID GULPING—take smaller sips and sip more slowly. Count the number of sips you take to finish your glass and then try to increase that on the next drink

- PUT DOWN YOUR GLASS BETWEEN SIPS—if it is in your hand you will drink from it more often

- DON'T REFILL YOUR GLASS UNTIL IT IS EMPTY—and don't let others (friends, waiters) refill it either

- ALTERNATE your drinks—try having an orange juice or a soft drink between alcoholic drinks

- COUNT your drinks

- DRINK LOW ALCOHOL BEVERAGES—try light or low alcohol beers in preference to regular beers

- DILUTE YOUR DRINKS by adding mixers to spirits, soda to wine, etc.

- NEVER DRINK ALCOHOL TO QUENCH YOUR THIRST—try drinking iced water or a soft drink first if you are thirsty

- AVOID SALTY NIBBLES such as crisps and nuts as they increase thirst

- EAT BEFORE DRINKING—this will mean that your drink will take longer to absorb and will have less effect on you. It will also mean that you won't be tempted to drink to stop hunger or simply to fill an empty stomach

- AVOID DRINKING IN 'SHOUTS'—buy your own drinks, explaining that you are trying to cut down. Alternatively, order soft drinks or skip rounds

- SAY 'NO THANKS'

- ORDER SMALLER SIZES of drinks, e.g, drink middies/half pints instead of schooners/pints

- DON'T HAVE YOUR FAVOURITE DRINK—try switching to a less favoured drink (although make sure it isn't a stronger one) to help break the habit, e.g. try a different beer to your usual. Drinking a less favoured drink might also mean you drink it more slowly

DAY DIARY

Day, Date Times	Where, with whom, doing what?	Feelings before drinking? Rate strength of craving (0–100)	What did you do (thoughts and actions)?	What happened? Behaviour, feelings, consequences	What did you drink?	Number of standard drinks
Mon 21/3 8pm–10pm	In a restaurant with friends, eating dinner, talking	Anxious, excited Craving (80)	Drank light beer. Recalled reasons for not getting drunk. Went home straight after meal	Stayed sober and had a good time. Felt proud of myself	4 glasses of light beer	2
Sat 26/3 8pm–1am	At a party with friends, dancing, talking	Feeling left out. Wanting to attract someone but afraid to make first move. Craving (90)	Drank to give myself the courage to join in	Got drunk. Next day, can't remember how I got home. Terrible hangover	375 ml bottle of rum, mixed	12½

Source: Adapted from Heather et al. (1989).

NUMBER OF STANDARD DRINKS AND BLOOD ALCOHOL CONCENTRATION (BAC) – MEN –

Decide on a BAC and find your weight. Read across to the time you would spend drinking. This tells you how many standard drinks it takes, on average, to reach the BAC you chose, in that time. Amounts above 8 drinks have been omitted from the chart because this would be binge drinking.

		TIME SPENT DRINKING				
BAC	WEIGHT	One hour	Two hours	Three hours	Four hours	Five hours
0.05% Cheerful & relaxed. Poor judgement, increased risk of accidents	Less than 70 kg (< 11 st)	2	3	4	4½	5
	70–80 kg (11–12 st 8 lbs)	2½	4	5	5½	6
	More than 80 kg (> 12 st 8 lbs)	3	4½	5½	5½	6
0.08% Warmth, well-being. Less self-control. Slow reactions, impaired driving	Less than 70 kg (< 11 st)	3½	4	5	5½	6½
	70–80 kg (11–12 st 8 lbs)	4	5	6	6½	7½
	More than 80 kg (> 12 st 8 lbs)	5	6	7	7½	8
0.12% Talkative, excited, emotional. Uninhibited, impulsive	Less than 70 kg (< 11 st)	5½	6	6½	7	7½
	70–80 kg (11–12 st 8 lbs)	6	7	8	—	—
	More than 80 kg (> 12 st 8 lbs)	7½	—	—	—	—

Source: Adapted from Heather *et al.* (1989).

NUMBER OF STANDARD DRINKS AND BLOOD ALCOHOL CONCENTRATION (BAC) – WOMEN –

Decide on a BAC and find your weight. Read across to the time you would spend drinking. This tells you how many standard drinks it takes, on average, to reach the BAC you chose, in that time. Amounts above 8 drinks have been omitted from the chart because this would be binge drinking.

TIME SPENT DRINKING

BAC	WEIGHT	One hour	Two hours	Three hours	Four hours	Five hours
0.05% *Cheerful & relaxed. Poor judgement, increased risk of accidents*	Less than 60 kg (< 9 st 6 lbs)	1½	2	2½	3	3½
	60–70 kg (9 st 6 lbs–11 st)	2	2½	3½	4	4½
	More than 70 kg (> 11 st)	2½	3	4	5	5½
0.08% *Warmth, well-being. Less self-control. Slow reactions, impaired driving*	Less than 60 kg (9 st 6 lbs)	2½	3	3½	3½	4
	60–70 kg (9 st 6 lbs–11 st)	3	3½	4½	4½	5½
	More than 70 kg (> 11 st)	3½	4½	5-1.2	5½	6
0.12% *Talkative, excited, emotional. Uninhibited, impulsive*	Less than 60 kg (< 9 st 6 lbs)	3½	4	4½	4½	5
	60–70 kg (9 st 6 lbs–11 st)	4½	5	5½	5½	—
	More than 70 kg (> 11 st)	5	6	—	—	—

Source: Adapted from Heather *et al.* (1989).

12

COUPLES THERAPY

RECOMMENDED USE

There are a range of different approaches to couples therapy. The methods presented here are derived from the work of O'Farrell and Cowles (1989) and from Montgomery and Evans (1983). This chapter describes how to use couples therapy when your client has a drinking problem as the effectiveness of couples therapy in the treatment of other drug use problems has not been tested. Couples therapy is only appropriate when there is agreement between you, your client and your client's partner that the partner's involvement would be beneficial.

The approach described in this chapter aims to enhance the couple's communication in a way that will *support changes in your client's drinking*. Although it is designed to improve the partners' communication, it is *not* aimed at solving entrenched relationship problems or counteracting violence.

Since couples therapy aimed at changing problem drinking requires that the partners are able to work together, it is most appropriate with couples who have moderate to low distress in their relationship, are living together, are at least high school educated and are employed. It is likely to be especially effective if the couple have sought help shortly after a crisis which has threatened the stability of their relationship.

The approach can be modified to include other significant people in your client's life, such as parents, flatmates or adult children. However, it is not recommended for solving family problems. If your assessment indicates that your client's family is in need of professional help or the children are in need of counselling, arrange for a referral to appropriate specialists.

Therapy with couples can be conducted either with individual couples or in group settings of up to four couples. In the group setting, two therapists are required. Groups provide individual couples with the opportunity to share their experiences and learn from the problems and solutions raised by others.

GOALS

The overall goal is to improve the couple's relationship in ways that will strengthen the capacity and commitment to achieve and sustain a change in drinking. This goal can be broken into several steps:

- To change alcohol-related interactional patterns and develop interactions that support the change in drinking behaviour
- To help the couple confront and resolve relationship conflicts without your client resorting to drinking
- To mend rifts in the relationship that have been aggravated as a result of the alcohol abuse
- To help the couple develop shared activities that are rewarding and do not involve alcohol or other drugs

Couples therapy emphasises interactions between people. It is very important to *avoid blame* when conducting this therapy. In particular, your client's partner should *not* be made to feel guilty or responsible for your client's drinking. The therapy should also emphasise that the *drinking* is the problem, rather than the drinker. Always focus on the behaviour as the problem on which the partners work together.

KEY CONCEPTS

Client and Partner

For the purposes of this chapter, the term 'drinker' refers to the person who has alcohol problems and the term 'partner' refers to that person's husband, wife or partner. It is important to keep in mind that both partners are your clients. Avoid the temptation to side with one or the other partner when a conflict arises. Ideally, once you have commenced couples therapy, you should only be seeing the drinker in the presence of his partner so that your relationship is with them as a couple rather than with one partner in particular.

Time-out

Escalating conflict can be interrupted by one or both partners calling 'time-out'. The conversation is then postponed until both partners feel calm or the circumstances are more favourable for a non-aggressive resolution of the conflict.

Positive interactions

Increasing the number of positive interactions between the partners will greatly strengthen the relationship as each partner experiences direct benefits from being in the company of the other. This chapter outlines two techniques to increase positive interactions: (a) *shared rewarding activities* where the partners negotiate and plan some leisure activities that they can enjoy together without drug use or drinking; and (b) *catch your partner doing something nice* where the partners increase their awareness of the benefits of their relationship.

METHOD

Assessment

Before proceeding to therapy, you will need to establish that both partners want to try couples therapy and that their relationship is stable enough to allow them to work together. You will also need to briefly assess the partner's drinking pattern in case she also has alcohol-related problems or dependence. Include a brief individual interview with the partner to identify any concerns that she is reluctant to express in the presence of the drinker. An impending crisis in the relationship such as a legal, vocational or financial crisis, warrants immediate attention. Couples therapy should not proceed until this situation has been stabilised.

You might also wish to include in the assessment a structured self-completion questionnaire such as the Dyadic Adjustment Scale (Spanier, 1976; see *Resource List*). The overall score of this questionnaire is a measure of the level of distress in the relationship. When both partners fill out the questionnaire separately, you can help them to identify areas in the relationship that are sources of disagreement or dissatisfaction (such as finances, sexuality, household roles, leisure, expression of affection, etc.). Encourage the couple to discuss which areas need change in order to (a) help the drinker to stay away from alcohol and (b) help increase satisfaction in their relationship.

In providing couples therapy, you should initially focus on changing the drinking behaviour, using the techniques discussed in other chapters of this book. Encourage the partner to participate in the negotiation of treatment goals. The couple will need to decide how they are going to structure their lifestyle so that the drinker is not exposed to high-risk situations during the first few weeks of therapy. Once initial change in the drinking behaviour has been achieved, concentrate on improving the quality of the couple's communication. This includes training them in methods to deal effectively with conflict, including decreasing alcohol-related arguments, and to increase their positive interactions. During the last few sessions, work with the couple in developing relapse-prevention strategies (Chapter 16).

Trouble-shooting

Couples therapy will be made more complicated if your assessment reveals that the partner also has a drinking problem. Murray and Hobbs (1977) developed a method to help partners who drink excessively together and reinforce each other's drinking. The method was designed for couples aiming at moderation and has not been tested with an abstinence goal.

If you wish to use this method, you should begin by getting the couple to agree on specific drinking limits (see Chapter 11, *Behavioural Self-management*). Encourage them to think of previous situations where they reinforced each other's excessive drinking. Explain that one way to avoid this mutual reinforcement is to drink together only when they are staying within the limits. If one partner decides to breach the limits, he should remove himself from his partner's presence and consume his drink in relative isolation (e.g. in the bathroom or in a corner of the bedroom). In this way, he avoids tempting his partner to lapse and his own excessive drinking is not rewarded by his partner's company. You should use this method in conjunction with the other strategies discussed in this chapter.

Dealing with Conflict

Explain to the couple that conflict itself is not a bad thing because it reminds us that we are different individuals with different needs. The problem with conflict is that it can escalate to a point where things that are said or done in anger can cause damage to the relationship that cannot easily be repaired. Conflict might also increase the chances of relapse by placing additional stress on the drinker.

Decreasing alcohol-related arguments

Discuss whether the couple ever experience conflict about drinking. For example, they might argue about incidents in the past where the drinker has had alcohol-related problems. Conflicts can also be about future situations where the partner fears that the drinker is going to relapse. Explore each partner's perspective about the meaning of this conflict. For example, if the partner brings up the past, the drinker might feel defensive at what he sees as 'nagging'. However, it is important to identify the partner's good intentions. She is probably trying to motivate her partner to change, or to protect their relationship by warning him about the dangers of drinking. Reframing the conflict in this way conveys your empathy for the partner's concerns and opens the way for the suggestion that these arguments might not be the most effective method for preventing her partner's relapse.

Get the couple to brainstorm (pp. 67–8) other ways for the partner to express her concerns and for the drinker to respond without defensiveness. One idea is to specify a particular period of time, each day, during which the drinker will reiterate his commitment to the treatment goal and will listen to his partner's queries or concerns. The partner should agree not to raise past incidents or future events beyond the activities of that particular day. Both partners should agree from the outset to listen to each other without interruption and to finish on a positive note. It would be helpful to role-play (p. 11) such a conversation during therapy.

Time-out

Time-out methods may help the couple to deal with conflict as it arises. The key to effective time-out is the ability to recognise that the conflict is escalating. Encourage the couple to think about how their physical arousal increases as the conflict escalates. Encourage each person to try to identify a point at which it is possible to walk away from the argument easily and compare this to later stages of the conflict when that person feels less in control and more compelled to continue arguing. It is useful to get the partners to identify the kind of negative self-talk (see below) that might contribute to this escalation.

Once the couple can identify that there are early stages of the conflict in which they both feel more in control, introduce the concept of 'time-out'. This is where either one of the partners might say 'I feel uncomfortable, I would like time-out for 15 minutes'. Each partner might go into a separate room and breathe deeply until he/she feels more calm. They should wait until they both feel safe to resume the discussion at a less antagonistic level.

Time-out also provides the opportunity for either partner to request a more appropriate time for dealing with the conflict. For example, one partner might say 'I feel unhappy about discussing this right now. How do you feel about waiting until after we've finished dinner to talk about this?' Explain to the couple that if one partner just leaves an argument without making a time-out statement, this might be experienced by the other person as an aggressive action. Emphasise the importance of keeping communication avenues open all the time.

When both partners feel that they have been able to express their feelings adequately, this clears the way for a practical resolution to the situation that produced the conflict. You can help the couple to achieve this by teaching them problem-solving skills (Chapter 5). Because the solution could require change in the behaviour of one or both partners, you will also need to help the couple to develop effective negotiation skills. You might need to devote some sessions to role-play communication skills such as positive specific requests (p. 95) and validation (p. 96).

Time-out agreements could be most helpful in dealing with negative interactions that escalate quickly towards the threat of violence. If violence has been a problem for the couple, it is important to negotiate a commitment from the violent partner not to hit or threaten the other person. This would involve monitoring personal levels of arousal and contracting to take time-out to calm down before violence becomes a possibility. The agreement would also include a plan for the non-violent partner to leave home and stay at some designated place for a specified amount of time if threat of violence occurs, thereby imposing an extended period of time-out.

Trouble-shooting

Couples therapy aimed at changing the drinking is not an adequate intervention for dealing with ongoing or serious violence problems. If the couple have problems of this magnitude, appropriate referral is advisable, including practical support for the non-violent partner. The couples therapy approach, as described in this chapter, would be unsuitable for a couple with these kinds of problems.

Positive Interactions

One of the aims of couples therapy is to increase the positive feelings, good will and commitment in the relationship. For the couple whose relationship has repeatedly been damaged by crises associated with the drinking problem, there is a need to repair that relationship through shared positive experiences. In the more stable relationship, the change in drinking behaviour can itself cause some tension and need for readjustment. You can assist them in this process by helping them to increase their positive interactions.

Shared rewarding activities

Get each partner to make a separate list of possible activities that the couple might enjoy sharing. These activities will obviously exclude drinking. If the couple have problems in their sexual relationship it's a good idea also to exclude sexual activity from this exercise to avoid unnecessary pressure on either partner. Encourage the couple to use their imagination to choose things they might have done before as a couple or have always wanted to try. Then use these lists to help the couple to plan their future activities together. They might need help in negotiating conflicts or problems relating to the activities. Help the couple to avoid potential pitfalls that could prevent the activities from getting started, such as waiting until the last minute before planning or getting side-tracked on trivial details.

Encourage the couple to choose one or two activities to do as home practice and then use the next session to discuss the way in which these activities were planned, any difficulties that arose and the experience of each partner when these activities took place. Discuss with the couple how these shared rewarding activities can be continued as an ongoing source of mutual enjoyment at least once a week.

Catch your partner doing something nice

Ask the couple 'What are some things that your partner does which show that he or she cares about you?' Give each partner a copy of the practice sheet 'Catch Your Partner Doing Something Nice'. This has been adapted from O'Farrell and Cowles (1989). Ask each of them to record one caring behaviour a day that they have observed their partner performing. Ask them not to show each other their sheets but to save them until the next session.

In the following session, get the partners each to read out the caring behaviours that they wrote down. Ask them how it felt to be the recipient of the caring behaviour. Introduce the concept of acknowledging the caring behaviour and model an example. This should be an 'I-statement' (pp. 94–5) and should be specific about what the partner did and how the recipient felt. For example, one partner might say 'I liked it when you . . . ' or 'When you . . ., I felt . . .'. Draw the couple's attention to the use of eye contact, smiles, a sincere and pleasant voice. Emphasise the importance of focusing on the positive feelings. Note that it is counter-productive to compare this positive experience with previous negative experiences. Get each partner to role-play acknowledging some of the caring behaviours on his/her list.

For home practice, ask the couple to hold a 2–5 minute daily communication session in which each partner acknowledges one pleasing behaviour noticed that day. Use the next session to further practise this skill and discuss any feelings or problems that might have arisen from the home practice. Encourage the couple to continue this practice at home throughout the treatment pro-gramme and after treatment.

Pleasing days

'Pleasing days' are days when one partner tries to do as many pleasing things for the other as possible. Each partner selects a day without announcing it to the other partner. The aim is to focus on learning what is helpful, pleasing and comfortable to each other. The lists compiled on the practice sheet for the previous exercise could be used for inspiration. These exercises might feel a little artificial for some couples. You may need to explain that this is part of the learning process and once the couple have adjusted to fit these activities into their relationship, they will become more spontaneous.

Self-talk

Self-talk is discussed in Chapter 8, *Communication Skills*. It is relevant to couples therapy because negative self-talk can undermine the couple's positive interac-tions, particularly when one person negatively interprets the intentions of an-other. Get the couple to compare the following examples of self-talk:

'Why is he being nice to me? What does he want from me?'
'That was really considerate of him to do that. I will tell him so.'

'The ungrateful so-and-so. She doesn't even notice the good things I do.'
'That's disappointing but I can't expect her to notice every time I do some good things for her. I'll let her know that I felt disappointed when she didn't notice.'

Emphasise the way in which the more constructive self-talk helps to expand the communication between the partners, rather than cutting off that com-munication. Encourage each partner to monitor his or her own self-talk and notice how it influences the couple's communication. Get the couple to brain-storm some other examples of helpful and unhelpful self-talk.

Relapse Prevention

Introduce the couple to the concepts involved in relapse prevention. Help them to identify high-risk situations and early warning signs of relapse for the drinker. Introduce the concept of a 'relapse drill' (p. 184) and help the couple to devise strategies to minimise the length and consequences of drinking in the event of a lapse. Get the drinker to role-play and cognitively rehearse these strategies and be sure to discuss any doubts that either partner has about the future.

Trouble-shooting

If the drinker relapses during therapy, help the couple to address this in the next session. Get the couple to explore what happened before, during and after the drinking and try to highlight the antecedents and consequences of the drinking (see Chapter 16, *Relapse Prevention*). The drinking might have been a reaction to some extra-marital stress (for example, work pressures). In this case, encourage both partners to come up with some ideas of how the drinker might handle this stress in the future, without resorting to alcohol.

Other drinking situations could arise out of some needs within the relationship. O'Farrell and Cowles (1989) have identified two ways in which this can occur.

- Drinking might have adaptive consequences for the relationship, for example, by making sexual or emotional interaction easier. If this seems to be relevant, encourage the couple to explore alternative ways of achieving positive interaction. You might need to devote more time to refining the couple's communication skills. Montgomery and Evans (1983) have provided some tips for couples wanting to improve their sexual relationship and there are two other self-help books dealing with sex in the *Resources List*. You might need to refer the couple for therapy which is specifically aimed at enhancing their sexual relationship.
- Drinking could be a response to recurring, intense conflicts between the partners. In this case, you should explore the chain of events that lead up to and unfold as a result of the conflict. You will also need to identify how the couple have attempted to deal with this and where their coping strategies have broken down. Encourage them to talk about the source of conflict during the therapy session where you can help them to practise time-out (see above), communication skills and problem-solving.

WHEN THE PARTNER PRESENTS ALONE

Sometimes the drinker will be reluctant to come to therapy but the partner will seek help alone. It is very important to reiterate that couples therapy or therapy involving the partner is not about blaming the partner for the drinker's problems. Although you will want to respond to the partner's request for information about how to help reduce the drinker's problems, your primary emphasis should always be on the partner's welfare. If the partner is feeling isolated, it may help to introduce the idea of getting support for the family from Al-Anon or Al-Teen (p. 173).

Encourage the partner to talk about her personal goals. Sometimes the partner will have suspended the satisfaction of personal needs until the time when the drinker achieves recovery. Empathic counselling can help her to identify her needs and problem-solving techniques might be used to devise strategies for change.

Encouraging the partner to focus more on her own needs will in fact have an impact on the couple's relationship. As the partner becomes less focused on the drinking, the drinker may be forced to take more responsibility. Encourage the partner to take less responsibility for the protection of the drinker from alcohol-related consequences. The partner might like to try an experiment where she stops doing certain things which she normally does to ensure the drinker's comfort. For example, she might *refrain from*: (a) keeping missed meals for the drinker; (b) making the drinker comfortable when he has fallen into intoxicated sleep in the lounge room; (c) making excuses to employers for the drinker's absence from work; (d) cleaning up when the drinker has been sick; or (e) apologising to friends for the drinker's anti-social behaviour. Obviously, this list excludes situations where the consequences of drinking are potentially dangerous (e.g. where the drinker has passed out under potentially dangerous circumstances or where there is a risk of drink-driving).

Communication skills will also be useful for the partner. Discuss whether she and the drinker ever get caught up in alcohol-related arguments (see above). Discuss how certain ways of communicating may be aimed at protecting the drinker but seem to result in conflict. Self-talk and 'I-statements' are useful concepts to assist the partner to communicate to the drinker how she feels without becoming trapped in a no-win alcohol-related argument. Once again, the emphasis is on encouraging the partner to take responsibility for her own needs and give back the responsibility for the drinking to the drinker.

If the partner has experienced physical violence from the drinker, you will need to help devise a strategy for her own protection. For example, the partner might inform the drinker that the next time this occurs, she will call the police. Alternatively, the strategy might be for the partner to leave the home and stay at a designated place for a specified amount of time. Once the drinker has been informed of the chosen strategy, any physical violence should be met with immediate action so that the drinker realises that the partner is serious and will take action to protect herself.

RESOURCES LIST

Heiman, J., LoPiccolo, L. & LoPiccolo, J. (1976). *Becoming Orgasmic: A Sexual Growth Program for Women*. Englewood Cliffs, NJ: Prentice-Hall.
—A practical guide for women who want to improve their sexual satisfaction.

Kadden, R., Carroll, K., Donovan, D., Cooney, N., Monti, P., Abrams, D., Litt, M. & Hester, R. (1992). *Cognitive Behavioral Coping Skills Therapy Manual: A Clinical Research Guide for Therapists Treating Individuals with Alcohol Abuse and Dependence*. Project MATCH Monograph Series, Volume 3. Rockville, MD: National Institute on Alcohol Abuse and Alcoholism.
—This session-by-session manual provides brief guidelines on couples/family involvement in therapy.

Montgomery, B. & Evans, L. (1983). *Living and Loving Together*. Ringwood, Australia: Penguin.
—An excellent self-help book on improving relationships. It includes chapters on communication and conflict resolution, problem-solving and improving sexual satisfaction.

Murray, R.G. & Hobbs, S.A. (1977). The use of a self-imposed timeout procedure in the modification of excessive alcohol consumption. *Journal of Behavior Therapy and Experimental Psychiatry*, **8**, 377–380.
—Describes in detail a time-out procedure designed to assist couples where both partners wish to reduce their excessive drinking.

O'Farrell, T.J. & Cowles, K.S. (1989). Marital and family therapy. In R.K. Hester & W.R. Miller (Eds), *Handbook of Alcoholism Treatment Approaches: Effective Alternatives* (pp. 183–205). New York: Pergamon.
—Comprehensive guidelines for the behavioural approach to couples therapy on which this chapter is based.

O'Farrell, T.J. & Cutter, H.S.G. (1984). Behavioral marital therapy couples groups for male alcoholics and their wives. *Journal of Substance Abuse Treatment*, **1**, 191–204.
—Session-by-session guidelines for a 10-week couples therapy programme.

Sisson, R.W. & Azrin, N.H. (1986). Family-member involvement to initiate and to promote treatment of problem drinkers. *Journal of Behavior Therapy and Experimental Psychiatry*, **17**, 15–21.
—An approach for assisting partners of problem drinkers when they seek help alone.

Spanier, G.B. (1976). Measuring dyadic adjustment: New scales for assessing the quality of marriage and similar dyads. *Journal of Marriage and the Family*, **38**, 15–28.
—A validated scale for assessing couples' satisfaction with their relationship.

Zilbergeld, B. (1978). *Men and Sex: A Guide to Sexual Fulfilment*. London: Fontana.
—A practical guide for men who want to improve their sexual satisfaction. The book challenges common myths about sexuality.

PRACTICE SHEET

CATCH YOUR PARTNER DOING SOMETHING NICE!

Here are some examples of pleasing behaviours that you might catch your partner doing.

DAY	DATE	PLEASING BEHAVIOUR
Monday	2/2	Saved my dinner for me when I worked late
Tuesday	3/2	Took the kids for a drive while I had a sleep
Wednesday	4/2	Told me what a good job I did

Use the table below to record one nice thing your partner does for each day of the coming week. Don't show your partner your record until your next therapy session.

Name: _____ **Partner's name:** _____

DAY	DATE	PLEASING BEHAVIOUR
Monday		
Tuesday		
Wednesday		
Thursday		
Friday		
Saturday		
Sunday		

Source: Adapted from O'Farrell & Cowles (1989).

13

ANTABUSE

RECOMMENDED USE

Antabuse is the trade-name for the prescription drug disulfiram, which reacts chemically with alcohol in the body to produce unpleasant sensations. As a deterrent against further drinking, it is an appropriate treatment if your client wishes to abstain from alcohol and accepts the idea of external therapy to control her drinking. She must also be willing to cooperate with regular supervision of the daily Antabuse dosing because unsupervised treatment is far less effective. Antabuse treatment might be particularly useful if your client has tried other forms of treatment but has been unable to maintain abstinence from alcohol. It is also useful when further drinking by your client could lead to marriage breakup, loss of job, legal repercussions or immediate danger to health. For effective use, the treatment requires cooperation between you, your client and the prescribing doctor.

Termination of Antabuse treatment will depend upon your client's plans for the future. If she wishes to learn to drink in moderation, the Antabuse treatment may be only a short-term feature, lasting about a month. After that your client might move into a behavioural self-management programme (Chapter 11). If, on the other hand, your client wishes to continue with abstinence, you should review the Antabuse treatment at three and six months. A severely alcohol-dependent client may need to continue on Antabuse for twelve months or more. However, you should prepare your client for abstinence without Antabuse by training her in other skills such as drink refusal and relapse prevention (Chapters 6 and 16).

Antabuse treatment is not appropriate if your client has: (a) shown hypersensitivity to Antabuse; (b) heart disease; (c) advanced liver or renal disease; (d) psychotic states; and/or (e) is pregnant. Antabuse should not be administered until your client has abstained from alcohol for at least 24 hours. It is a prescribed medication and therefore it is a medical matter to determine your client's suitability and the potential adverse effects of drug interactions.

GOALS

Antabuse treatment aims to ensure that your client:

- Is deterred from any further drinking during treatment. Because Antabuse stays in her body for up to seven days after the last dosage, it assists your client to avoid impulsive drinking.
- Is assisted in the maintenance of abstinence over several months.
- Has a period of 'time-out' from alcohol, during which she can stabilise her lifestyle and learn skills that will assist in the long-term maintenance of abstinence.

KEY CONCEPTS

Antabuse–Alcohol Reaction

When alcohol is taken during Antabuse treatment, the Antabuse drug, disulfiram, interferes with the breakdown of alcohol in the digestive system. A toxic reaction causes the drinker to experience unpleasant sensations such as skin-flushing, sweating, nausea, vomiting, bad headaches and breathing difficulties. Other effects include thirstiness, coughing spasms, palpitations, dizziness, blurred vision, numbness of the hands and feet and insomnia. The drinker might also experience uneasiness or fear. The effects can last from 2 to 4 hours.

Dosage

All decisions about the appropriate dosage will need to be made after negotiation between you, your client and the prescribing doctor. The usual dosage of Antabuse is around 250 mg per day. The drug is taken in tablet form on a daily basis. If your client risks drinking during treatment and finds that she is able to do so without an Antabuse–alcohol reaction, the dosage may need to be increased and can be safely increased to 500 mg per day under medical supervision.

Antabuse might produce some side-effects such as drowsiness, psychotic reactions, or sensorimotor reactions such as numbness, tingling, or pain or weakness in the hands or feet. Other potential side-effects include impotence, headache, fatigue, dermatitis, stomach upset, or a metallic or garlic-like taste. These symptoms should subside in the first two weeks of treatment. If they persist beyond this time, the dosage might need to be reduced by the prescribing doctor.

Supervision

Supervision is a very important aspect of Antabuse treatment. Antabuse will only work if your client is regularly taking the prescription. You will need to have regular contact with your client, at least two or three times a week, to ensure that she is taking her prescription and to discuss any problems that have arisen. These meetings will also provide an opportunity for additional therapy such as skills training or relapse prevention. To strengthen the supervision arrangements, you and your client might wish to enlist further assistance from a third person who is close to your client (such as your client's partner or flatmate) depending upon her personal circumstances (see below).

METHOD

Rationale for Your Client

Begin by explaining to your client how Antabuse can help her to stay away from drinking. Focus on the advantages that Antabuse provides such as:

- The removal of the pressure to drink so that she can concentrate on therapy and on restoring order to her lifestyle.
- A concrete reason to give to herself and others for not drinking.
- A 'cooling down' period so that even if she decides to resume drinking, she will have to wait for up to seven days before the Antabuse leaves the body. Rather than drinking on impulse, your client therefore has time to consider carefully whether or not she really wants to resume drinking.

Before referring your client for prescription, explore her feelings about taking an external substance to cope with drinking problems. Explain that Antabuse is a useful aid in the process of achieving change but that does not, however, take away her choice or responsibility in learning to maintain abstinence. You should discuss with your client how long she would like to stay on Antabuse and what other strategies you could develop so that she can continue to abstain after she stops using Antabuse.

You will need to explain the unpleasant effects of drinking while on the Antabuse treatment. Your explanation of these effects is as much a deterrent as the drug itself! However, do not try to instil fear in your client as this may interfere with her willingness to comply with the treatment. Instead emphasise that these effects take away the desirability of drinking and therefore assist her in achieving and maintaining abstinence.

You should advise your client to seek medical attention if she experiences a reaction as a result of intentional or inadvertent alcohol consumption. Warn her to avoid all alcohol-containing preparations that might lead to ingestion of alcohol or absorption through the skin. Some examples are: certain cough syrups, sauces, vinegar, foods prepared with wine; alcohol-based cosmetics such as astringents, perfumes, after-shave lotions and alcoholic back rubs.

Referral for Prescription

When you refer your client to a general practitioner for a prescription of Antabuse, explain briefly your plan for treatment including how long you expect her to be using Antabuse. Indicate to the doctor that you hope to maintain communication regarding your client's treatment in case the prescription needs to be adjusted at any stage.

Trouble-shooting

If your client has a history of several previous failures with Antabuse treatment or is sceptical about the effects of Antabuse after several weeks of treatment, you may need to demonstrate the effects of the treatment by carrying out a medically supervised 'challenge'. Brewer (1984) proposed that the following procedure be carried out between one and two weeks after your client first starts taking Antabuse. Firstly, give your client the equivalent of 5 ml of ethanol (for example, 12 ml of brandy) and wait for 20 minutes. If she shows no reaction, give her a further 10 ml of ethanol (approximately 25 ml of brandy). At this stage, your client should start to experience some flushing and increased heart rate. If there is still no reaction, the dosage of Antabuse will need to be increased and the challenge repeated after another week of treatment. The main objective is to demonstrate to your client that Antabuse treatment is not all therapist 'bluff' but is actually a physical deterrent against drinking. The general practitioner should be aware that the challenge is being carried out and should be present.

Supervising the Dosage

Take an active role in supervising your client while she is receiving Antabuse treatment. Encourage your client to tag the daily dose of Antabuse to another routine event such as a mealtime or cleaning teeth before bed. This will help her to remember to take the dose daily. Explain that it is important that she tell you if a daily dose was missed so that you can both explore why this occurred and develop a new strategy for ensuring that future doses are taken every day.

Try to see your client at least twice, if not three times, a week for the first few weeks of treatment. This will assist her in her initial adjustment to the use of Antabuse. Depending upon your client's situation, you might wish to wait for two or three weeks of abstinence before commencing any other therapy. Many alcohol-related problems subside with abstinence and your client could experience considerable improvement in her physical and psychological health and social relations during the initial stages of treatment. Once she has been abstinent for two or three weeks she might be more willing and able to work with you in learning new coping skills and discussing relapse-prevention strategies. Be sure to maintain regular contact in session and/or by telephone throughout the whole Antabuse treatment programme.

Antabuse Agreements
Negotiating an agreement

Studies have found that the effectiveness of Antabuse treatment can be greatly enhanced by enlisting the help and cooperation of a third person (Azrin, Sisson, Meyers & Godley, 1982; O'Farrell & Bayog, 1986). This person might be the community nurse or health worker, the local clergyman, a close friend, a room mate, or your client's partner. If you are going to work with a third person, you will need to make sure that:

- Your client is willing and able to see this person every day
- The person is willing to be involved in an Antabuse agreement
- Involvement in the Antabuse supervision will not aggravate existing problems in the relationship between this person and your client

A method of supervision used with couples that has been found by O'Farrell and Bayog (1986) to enhance the outcome of Antabuse treatment is the *Antabuse agreement*. Although you will need to negotiate the contents of the Antabuse agreement according to the needs of your client and her partner, their method provides some basic features that you might like to include in your agreement. A sample agreement is presented at the end of this chapter.

Begin by establishing with the couple the objectives of the Antabuse agreement, with the view that it should be designed for the benefit of both partners. For example, the overall aim might be to ensure that the Antabuse treatment is successful without putting undue pressure on your client. To achieve this aim, you will need to help each partner define his or her role in the agreement. For example, they might agree that your client will take the Antabuse each day while her partner observes. Explain that this means your client's partner must be present and see the medication being taken. He should also record these observations on a calendar.

Ensure that the agreement provides ongoing support for the couple. For example, you might arrange to see them on a weekly basis, at least for the first month. You should also make a commitment to contact the couple by telephone at a specified time to monitor their progress and discuss any problems they may have.

Minimising alcohol-related conflict

The agreement should also aim to minimise any confrontation about drinking. For example, you might ask your client's partner to agree not to mention any past drinking episodes or any fears he has about future drinking episodes. Your client might also agree to refrain from discussion about drinking and, if necessary, request that her partner avoids such discussion. For further details about helping them to avoid alcohol-related conflict, see Chapter 12, *Couples Therapy*.

The agreement to minimise confrontation has two goals. Firstly, any discussion or arguments about your client's drinking might arouse anger or fear in your client that could precipitate relapse. Secondly, this part of the agreement will help the couple to avoid unpleasant interactions and may assist them in building mutual trust. The agreement might also include a provision for positive interactions. For example the couple might agree to thank each other at the time of the daily Antabuse observation as a way of acknowledging each partner's contribution to solving the drinking problem.

Recording the agreement

Details of the agreements should be in written form, such as in the example provided at the end of this chapter, and kept with the calendar and the Antabuse medication in the place where your client intends to take the Antabuse. The written agreement should include an expiry date that defines how long it will be in effect. When it is due to expire, make an appointment for the couple to come and see you to discuss their progress and decide whether a new agreement is necessary.

At all times stress that the agreement will only work if it is entered into freely by both people. It is *not* the responsibility of your client's partner to police the Antabuse dosing. Rather, his part of the agreement is simply to witness the dosing and refrain from discussion about drinking, while your client agrees freely to take the Antabuse in her partner's presence.

Apart from negotiating an agreement, you might want to provide additional assistance to the couple during your weekly meetings. If your client's drinking has been the central issue concerning the family for some time, the couple might need assistance in dealing with other issues that have become visible in the light of your client's new abstinence. The couple might benefit from learning some of the skills outlined in Chapter 12, *Couples Therapy* or a referral for specialist family assistance could be appropriate.

Trouble-shooting

Encourage both partners to agree to contact you if the taking of Antabuse is not observed for two consecutive days. This will give them the opportunity to discuss the reasons for this slip and work out strategies to prevent further slips.

RESOURCES LIST

The manufacturers of Antabuse provide informative leaflets that might be available from the prescribing practitioner. Other useful resources are listed below.

Azrin, N.H., Sisson, R.W., Meyers, R. & Godley, M. (1982). Alcoholism treatment by disulfiram and community reinforcement therapy. *Journal of Behavior Therapy and Experimental Psychiatry*, **13** (2), 105–112.
—This study gives evidence that the effectiveness of Antabuse increased for married clients when there was a supervision agreement and for single clients when the medication was given in the context of other skills training.
Brewer, C. (1984). How effective is the standard dose of disulfiram? A review of the alcohol–disulfiram reaction in practice. *British Journal of Psychiatry*, **144**, 200–202.
—This article argues that sufficiently high doses need to be prescribed in order for Antabuse therapy to be effective.
Brewer, C. (1986). Supervised disulfiram in alcoholism. *British Journal of Hospital Medicine*, **35** (2), 116–119.
—Reviews the evidence regarding the effectiveness of Antabuse and addresses common concerns about its potential toxicity.
Fuller, R.K. (1989). Antidipsotropic medications. In R.K. Hester & William R. Miller (Eds), *Handbook of Alcoholism Treatment Approaches: Effective Alternatives* (pp. 117–127). New York: Pergamon.
—Provides detailed guidelines on the contra-indications of Antabuse, the procedures for its use, and research results regarding its effectiveness.
Heather, N. (1993). Antabuse treatment for alcohol problems: Is it effective and if so, why? In C. Brewer (Ed.), *Medical Management of Alcohol and Opiate Abuse* (pp. 1–18). London: Gaskell Monographs, Royal College of Psychiatry.
—Examines general evidence on the effectiveness of Antabuse and considers how it works in terms of learning theory.

O'Farrell, T.J. (1990). *Marital and Family Therapy in Alcoholism Treatment.* Workshop presented at Fifth International Conference on the Treatment of Addictive Behaviours. Sydney, Australia, February 7.

O'Farrell, T.J. & Bayog, R.D. (1986). Antabuse contracts for married alcoholics and their spouses: A method to maintain Antabuse ingestion and decrease conflict about drinking. *Journal of Substance Abuse Treatment,* **3,** 1–8.

—A detailed guide to helping partners assist in Antabuse supervision.

ANTABUSE AGREEMENT

In order to help _____ **to claim self-control**
NAME OF CLIENT

and to bring peace of mind to _____
NAME OF PARTNER

_____ **agree to the following arrangement.**
BOTH NAMES

_____ **agrees to:** _____ **agrees to:**
CLIENT'S FIRST NAME   PARTNER'S FIRST NAME

1) Take Antabuse each day at   1) Observe the Antabuse being taken and
SPECIFY TIME _____   record this observation on a calendar.

AND PLACE _____

2) Thank partner for observing the   2) Thank client for taking the Antabuse.
Antiabuse.

3) If necessary, ask partner to   3) Avoid mentioning client's past drinking
avoid mentioning past drinking   or any fears about future drinking.
or fears about future drinking.

4) Refill Antabuse prescription   4) Remind client when prescription needs
before it runs out.   filling.

EARLY WARNING SYSTEM: If at any time, Antabuse is not taken for two days

in a row, _____ agree to contact
BOTH NAMES

_____ immediately.
THERAPIST'S NAME AND PHONE NUMBER

LENGTH OF AGREEMENT: This agreement covers the time from today until

_____ . It cannot be changed unless all three parties
AGREED DATE FOR REVIEW

discuss the changes in a face-to-face meeting of at least 30 minutes.

Signed: _____ _____
PARTNER'S SIGNATURE   CLIENT'S SIGNATURE

_____ Dated:_____
THERAPIST'S SIGNATURE

Source: Adapted from O'Farrell (1990).

14

COVERT SENSITISATION

RECOMMENDED USE

Covert sensitisation is an aversive therapy where an imaginary association is made between drinking alcohol and some unpleasant experience. It is appropriate to use this technique in conjunction with relapse prevention (Chapter 16) to assist clients who wish to achieve abstinence from drinking. To be effective, it needs to be conducted on a one-to-one basis. It is important for you to make sure that the unpleasant side of this therapy is not experienced by the client as a punishment for drinking but rather as a tool to assist him in his decision to stop drinking. Covert sensitisation may not be suitable for clients who have: (a) a history of or current gastro-intestinal disorders; (b) a history of or current heart disease; (c) a current severe depression or suicidal ideation; and/or (d) a current psychosis.

The approach to covert sensitisation that is described here is based on the work of Rimmele, Miller and Dougher (1989). To ensure that the method is effective, you will need to provide your client with a number of structured sessions where you systematically shape imaginary scenes according to his reactions. Rimmele, Miller and Dougher (1989) have recommended that you conduct eight sessions with two 60-minute sessions per week. In each of these sessions, around seven scenes lasting approximately 8 minutes can be presented. Alternatively, shorter sessions presented more frequently have been found to be effective (Maletzky, 1974).

GOALS

As a result of covert sensitisation, your client should:

- Acquire a conditioned response of nausea (or some other unpleasant feeling) associated with imaginary scenes of drinking alcohol, and consequently
- Feel less desire to drink and take action to avoid drinking alcohol

KEY CONCEPTS

Conditioned Response

Thoughts about vomiting usually arouse an unpleasant feeling such as nausea. After you have repeatedly paired these unpleasant thoughts with images of drinking, your client might begin to feel nauseated as soon as he imagines drinking. This is known as a 'conditioned response'.

Pairing

An important part of this procedure is pairing, which means presenting two scenes so that one always follows the other.

Imaginary Scenes

There are five types of imaginary scenes used in covert sensitisation.

- In *drinking scenes,* your client imagines his typical drinking occasions.
- In *aversive scenes,* your client imagines experiencing unpleasant physical consequences of drinking in his typical drinking setting. The aversive scene should always be paired with a preceding drinking scene.
- In *relief scenes,* your client imagines relief and recovery after imagining the aversive scenes. This allows him to relax before you present the next pairing of drinking and aversive scenes.
- In *escape scenes,* your client starts to imagine the typical drinking occasion but once a conditioned response occurs, the scene is switched to one of relief and of choosing a pleasant alternative to drinking.
- In *avoidance scenes,* your client imagines choosing an alternative to drinking *before* experiencing the conditioned response.

Timing

In order to achieve a conditioned response, your timing of the presentation of specific images must be fairly precise. Therefore it is important that you carefully read the guidelines described under the heading *Method* below.

Generalisation

To ensure that the therapy 'generalises' to all possible drinking situations, try to include as many aspects of your client's typical drinking pattern as possible.

You will need to focus on each beverage your client favours and each of his usual drinking settings (for example, in the hotel, at a party or at home).

METHOD

This description is based largely on the work of Rimmele, Miller and Dougher (1989), details of which are given in the *Resources List*.

Rationale for Your Client

Begin by explaining to your client that the therapy is designed to reduce his desire to drink by linking unpleasant feelings with drinking in his imagination. An example such as 'think of how you'd feel if you bit into a piece of lemon' might help to show how imagination can affect feelings. However, it might be important to reassure your client that he will *not* be 'hypnotised'. Because the therapy depends on how vividly your client imagines the scenes, he is in control of the procedure.

It is important that you do not tell your client how he should respond to the scenes. Explicit explanations will place demands on your client to behave in a certain fashion which will make it difficult for you to judge whether the therapy is being effective. Instead, explain to your client that he might feel varying degrees of 'discomfort' at times throughout the session and that whenever he feels that way he can let you know by means of a mutually agreed signal (see below).

Before Starting Treatment

To monitor responses to the aversive scenes, work out a signal with your client before the first covert sensitisation session begins. These signals should be used *whenever* he feels *any* discomfort throughout the entire session. For example, your client might raise one finger at the first feeling of discomfort, two fingers when he feels moderate discomfort and three fingers when discomfort becomes so great that vomiting might occur. Explain to your client that it is important for him to report his feelings of discomfort as accurately as possible so that you can determine how the therapy is going. You will also need to look for other signs of discomfort such as choking, coughing, gagging, eyes watering, grimacing, moaning, gasping, panting, swallowing or burping.

If your clinic has access to equipment which measures the skin conductance level, the heart rate or changes in respiration, these could be used to monitor physiological signs of nausea during treatment. Rimmele, Miller and Dougher (1989), have provided detailed guidelines for the use of such equipment.

Creating the Scenes

Work together with your client to create the imagery for drinking and escape scenes so that the images are *relevant* and *personal*. For example, *drinking scenes* should describe your client's favourite alcoholic drinks and places, and *escape scenes* should describe his preferred alternatives to drinking. Several different scenes may be needed to cover all your client's preferences. When you write the scripts for the scenes use your *client's own words* whenever possible.

Typically, some standard scripts involving nausea have been used as the *aversive scenes* in covert sensitisation procedures and an example of one is shown below. However, before you write the script, you might want to ask your client to describe some experiences that he has found revolting so that you can include some personally salient details in his own words. All scenes must be as specific, detailed and alive as possible, concentrating on *smells, sounds, tastes, colours and textures*. The use of real beer cans, the smell of alcohol or awful smells (for example, valeric acid) may help to enhance the credibility and vividness of the fantasies (Maletzky, 1974).

You might need to allow an entire session to work out these details with your client. It is useful for you to keep a record of the scenes in an exercise book, as well as recording a list of your client's favourite alcoholic drinks and drinking settings. Also use this book to carefully record signs of your client's reactions to the scenes you present. This information will be crucial in determining when a conditioned response occurs and when to appropriately introduce an *escape scene* (see below).

Presenting the Scenes

Arrange for your client to be seated in a quiet room with a comfortable chair. Instruct him to close his eyes and to actively imagine the scenes as if they were *really happening*. Stress to your client the importance of imagining himself actually experiencing the events as you describe them. During your first few presentations of the scenes, you should check regularly with your client that these are relevant and detailed enough for him to imagine them as if they were really happening.

Drinking scenes

Start by presenting the typical drinking scenes a few times to check on their reality for your client. These scenes should vividly describe your client drinking his favourite beverage in his usual drinking setting and should *last about 2–3 minutes*. If the scene is too short, it will not be vivid enough to involve him emotionally. If the scene lasts too long, your client might get distracted by aspects of the story other than the drinking. Here is an example of a *drinking scene*:

'You have had a hard day's work. Some of the jobs have been frustrating and the boss has been giving you a hard time. You feel like you need a beer to wind down. At knock-off time you and two friends agree to go over to the pub. As you walk across to the pub, you are feeling really thirsty. You swallow and your mouth feels dry. You think to yourself how good a beer would be right now. You reach the pub and go inside. It's cool and dark inside. Your friends get a table and you go over to the bar and order three schooners. You watch as the bartender pours the amber liquid from the tap. The glasses are filled to the brim and the foam overflows as the bartender puts them onto the towel in front of you. The glasses feel cool and wet in your hands as you carry them over to the table. You put your schooner down on the coaster in front of you. Your friends are already drinking and licking their lips. As you look at the amber liquid you can almost taste it running down your throat. You raise the glass to your mouth and feel the bubbles of foam bursting against your lips. You smell the beer aroma distinctly. You take a long sip and the beer fills your mouth. You feel how cold it is in your mouth. You taste the sharp, bitter, malty flavour of the beer on your tongue. You savour the smell and taste the beer and the alcohol. You swallow it and feel the cool sensation as the beer runs down to your stomach. You feel yourself swallowing the beer and it runs down towards your stomach.'

Aversive scenes

After you have established that the drinking scenes are vivid and real for your client, introduce the aversive scene. Present the aversive imagery immediately after your client has imagined the first taste or swallowing of alcohol. This scene should also *last about 2–3 minutes*. It should be long and graphic enough to allow for an intensification of your client's discomfort without him actually vomiting. *Signs that a scene is producing a major effect include a signal of moderate discomfort (two fingers)(!) from your client together with any other visible signs of discomfort such as gagging and other signs mentioned above.* Here is an example of an *aversive scene*:

'Then you feel an odd sensation. You are feeling a little bit queasy. You feel a little bit nauseated. You decide to take another sip to settle yourself. You take a big gulp and your mouth fills with beer but the taste of it seems to be making you feel worse. You start to feel warm fluid moving in your stomach. You feel it moving up towards the back of your throat. You are feeling waves of nausea. Now you can taste a sour taste and feel a burning sensation at the back of your throat. You realise that it is vomit forcing its way up out of your stomach. Vomit and the partially digested food from your last meal are mixing with the beer in your mouth and you start to gag. You taste the bitter taste of this mixture on the back of your tongue. There are slimy lumps of half-digested food sloshing into your mouth. The vomit is rising up into your nostrils and choking you. You open your mouth a little bit and the spew seeps out and runs down your chin. Your stomach is churning and you are feeling more and more sick. You look down at the beer in your glass and the nausea feels worse. You open your mouth and your stomach heaves uncontrollably as you spew out the vomit. Lumpy vomit splatters over the beer glass and up into your face. You smell the stench of spew mingled with the smell of beer. You are shaking all over and heaving with nausea until there is nothing left in your stomach. Then you taste the foul taste of green bile. Your eyes are watering and your nose and throat are burning. You can still taste the beer and you try and spit it out. You are feeling weaker and weaker, more and more sick. You look at your friends and they seem to be spinning around. You can't get a hold on things and you're feeling really scared.'

Trouble-shooting

It is important that your client does not actually vomit during therapy. Vomiting signals the end of the nausea bout and may provide premature relief which could undermine the effectiveness of the therapy (Clarke & Saunders, 1988). It also creates practical problems for you! While in reality it is rare for someone actually to vomit, use the prearranged finger signals to indicate when vomiting is likely to occur so that the fantasy can be terminated before this happens.

If your client has shown *no signs of a major effect after four pairings of drinking and aversive scenes*, take a break to discuss the scenes. Perhaps the aversive scenes are not vivid or intense enough to produce an aversive response. If, after modifying the scene on the basis of your client's feedback, he still shows no signs of a major effect during the second session, it is advisable to choose a new form for the aversive scene. Nausea might not be the most effective emotional response for your client. Instead you might want to choose an aversive scene that arouses feelings of horror, anxiety, disgust or embarrassment. For example, Rimmele, Miller and Dougher (1989) described a scene involving a horrible drink-driving accident.

Relief scene

Conclude each aversive scene with a relief scene in which your client is removed from the unpleasant imagery associated with drinking and imagines recovering feelings of well-being. This allows your client to return to a more relaxed emotional state before the next paired scenes are presented. An example of a *relief scene* is provided below:

'You push out your chair and run out of the pub. Now you are outside and you are starting to feel better. Your stomach is starting to settle and you are feeling great relief. Now you arrive home and you clean yourself up. You clean your teeth and rinse out your mouth. Your mouth feels fresh again. You have a shower and put on clean clothes. You sit down in a comfortable chair and close your eyes. You are feeling relaxed and calm all over your body.'

Achieving a conditioned response

If the pairing of drinking with aversive scenes is successful, your client will eventually display a conditioned response to the drinking scene. A conditioned response can be said to have occurred when your client shows significant signs of discomfort or distress (see above) *during* the description of the drinking scene, that is, *before* you start to describe the aversive elements. Keep a record of all responses that indicate that your client is experiencing distress and, in particular, note down when he experiences a conditioned response.

Trouble-shooting

It is important to distinguish this *true* conditioned response from situations where your client starts to think about the aversive scenes while you are still presenting the drinking scene. This may result in signs that he is experiencing a major effect before you present the aversive scene. However, because the response of discomfort has followed thoughts about nausea and vomiting rather than the crucial automatic reaction of discomfort to the drinking scenes, it is *not* a conditioned response.

You can test this out by asking your client about his thoughts. Use a conversational approach and try to avoid giving him any impression that you are expecting a particular type of response. For example, you might say:

'I noticed that this time you gave the two finger signal before I described the vomiting and nausea images. Were you thinking about the nausea images before I got to them?'

If your client answers 'yes' to this question, next time you present paired scenes briefly remind him to concentrate *only* on the images that you are describing and not to race ahead of you.

If a conditioned response has not been achieved after 40 'paired' scenes (or at the end of six sessions), aversive therapy is unlikely to work. Even in this circumstance, finish off the covert sensitisation therapy with an avoidance scene (see below) so that your client is left with a mental image of the benefits of not drinking. You should then discuss other strategies with your client, such as Antabuse or skills training (Chapter 13).

Escape scenes

From the time that your client shows a conditioned response, you should start alternating paired scenes/escape scenes. Begin by presenting the drinking scene as usual but as soon your client indicates that he is experiencing moderate distress, move to the escape scene. This scene should describe your client choosing a healthy alternative to drinking, such as pouring away the drink, leaving the drinking setting, or drinking a non-alcoholic beverage. It might also include some pleasurable activity that excludes drinking, such as physical exercise. The details will reflect what your client sees as the most realistic and preferable alternatives. When presenting the escape scene, emphasise the wonderful feelings of relief from nausea, of the confidence and self-esteem associated with not drinking. Here is an example of an *escape scene*:

'You raise the glass to your mouth and then you stop. You don't like the smell of the beer. You don't feel like drinking it after all. Instead, you take it back to the bar and order an orange juice. You go back to the table and take a sip of the orange juice. You sip the icy cold drink of orange juice and relish its tangy taste. You drink it slowly, enjoying each sip. You notice how it quenches your thirst and tastes delicious. When you are finished you feel satisfied. You say goodbye to your friends and walk out of the pub. You are quite relaxed and you smile to yourself. You feel happy and confident about yourself. Your step is light as you walk down the street. You are feeling free and easy.'

Avoidance scenes

When you have observed your client experiencing three conditioned responses in a row, describe the avoidance scene. The avoidance scene may be constructed in the same way as the escape scene with your client choosing satisfying imaginary alternatives to drinking. However, in the avoidance scene, the non-drinking alternatives should be introduced *before* nausea (or distress) occurs. Your careful observations of your client's previous behaviour will help you to determine the precise timing. Once your client has experienced a block of three conditioned responses in a row for a second time, finish this phase of therapy.

Trouble-shooting

If you have any difficulty in predicting when a conditioned response will occur with your client (because his response doesn't consistently happen at the same time) then Rimmele, Miller and Dougher (1989) have suggested that you introduce the avoidance scene as soon as your client shows *any* signs of discomfort.

Conditioning Different Scenes and Beverages

Once your client has successfully achieved a conditioned response to one type of drinking scene, present some other drinking scenes based on his full range of drinks and preferred drinking settings. You will need to take him through the same process until a conditioned response is established for all the drinking possibilities to ensure that the conditioned response is generalised across situations.

Final Stages of Therapy

Finish the covert sensitisation sessions with an avoidance scene either (a) after your client has shown consistent conditioned responses to all possible drinking situations or (b) after 50 scenes (or eight sessions). While you might encourage your client to review the aversive images if he is facing a temptation to relapse, do not set any specific conditioning home practice as this might actually undermine the effectiveness of the treatment.

As covert sensitisation has been found to be effective mainly in the short term, always support it with other strategies such as training in drink-refusal skills and relapse prevention (Chapters 6 and 16). You might also want to provide booster conditioning sessions to ensure that the effects of covert sensitisation are lasting. Make follow-up appointments with your client for 6 and 12 months after treatment. During these appointments you will need to assess his progress in avoiding alcohol. If your client has shown a tendency to relapse, further scenes can be presented in order to re-establish the conditioned response. Alternate the paired drinking and aversive scenes with escape scenes several times and finish with an avoidance scene.

RESOURCES LIST

Clarke, C.J. & Saunders, J.B. (1988). *Alcoholism and Problem Drinking: Theories and Treatment* (pp. 124–145). Sydney: Pergamon.
—A theoretical and practical guide to covert sensitisation is provided, as well as general discussion of cognitive behavioural procedures. Clarke and Saunders argue, in contrast to the approach of Rimmele, Miller and Dougher (1989), that even imaginary vomiting is a source of relief. They therefore do not include vomiting in their imaginary scenes and, in fact, part of the discomfort described in their sample aversive scene is that the person is unable to vomit, despite considerable nausea. You may wish to consider their approach as an alternative to the approach we have presented in this chapter.

Elkins, R.L. (1980). Covert sensitisation treatment of alcoholism: contributions of successful conditioning to subsequent abstinence maintenance. *Addictive Behaviors*, 5, 67–89.
—Provides research evidence and methods for covert sensitisation.
Maletzky, B.M. (1974). Assisted covert sensitisation for drug abuse. *International Journal of the Addictions*, 9, 411–429.
—Provides research evidence and methods for covert sensitisation.
Rimmele, C.T., Miller, W.R. & Dougher, M.J. (1989). Aversion therapies. In R.K. Hester & W.R. Miller (Eds), *Handbook of Alcoholism Treatment Approaches: Effective Alternatives* (pp. 128–140). New York: Pergamon.
—The details outlined in this chapter are partly drawn from this excellent resource which is highly recommended reading.

MAINTAINING CHANGE

15

SELF-HELP GROUPS

RECOMMENDED USE

The self-help services offered by Alcoholics Anonymous (AA) and Narcotics Anonymous (NA) are widely available. Although their 12-Step philosophy is sometimes incorporated in drug and alcohol treatment, AA and NA are not considered by their members to be a form of treatment. Rather, they are fellowships of men and women who share the experience of alcohol or drug dependence and want to help each other to stay drug-free.

AA might be suitable if your client has alcohol dependence and chooses abstinence as her treatment goal. Because of the abstinence philosophy of AA, it is counter-productive to recommend them if your client has a goal of moderation. NA may be appropriate if your client is dependent on other drugs, particularly if she is undergoing a drug-free method of treatment. Individual AA/NA groups determine their own guidelines and some groups are happy to accept members who are on methadone maintenance.

Self-help groups offer your client highly accessible and ongoing social support from others who have had similar experiences. The following chapter outlines the basic principles of AA and recommends the ways in which you might incorporate referral to AA/NA in your treatment plan.

GOALS

Self-help groups in the tradition of AA share the view that dependence on alcohol or drugs results from a person's genetic or constitutional make-up rather than from the qualities of the drug itself. They therefore distinguish 'alcoholics' and 'addicts' from 'social drinkers' or 'experimenters'. True addiction is seen as being an illness that cannot be cured but can be arrested. The 12-Step programme is designed to arrest the addiction by assisting the person to stay abstinent one day at a time with the consistent social support provided in meetings. The *primary purpose of AA* is the achievement of day-to-day abstinence from alcohol and to help others with alcohol dependence. The *primary purpose of NA* is to stay drug-free and offer assistance to other drug-dependent people.

KEY CONCEPTS

The 12 Steps

The process of recovery defined by AA/NA is based on 12 steps that are presented in two charts at the end of this chapter. The commitment to a drug-free lifestyle requires that your client accepts that she is powerless over her drinking or drug-taking. This first step is the essential foundation on which the remaining steps are built. Your client works through each step at her own pace, with the encouragement and support of her sponsor and other members.

The 12 Traditions

The 12 traditions outline the philosophy for the organisation within which 12-Step groups run. These traditions ensure that the personal ambitions of any AA/NA member or any influence outside AA/NA cannot distract the group from the primary goal, which is to give the 12-Step message to other alcohol-dependent people. For example, so that they do not become involved in disputes about money, AA and other 12-Step groups are totally self-supported via voluntary donations from their membership. Similarly, there is a major emphasis on setting aside personal egos for the common good. This is expressed in Tradition 12: 'Anonymity is the spiritual foundation of our traditions, ever reminding us to place principles before personalities.'

Member

Tradition 3 of AA/NA states that: 'The only requirement for AA membership is a desire to stop drinking/using.'

Open and Closed Meetings

Open meetings are available to any interested person, regardless of whether or not she has a drinking problem. The open meeting often involves one or more members telling their stories to the group and the newcomer or visitor is not usually required to speak or identify herself as an 'alcoholic'. In contrast, closed meetings are open only to people wanting to change their drinking behaviour. They are more likely to involve discussions in which everyone is encouraged to contribute.

Sponsor

Newcomers are assisted in their adjustment to the 12-Step group through sponsorship by a longer-term member. The sponsor is someone who has achieved ongoing recovery and can therefore serve as a role model for your client and introduce her to the concepts and practices of the 12-Step pro-gramme. As trust develops, the sponsor may also act as a confidant for your client. According to McCrady and Irvine (1989), the ideal sponsor is someone who is the same gender as the person being sponsored and who can be con-tacted as often as needed. This accessibility is particularly important in helping the sponsored person to cope effectively with cravings, lapses or relapses.

METHOD
Rationale for Your Client

When introducing your client to 12-Step groups, emphasise the value of being able to meet others who have had similar problems and experiences and can therefore give her understanding and support. Stress that this support is avail-able from other members whenever your client needs it. It is ongoing and therefore available for as long and as often as she wants to attend. Make sure your client knows that her attendance at meetings is free and totally voluntary. She should also be aware that what is said during meetings is kept confidential and anonymous. Encourage your client to attend AA/NA meetings at least three times so that she can make an informed decision about whether or not to continue involvement with the group.

12-Step groups are not just about recovery but they also provide an oppor-tunity for having fun and making friends, without needing to drink or use drugs. People who attend AA/NA come from all walks of life, so your client should be able to meet others with similar interests. It may be a new experience for your client to join a social network that does not involve drinking or using.

Before Starting

Increase your awareness of the activity of self-help groups in your local area. Most (if not all) of these groups will be based on the 12-Step model. The easiest way to find out more about 12-Step groups is to attend some of the open meetings. Try to develop some acquaintances with AA/NA hospital or institution committee members and the local general service officers. Be aware that there are AA/NA meetings especially for particular groups, such as women, gay men or lesbians, and for people who are attending for the first time. Being able to contact a variety of people in the self-help network and having awareness of meetings for special interest groups will allow you flexibility when you are advising your client. Besides AA and NA, there are also other kinds of 12-Step groups which you might want to investigate, such as Pills Anonymous.

You should familiarise yourself with the self-help literature and telephone services. Ensure that pamphlets and booklets produced by AA/NA are available in your clinic for clients to peruse. In particular, both AA and NA provide listings of the days, times, locations and types of meetings being held in your local area. This information will be invaluable in helping your client to plan her first meeting attendance. You can get a copy of the list at a meeting or by telephoning AA/NA. You might also want to give your client a copy of either the NA or AA 12-Steps, listed at the end of this chapter.

Linking AA with Therapy

You might choose to recommend AA/NA to all of your clients (who are aiming for abstinence or a drug-free lifestyle), by highlighting the advantages of social support, accessibility and self-help. AA/NA can easily be incorporated into your treatment plan. For example, attending meetings or telephoning her sponsor might be one of the methods that your client uses for relapse prevention (p. 184). The 12-Step groups in turn provide support for members' involvement in treatment programmes. NA also provides education about HIV and harm-reduction strategies.

AA/NA offers your client an opportunity for reassurance that other people have survived the uncomfortable, initial side-effects of quitting and have been able to maintain abstinence. This can help to increase your client's confidence in her own ability to abstain from alcohol or drugs. The group's encouragement can also reinforce her progress towards long-term abstinence.

Your client might also experience a sense of relief at meeting others who have had similar alcohol- or drug-related problems. She might have thought that she was the only person ever to go through these negative experiences. The meetings provide a supportive environment for your client to share these personal thoughts and feelings with others. Also fundamental to the 12-Step approach is a spiritual outlook which can inspire in your client a new sense of purpose and hope.

Trouble-shooting

You might need to dispel any myths that your client has about AA/NA. For instance, she might think that AA/NA is suitable only for people with very severe dependence or alcohol- or drug-related problems. Explain that AA/NA can be used to help anyone, regardless of how severe their alcohol- or drug-related problems have been.

Your client might consider that the 12 Steps or their emphasis on spirituality are not relevant for her. Clients might also have different reactions to the message that alcohol dependence is a disease. For example, the idea that she is powerless over alcohol might undermine your client's confidence in her ability to change. Alternatively, by accepting that she is powerless over alcohol or drugs, your client might feel less shame and be more able to ask for help from others. McCrady and Irvine (1989) have suggested that 'powerlessness' in the 12 Steps might be experienced as a strength rather than a weakness. Ultimately, however, it is important that you respect your client's decision about whether or not AA/NA is suitable for her. Bear in mind that the 12-Step philosophy might not be effective for everybody.

SELF-HELP GROUPS FOR THE FAMILY

Based on the 12 Steps of AA, Al-Anon Family Groups is a fellowship aimed at assisting families and friends of alcohol-dependent people. Regular meetings of Al-Anon offer opportunities for friendship and for sharing the experience of coping with alcohol dependence in the family with others who have had similar experiences. Al-Anon provides tips about how to minimise drink-related conflicts or over-involvement with the drinking problem. It also provides a programme for self-growth centred on the 12 Steps. Al-Anon could be particularly helpful for other family members when your client is attending AA on a regular basis. It might also be a useful source of support for family members even when the drinker is not attending AA. If an Al-Anon group is not available in your area, the General Service Office will provide a free starter kit to assist people to start their own group.

Other 12-Step family support groups include Al-Teen, a self-help group for teenagers who have an alcohol-dependent parent, and Nar-Anon, a self-help group for the family and friends of narcotic-dependent people.

RESOURCES LIST

AA World Services Inc. (1975). *Living Sober*. New York: AA World Services Inc.
—Provides strategies for preventing relapse.
AA World Services Inc. (1978). *Twelve Steps and Twelve Traditions*. New York: AA World Services Inc.
—Explains each AA Step and Tradition.
AA World Services Inc. (1988). *Alcoholics Anonymous: The Big Book* (3rd edn). New York: AA World Services Inc.
—Detailed description of the AA programme. Explains AA's perception of alcohol problems and presents personal stories of recovery through AA.
Edwards, G. (1982). *The Treatment of Drinking Problems: A Guide for the Helping Professions*. London: Grant MacIntyre.
—A classic, brief overview of the organisation. Recommended reading for all professionals in the drug and alcohol area.
McCrady, B.S. & Irvine, S. (1989). Self-help groups. In R.K. Hester & W.R. Miller (Eds), *Handbook of Alcoholism Treatment Approaches: Effective Alterntives* (pp.153–169). New York: Pergamon.
—Chapter 16 gives a comprehensive account of the principles and practices of AA.
Nowinski, J., Baker, S. & Carroll, K. (1992). *Twelve Step Facilitation Therapy Manual: A Clinical Research Guide for Therapists Treating Individuals with Alcohol Abuse and Dependence. Project MATCH Monograph Series, Volume 1*. Rockville, MD: National Institute on Alcohol Abuse and Alcoholism.
—A session-by-session manual aimed at supporting clients' active involvement in AA.
Peyrot, M. (1985). Narcotics anonymous: Its history, structure, and approach. *International Journal of the Addictions*, **20**, (10), 1509–1522.
—An overview of NA.
Robertson, D. (1979). *Talking Out of Alcoholism: The Self-help Process of Alcoholics Anonymous*. London: Croom Helm.
—Detailed introduction to AA.
World Service Office Inc. (1988). *Narcotics Anonymous — The Basic Text*. California: World Service Office.
—Description of the NA programme, including personal stories of recovery through NA.
World Services Office Inc. (1991). *Just for Today*. California: World Service Office.
—Provides daily meditations for recovery.
World Services Office Inc. (1993). *NA: It Works, How and Why?* California: World Service Office.
—Detailed description of the NA Steps and Traditions.

THE TWELVE STEPS OF ALCOHOLICS ANONYMOUS

1. We admitted we were powerless over alcohol—that our lives had become unmanageable.

2. We came to believe that a Power greater than ourselves could restore us to sanity.

3. We made a decision to turn our will and our lives over to the care of God *as we understood Him.*

4. We made a searching and fearless moral inventory of ourselves.

5. We admitted to God, to ourselves, and to another human being the exact nature of our wrongs.

6. We were entirely ready to have God remove all these defects of character.

7. We humbly asked Him to remove our shortcomings.

8. We made a list of all persons we had harmed, and became willing to make amends to them all.

9. We made direct amends to such people wherever possible, except when to do so would injure them or others.

10. We continued to take a personal inventory and when we were wrong promptly admitted it.

11. We sought through prayer and meditation to improve our conscious contact with God *as we understood Him*, praying only for knowledge of His will for us and the power to carry that out.

12. Having had a spiritual awakening as the result of these steps, we tried to carry this message to alcoholics, and to practise these principles in all our affairs.

THE TWELVE STEPS OF NARCOTICS ANONYMOUS

1. We admitted we were powerless over our addiction—that our lives had become unmanageable.

2. We came to believe that a Power greater than ourselves could restore us to sanity.

3. We made a decision to turn our will and our lives over to the care of God *as we understood Him.*

4. We made a searching and fearless moral inventory of ourselves.

5. We admitted to God, to ourselves, and to another human being the exact nature of our wrongs.

6. We were entirely ready to have God remove all these defects of character.

7. We humbly asked Him to remove our shortcomings.

8. We made a list of all persons we had harmed, and became willing to make amends to them all.

9. We made direct amends to such people wherever possible, except when to do so would injure them or others.

10. We continued to take a personal inventory and when we were wrong promptly admitted it.

11. We sought through prayer and meditation to improve our conscious contact with God *as we understood Him*, praying only for knowledge of His will for us and the power to carry that out.

12. Having had a spiritual awakening as the result of these steps, we tried to carry this message to addicts, and to practise these principles in all our affairs.

16

RELAPSE-PREVENTION TRAINING

RECOMMENDED USE

Relapse-prevention training should be part of any treatment programme aimed at modifying drug or alcohol use. It is equally relevant for those pursuing abstinence or moderation goals. Relapse-prevention strategies are also easily adapted for clients with harm-reduction goals who wish to abstain from needle-sharing or unsafe sexual practices. You can conduct relapse-prevention training in either group or individual settings, although the skills training procedures incorporated in this approach are often facilitated by group learning. As previously mentioned (p. 9), it is not a good idea to include clients with different goals in the same group.

GOALS

The general goals of relapse-prevention training are to ensure that your clients have:

- A variety of skills and the confidence to avoid lapses to alcohol or drug use
- A set of strategies and beliefs that reduce the fear of failure and prevent such lapses turning into relapses

KEY CONCEPTS

High-risk Situations

These are situations that your client identifies as those in which he is most likely to find it difficult to resist drinking or drug use. The research literature suggests that (re)lapses commonly occur in response to: (a) negative emotional states, such as anxiety or depression; (b) interpersonal conflict; or (c) social pressure (Cummings, Gordon & Marlatt, 1980).

Lapses or 'Slips'

In the context of relapse-prevention training these terms are used to refer to an initial, relatively isolated use of drugs or alcohol after a period of abstinence, or alternatively, the first or an isolated instance of heavy use after a period of controlled substance use. These terms are used to distinguish between *some* use and a return to constant, heavy use.

Relapse

This term is generally reserved for a return to constant and/or heavy use of a substance.

METHOD

This section is based on the work of Marlatt and Gordon (1985) and in particular, draws on the relapse-prevention strategies described by Saunders and Allsop (1989, 1991).

Allsop (1994, pers. comm.) has stated that relapse-prevention training is about 'demystifying' relapses. That is, it aims to help clients move away from the belief that staying abstinent is only about having a sufficient amount of 'willpower'. While a strong resolve to change is essential, successful relapse prevention is also about ensuring that your client has sufficient 'skill power' to recognise and effectively deal with triggers in the environment that can contribute to slips or relapses. These triggers occur in 'high-risk' situations and can involve particular emotions, or be related to other aspects of the situation such as the presence of drinking or drug-using friends.

Relapse-prevention training also attempts to change common beliefs about giving up addictive behaviours. It aims to reduce the overwhelming dread of 'failure' by emphasising that behaviour change is not an 'all or nothing' event. The goal is to help your client to see changing his substance use in the same way as giving up other fond habits by recognising that change is a process whereby learning from mistakes and lapses forms part of the progress toward reaching a final goal.

Finally, the maintenance of an initial change in addiction behaviour is largely influenced by lifestyle issues. Saunders and Allsop (1989) made a clear distinction between deciding to change or stop drug or alcohol use and deciding to change one's lifestyle, noting that the former is probably not possible without the latter. Therefore relapse-prevention training also involves examining lifestyle factors that can either hinder or support behaviour change.

Accordingly, this section divides relapse-prevention training into the following areas which should be considered in the course of any programme:

(1) Enhancing the commitment to change
(2) Identifying high-risk situations
(3) Teaching coping and other useful skills
(4) Other helpful hints to avoid temptation
(5) Preparing for a lapse
(6) Other lifestyle issues important to maintaining change

Before Starting

You may wish to start by explaining the general rationale for relapse-prevention training. In doing so cover the points that were discussed in the paragraphs above. We have also offered more details about the specific rationale for learning how to deal with a lapse in a separate section below, as this is often a more threatening notion for many clients.

Enhancing a Resolution for Change

It is important to acknowledge that a high-quality resolution to change is an important aspect of maintaining abstinence or moderation. It will not matter very much how skilled or confident your client might become about coping with high-risk situations if he does not have a strong commitment to maintain behaviour change. Therefore it might be important for your client to review both the negative reasons for changing drug-use patterns and the expected rewards of making such changes. If you haven't already done so, it might also be useful to get your client to write down his reasons for change so that they can be easily accessed as reminders and motivators when needed (see p. 61).

Identifying High-risk Situations

Identifying high-risk situations involves detailing the 'where, when, with whom, doing what, and feeling what' of situations where your client feels most tempted to use drugs or alcohol. There are a variety of ways of identifying high-risk situations. These include pencil and paper questionnaires and/or self-monitoring forms. Some pencil and paper tools include the *Inventory of Drinking Situations* (Annis, 1982), the *Relapse Precipitants Inventory* (Litman, Stapelton, Oppenheim, Peleg & Jackson, 1983) and the *Situational Confidence Questionnaire* (SCQ) (there is a form of this questionnaire both for alcohol and for heroin: Annis, 1987; Barber & Cooper, 1991). Sitharthan and Kavanagh (1990) have also developed a questionnaire for assessing the confidence of clients with moderation goals.

Alternatively, high-risk situations can be identified from the self-monitoring forms of clients who are attempting to moderate their drinking (described in Chapter 11, *Behavioural Self-management*) or from discussion with clients about those situations which have caused difficulty in the past. Similarly, valuable information can also be gained by encouraging clients who are abstinent to self-monitor urges and cravings to drink or use drugs. An example of a day diary which can be used for monitoring urges and cravings is included at the end of this chapter.

Your client's high-risk situations can then be graded from the least to the most threatening situations. This hierarchy should be used as a basis for exercises and home practice throughout the remaining sessions.

Teaching Coping Skills

A note on avoidance

Particularly in the early stages of changing behaviour, advise your client to avoid high-risk situations whenever possible. Indeed there may be certain situations for some clients in which avoidance will often or always be the best solution. However, it is not always possible to avoid some potential high-risk situations. For example, it will be difficult to avoid ever feeling upset or to permanently avoid social occasions where alcohol is served. Therefore other strategies also need to be addressed.

Teaching problem-solving skills

At this stage, if you have not already done so, you might choose to teach your client problem-solving strategies. Saunders and Allsop (1991) suggested that this approach has the advantage of providing your client with a general skill which he can apply to a variety of situations which challenge his resolve. The details of how to teach problem-solving skills are dealt with on in Chapter 5 and will not be dealt with here. In brief, the basic tenets of problem-solving include:

(1) Defining *exactly* what the problem is
(2) Brainstorming options to deal with the problem
(3) Choosing the best option(s) by examining the pros and cons of each potential solution
(4) Generating a detailed action plan
(5) Putting it into action—mentally rehearse, role-play, and actually carry out the plan
(6) Evaluating the results to see how well the selected solution worked

Begin by working on easier high-risk situations first. Brainstorm a number of possible alternative ways of dealing with the high-risk situation without using drugs or alcohol. Then get your client to select his best solution and practise it either by thinking the solution through or by trying it out in a role-play (p. 11). It is useful to encourage your client to write down his possible options and the final selected solution so that these can also be referred to later if necessary.

Home practice exercises can include brainstorming and selecting solutions to other risky situations on the list, as well as carrying out the solution to situations that have been 'problem-solved' during the session. Review practice exercises at the beginning of each session, rewarding success and discussing any problems experienced by your client. Ensure that easier situations are dealt with first, remembering that success breeds success. The aim is that your client should become confident about his ability to cope with known high-risk situations. It is also important that he becomes practised enough in using problem-solving strategies to be able to use them to cope with unexpected events that challenge his commitment to change (see below).

Other skills

You might find that there are common themes among the types of relapse situations that have been identified by your client. For example, your client might be particularly prone to using drugs to help him cope with stress. Problem-solving techniques might offer a number of potential solutions, among them a need to learn relaxation skills (Chapter 10). You might then decide to focus some specific training in that area.

Given that there is evidence to suggest that negative emotional states, interpersonal conflict and social pressure are very common precipitants of (re)lapse, you might wish, particularly in a group setting (where there is less flexibility to tailor to individual needs), to spend a session(s) addressing other specific strategies to cope with these issues in more detail. Areas to address may include:

- *Coping with social pressure:* Almost all clients will at some time need to be able to refuse drinks or drugs offered to them by others. Therefore, you might wish to practise appropriate refusal skills (Chapter 6) using role-play.
- *Coping with anxiety:* You might wish to introduce basic relaxation skills to clients.
- *Coping with depression and anger:* The skills covered in this area are addressed in Chapter 9, dealing with *Cognitive Restructuring*. Monti, Abrams, Kadden and Cooney (1989) also describe sessions outlining anger-management techniques (see *Resources List*).
- *Coping with urges/craving:* It might be useful to directly address the issue of craving or urges with your client. He should be reassured that feelings of craving are: (a) natural reactions following a change in drinking or drug use; (b) often a response to situations, people, and even moods which used to be part of drinking or drug taking; and (c) probably a good warning sign that he might be in a high-risk situation and should take care! Some clients might also have a fear of being overwhelmed by craving and/or expect that the craving will get more and more unbearably intense if it is not relieved by drinking or drug use. To allay such fears introduce your client to the analogy of an ocean wave and explain that, like a wave, craving builds to a peak but then subsides and fades. Also introduce the imagery of 'urge surfing', and suggest that it is possible to 'ride' out an urge, mastering rather than being swamped by it. Stress that the more often he successfully copes with a craving, the less frequent and/or intense the cravings will become.

Other Helpful Hints for Avoiding Temptation

Planning ahead

You should also stress to your client that one of the most useful strategies for dealing with high-risk or other potentially difficult situations is to plan ahead. That is, he should think about possible difficulties or pitfalls that might arise and plan strategies to cope with them in advance.

Apparently irrelevant decisions

Often clients either fail to recognise or deliberately choose to ignore warning signs of an approaching high-risk situation. This aspect of relapse-prevention training aims to highlight an awareness of such warning signs. It again emphasises that slips don't just happen 'out of the blue' but rather, that choices are always present. In fact, Saunders and Allsop (1991) have stressed that there is always *a strong element of personal responsibility* involved when a client resumes drinking or drug use.

It is useful to illustrate this point by describing an imaginary client and the chain of events leading to drinking or drug using. For example, an ex-user chooses to walk by a cafe known to be a meeting place for users. An old friend who is just leaving sees him and invites him back to her house for a meal. While he is at her house, some other people, who have just scored, drop by and the ex-user finds himself hitting up with the group.

Another more detailed example of a script is provided below. You can also create your own script that is relevant to your client's problems.

---

* John has just had a bad day at work, he skipped lunch and feels 'strung out'. In recent months, since he left treatment, he has been going swimming after work to relax. However, today he thinks that he is too tired to go swimming. * Just as he is about to leave work a friend and business associate (known to be a heavy drinker) phones and invites him to dinner with a group of his colleagues. * John decides to go straight from work and wait for the others at the club. * He has an important meeting early the next morning and does not want to overdrink. He feels quite confident about keeping within his four drink maximum. * He arrives early, thirsty from his walk, orders a pint of beer, gulps it down and without thinking orders another. * Friends arrive soon after, with a third round in hand. * John and his colleagues go in to dinner and his business associate immediately orders three bottles of wine among four people. * Already feeling lightheaded, John thinks: 'I'll just sit on one or two glasses over dinner'. * The conversation gets lively and John's glass keeps getting refilled before it is empty.

Ask your client if he believes that the imaginary drinker or drug user was 'unable to cope' or had actually made choices that led him to drink or use drugs! Get him to identify all the warning signs or decision points in the script. In the example script above, the various decision points are all marked by an asterisk. Encourage your client to use a problem-solving approach to generate alternative choices at each of the identified decision points. Ask your client how difficult he thinks the solution to the first event in the chain would be in comparison to an alternative solution at the last decision point before drinking or using drugs. This is a useful way of demonstrating the advantages of dealing with a potential slip by altering events early in the chain.

As a follow-up practice exercise, ask your client to describe a similar 'slippery slope' situation that he has experienced and examine it in the same way as above.

Preparing for a Lapse

Rationale for your client

The next stage in relapse-prevention training is concerned with responding to a 'slip', should it happen. Saunders and Allsop (1991) noted that some clients might feel that you are showing a lack of confidence in them or even condoning a return to (heavy) use by talking about lapse management. They therefore suggested that clients might be introduced to the analogy of the 'fire drill'. They explained that a 'fire drill' neither condones nor increases the likelihood of a fire, though it acknowledges that there *is* some risk it might happen. More importantly, the drill ensures that the harm can be minimised if a fire occurs. A 'relapse drill' therefore serves the same purpose by creating a contingency plan for preventing a slip from becoming a full-scale relapse.

The 'relapse drill'

Saunders and Allsop (1991) have suggested that you begin by getting your client to list the conditions (both situational and emotional) under which he would be most likely to continue to drink or use drugs after an initial slip in his resolve. For example, situational factors might involve the ready availability of the drug or alcohol. Very common emotional factors you might discuss would include feelings of guilt, a sense of failure, disappointment and self-blame. It is important that you acknowledge that lapses can produce these very powerful negative emotions for clients. Marlatt and Gordon (1985) have also referred to the 'abstinence violation effect'. This is the overwhelming feeling or belief that one slip inevitably leads to an uncontrollable and permanent return to use. You should strongly discourage your client from any belief that a slip is tantamount to total disaster or defeat. The emotional and situational conditions that might cause your client to keep on drinking or using should instead be seen as posing specific problems that could be resolved by using a problem-solving approach.

Encourage your client to brainstorm a number of different strategies that he could use to stop further drinking or drug use after an initial lapse. Then help him to generate *detailed* action plans for putting these strategies into operation. For example, one potential strategy for dealing with a slip might be to 'call someone'. However, as Saunders and Allsop (1991) have stressed, this response by itself lacks detail. Instead the client should decide on who to call, have their telephone number ready and be realistic about how that person might help. Where appropriate, 'relapse drills' could also be practised in session using role-play. The relapse drills should also be written down by your client and kept in a handy place for future reference.

Talking about the bigger picture of lapses and relapses

You should also further reinforce the notion that learning anything new involves making slips and mistakes. Encourage your client to see 'slips' as a natural part of the process of learning to change his behaviour. In this way you can also suggest that it is possible to learn from a slip by looking at what did or didn't work, using that information to devise better strategies to cope with similar situations in the future.

Other Lifestyle Issues Important to Maintaining Change

It is essential to remember that treatment does not happen in a vacuum. Lifestyle and other factors in the environment can be crucial determinants of the success of your client's attempt to change his behaviour. Clearly, also, it will be necessary to find new ways of achieving the positive effects that your client formerly derived from his drug use. Work with your client in identifying new, rewarding activities that could replace drinking or drug use. At the simplest level this might involve taking up new hobbies, joining clubs or taking up a sport or other physical exercise. However, on a more general level you might also need to involve the family and friends in ways of supporting the client's behaviour change, or to help him to cultivate new friends. You might also need to consider linking him up with agencies that could help him to find a job or a new job, or help him to move to a new geographical location.

Trouble-shooting

Needless to say, many relapses happen after treatment has ended. An appropriate aftercare plan (Chapter 17) will help your client to feel more comfortable about the possibility of returning to see you in the event of a relapse. It might be important to address feelings of 'failure' by reviewing once again the cyclical model of change according to which relapse is part of the learning process (see Figure 1, p. 26). In the context of this model you can reassure your client that all he has learnt will not be lost but can be drawn upon next time he decides to make a change.

RESOURCES LIST

Annis, H.M. (1982). *Inventory of Drinking Situations*. Toronto, Canada: Addiction Research Foundation.
   —This is a 100-item (or 42-item short form) self-report questionnaire which provides a profile of situations in which your client drank heavily over the past year.

Annis, H.M. (1987). *The Situational Confidence Questionnaire (SCQ-39)*. Toronto, Canada: Addiction Research Foundation.
—This self-completion questionnaire is designed to assess the self-efficacy of clients to cope with situations that involve resisting alcohol.

Annis, H.M. & Davis, C.S. (1988). Relapse prevention. In R.K. Hester & W.R. Miller (Eds), *Handbook of Alcoholism Treatment Approaches: Effective Alternatives* (pp.170–182). New York: Pergamon.
—Provides a detailed explanation of a relapse-prevention approach differing slightly from that presented in this chapter.

Barber, J.G. & Cooper, B.K. (1991). The Situation Confidence Questionnaire (Heroin). *International Journal of the Addictions*, **26**, 565–575.
—Adapted from the version for alcohol, this questionnaire might be useful in assessing high-risk situations with opiate-dependent clients.

Cummings, C., Gordon, J.R., & Marlatt, G.A. (1980). Relapse: Prevention and prediction. In W.R. Miller (Ed.), *The Addictive Behaviours* (pp. 291–321). Oxford: Pergamon.

Gorski, T. (1986). Relapse prevention planning: A new recovery tool. *Alcohol and Research World*, **11**, (1), 6–11, 63.
—This article describes an approach to relapse prevention of particular interest to those who work within a disease model formulation of addictive behaviours.

Gossop, M. (Ed.) (1989). *Relapse and Addictive Behaviour*. London: Tavistock/Routledge.
—This book provides an overview of relapse across a variety of addictive behaviours from both clinical and research perspectives.

Kadden, R., Carroll, K., Donovan, D., Cooney, N., Monti, P., Abrams, D., Litt, M. & Hester, R. (1992). *Cognitive Behavioral Coping Skills Therapy Manual: A Clinical Research Guide for Therapists Treating Individuals with Alcohol Abuse and Dependence. Project MATCH Monograph Series Volume 3*. Rockville, MD: National Institute on Alcohol Abuse and Alcoholism.
—This session-by-session manual includes sessions on coping with urges, coping with a lapse, and seemingly irrelevant decisions.

Litman, G.K., Stapelton, J., Oppenheim, A.N., Peleg, M. & Jackson, P. (1983). Situations related to alcoholism relapse. *British Journal of Addiction*, **78**, 381–389.
—Describes the development of the *Relapse Precipitants Inventory*, designed both to identify potential relapse situations and estimate an overall danger of relapse.

Marlatt, G.A. & Gordon, J. (Eds) (1985). *Relapse Prevention: Maintenance Strategies in the Treatment of Addictive Behaviors*. New York: Guilford Press.
—One of the most comprehensive texts in the area of relapse prevention. Also provides a comprehensive theoretical and research overview of the area.

Monti, P.M., Abrams, D.B., Kadden, R.M. & Cooney, N.L (1989). *Treating Alcohol Dependence: A Coping Skills Training Guide* (pp. 116–122). New York: Guilford Press.
—Outlines sessions dealing with seemingly irrelevant decisions and planning for emergencies.

Saunders, B. & Allsop, S. (1989). Relapse: A critique. In M. Gossop (Ed.), *Relapse and Addictive Behaviour*. London: Tavistock/Routledge.
—A critique of aspects of the relapse model presented by Marlatt and Gordon.

Saunders, B. & Allsop, S. (1991). Helping those who relapse. In R. Davidson, S. Rollnick & I. MacEwan (Eds), *Counselling Problem Drinkers*. London: Tavistock/Routledge.
—In combination with the reference above, this chapter outlines much of the relapse-prevention approach described in this chapter.

Sitharthan, T. & Kavanagh, D.J. (1990). Role of self-efficacy in predicting outcomes from a programme for controlled drinking. *Drug and Alcohol Dependence*, **27**, 87–94.

—Describes the development of a scale to assess your client's confidence in maintaining moderation across a range of situations.

Wanigaratne, S., Wallace, W., Pullin, J., Keaney, F. & Farmern R. (1990). *Relapse Prevention for Addictive Behaviours: A Manual for Therapists*. Oxford: Blackwell Scientific Publications.

—Provides a comprehensive session-by-session description of a treatment programme based on relapse-prevention principles.

URGES AND CRAVINGS DIARY

Day, Date, Time:	Where, with whom, doing what?	Rate strength of craving (0-100)	Thoughts and feelings associated with craving	Response to craving (thoughts and actions)	Rate strength of craving (0-100)
Mon 11/5 8.30pm	In a restaurant with friends	(80)	Happy and excited. I'd love to have a drink now	Thought about my reasons for not drinking, had mineral water instead	(20) Stayed sober and had fun. Felt proud of myself

$\boxed{17}$

AFTERCARE

RECOMMENDED USE

Clients who have received your assistance in changing their drinking or drug use will require your support for some time after the formal programme has finished. Because relapse is very common among people who are trying to maintain abstinence or moderation, it is most important that you have a structured programme in place for aftercare. Although relapse-prevention techniques and referral to self-help groups are both important aspects of aftercare, they are not enough. Research has shown that a well-planned programme for continued assistance will increase your client's chances of a successful long-term outcome (Ito & Donovan, 1986). Most clinics have some kind of follow-up but this often involves an informal approach that only attracts successful clients. *Take some time to assess the strengths and limitations of your own aftercare arrangements.* You will need to look at both therapist- and client-initiated follow-up.

Therapist-initiated Follow-up

Therapist-initiated follow-up can serve several functions. It allows you to monitor your client's progress and discuss any problems she might have encountered. It is also an opportunity for you to reinforce her successes. When organised on a one-to-one basis, follow-up appointments allow you to work on strategies to cope with any new situations that might have arisen to challenge your client's resolve to maintain her behaviour change. You might also want to organise some extra 'booster sessions' to strengthen the skills that your client has learnt in treatment.

When aftercare is organised on a group basis, there is the opportunity for clients to form important support networks and to learn from each other's mistakes and successes. However, you should also make time to review each individual client's experiences.

The following guidelines will help you to tighten the structure of your aftercare plans:

(1) Your arrangement for continued contact with your client after the completion of therapy should be part of an overall package, *not an optional extra*. This will be the case regardless of the type of therapy your client has received. A structured follow-up plan is particularly important for clients leaving the relative security of residential programmes.

(2) Prepare your client for aftercare while she is still in therapy. Stress that follow-up appointments are an important part of her therapy programme. Explain to her that clients *can benefit from these appointments, regardless of whether or not they have successfully maintained their goals*. You are not expecting her to relapse but if she does, the follow-up appointment will offer an opportunity for her to discuss this with you.

(3) *Do everything you can to ensure that your client keeps her appointments*. For example, you could provide her with a calendar indicating the appointment dates. You should also telephone her or write to her the week before, reminding her about the appointment.

(4) If your client misses an appointment, *reschedule the appointment for another time as soon as possible*. When she next comes to see you, use a motivational interviewing approach (Chapter 3) to explore her reasons for missing the appointment. She might, for example, have felt reluctant to see you because of a lapse or a relapse.

(5) Follow-up appointments can vary greatly in terms of frequency. You might want to have standard follow-ups at three, six and twelve months after therapy. Some clients will need more support and could benefit from frequent, brief appointments or even phone calls in the months after therapy. Your plan for aftercare should be *both structured and flexible*.

Client-initiated Aftercare

In addition to follow-up appointments, make arrangements with your client to contact you if she needs your help. As your client adjusts to life without drugs and without the support of ongoing treatment, she will encounter temptations, pressures and unexpected problems. She might need to contact you for assistance when these situations arise. The following guidelines will help you to organise a system that is convenient for you both:

(1) Your client might feel embarrassed to contact you if she has had a lapse in her drinking or drug-using behaviour. Emphasise to her that *the event of a lapse is a critical time for seeking help*.

(2) There will also be times when you will not be available for contact. Help your client to brainstorm some ideas for getting assistance from other sources. *A plan of action should be in place for your client to use when her need arises.* For example, she could put the number for telephone counselling services near the phone for ready access or arrange for a sympathetic friend to be available (see p. 184). Another alternative for clients in group therapy is the 'buddy system'. This is where clients who have been in therapy together pair up and agree to telephone each other from time to time, to lend support.

RESOURCES LIST

Ito, J. R. & Donovan, D. M. (1986). Aftercare in alcoholism treatment: A review. In W. R. Miller & N. Heather (Eds), *Treating Addictive Behaviors: Processes of Change*. New York: Plenum Press.
—Excellent unbiased review of the then extant evidence on the value of aftercare.
McAuliffe, W.E. & Ch'ien, J.M.N. (1986). Recovery training and self-help: A relapse prevention program for treated opiate addicts, *Journal of Substance Abuse Treatment*, **3**, 9–20.
—Provides clear evidence of the value of scheduled and structured aftercare. Recommended reading on designing such an aftercare programme.

IV

DESIGNING AN INTERVENTION

PUTTING IT ALL TOGETHER

MATCHING TREATMENT TO YOUR CLIENT'S NEEDS

As we have stressed throughout this book, the techniques that you include in your treatment plan should be chosen through *negotiation* with your client, and should reflect his unique *needs* and *preferences*. We also recommend that you frame any intervention within an empathic counselling style that supports your client's commitment to, and confidence in, change. The length and intensity of your intervention will also be shaped to some extent by other factors such as the setting in which you work and, realistically, the time you have available. Below we outline a 'therapeutic skeleton' to use when planning your intervention.

Outpatient Interventions

For some clients a relatively brief intervention over a few sessions (e.g. up to five sessions) will be all that is required, and might often be all that is wanted. These clients in general will probably have shorter histories of use, stable backgrounds and low levels of dependence or drug- or alcohol-related problems. With such a client your treatment should incorporate all of the following:

- An assessment of dependence and, if there is time, of other areas of his functioning, especially psychiatric status
- Brief motivational interviewing if he appears to be unsure or ambivalent about changing his drug use or drinking behaviour
- The negative health effects of excessive consumption should be described in a fashion that personalises them for your client
- Methods of limit-setting and general self-management procedures should be set out
- If resources allow, a self-help manual/pamphlet should be made available
- The identification of high-risk situations and an explanation of relapse-prevention strategies, including the identification of strategies such as drink-refusal skills to minimise the risk of relapse

- The firm offer and arrangement of a follow-up visit and aftercare sessions

If your client has a more complicated drug- or alcohol-use history, you will need to consider a longer intervention. This form of intervention might occur for up to 15 or more sessions, and no precise guide can (or should) be made about the length of intervention required. However, your intervention should include the following:

- A comprehensive assessment
- Arrangements should be made for detoxification if your client is likely to experience physical withdrawal symptoms
- Motivational interviewing if your client is unsure or ambivalent about changing his drug-use or drinking behaviour
- The negative health effects of excessive consumption should be described in a fashion that personalises them for your client
- Referral for intervention for any psychiatric or psychological disorders that are detected
- Either, pharmacotherapy such as methadone maintenance or disulfiram dosing under supervision for some dependent clients
- Or, methods of limit-setting and general self-management procedures
- Selected training in skills-based approaches as necessary to deal with communication skills deficits, lack of assertiveness, relaxation and relationship difficulties
- Covert sensitisation might also be an option for some clients who are aiming for abstinence from alcohol
- Relapse-prevention training should be undertaken to minimise the risk of a return to problem drug use or drinking
- Appropriate assistance and referral to help your client remedy other lifestyle problems
- An introduction to self-help groups should be arranged for those clients pursuing abstinence goals
- Scheduled aftercare or booster sessions should form an integral part of the intervention

Inpatient/Residential Interventions

The techniques in this book are as equally applicable to residential/inpatient as outpatient settings. In general, for clients with alcohol dependence *per se*, we believe that there is no evidence to suggest that a residential treatment is superior to outpatient treatment. However, residential care might be useful if your client is homeless or his home environment is extremely conducive to drinking. Inpatient treatment might also suit clients whose extreme severity of dependence requires an intense form of supervised intervention. In the case of severe dependence on opiates, a residential drug-free therapeutic community is more likely to produce benefits than drug-free outpatient care.

When an inpatient/residential intervention is desirable, your treatment should incorporate all of the procedures described in the section above with one further addition. In order to maintain abstinence or moderation, your client must be able to effectively apply skills learnt in treatment to his everyday environment. The opportunity to practise at home is one of the main advantages of outpatient treatment. Therefore, in the case of an inpatient or residential treatment programme, it is strongly recommended that there be a gradual 're-entry phase' following treatment, where your client is assisted in returning to his usual environment, while not relapsing.

VIGNETTES

In the remaining part of this chapter, we present four examples of how the techniques included in this book might be used to provide effective treatment for people with different drug-related problems. These case histories are broadly based on the problems presented to therapists by real clients, but are not intended to represent actual people and, therefore, any such resemblance is purely coincidental.

Case 1: Severe Alcohol Dependence with Psychiatric Condition: The Case of the Unhappy Drinker

Assessment

Background information: Roy was 39 years old. He had completed a high school education and then worked in the public service. At the time of seeking treatment, he was supervising a staff of three. He was also living in a *de facto* relationship with his partner, Tracey. Roy was referred by his local doctor because of physical signs of excessive drinking, he had memory problems and he was facing the potential loss of his job.

Pattern and context of drinking: Roy began drinking at the age of 15 years and started regular consumption at 16. At that time, he lived in the country with his family and it was considered acceptable for him to drink alcohol. By the time he was 20 years old, he was drinking four to six large beers regularly through the week and on Friday and Saturday nights.

In his mid-twenties, he travelled to the city and joined the public service. In the company of male friends, he began to binge, drinking up to 15 or more large beers. Gradually, this pattern of heavier drinking became regular and he started drinking on the next day to recover from the effects of his hangover. He noticed that if he did not drink, he would feel shaky, sweaty and generally apprehensive after a heavy night. Over the years, as his drinking increased, Roy became tolerant to the effects of alcohol. Except on those occasions when he drank in a binge pattern, he rarely appeared to be drunk.

Roy would usually have a drink quite early in the morning. He would often get up before his partner, as she was a shift worker, and he was therefore able to drink without her knowledge. Whether or not he was able to consume alcohol at home, he would typically have had at least two beers by 10.00 a.m. in a tavern near his work. He would slip out on the pretext of buying some morning tea and consume the beers quite quickly, returning within 10 or 15 minutes. At lunchtime, he would usually consume four large beers which, he felt, helped him to get through the afternoon until his next opportunity to drink. After work, he would return to the tavern and have another five large beers. He then typically purchased some beer to take home with him. At home, in the evenings, it would not be unusual for him to drink another five beers before falling asleep on the couch. He would typically follow this pattern throughout the working week and increase the amount he drank on the weekends. On some days, he would consume up to two dozen cans of beer, although this was a rare occurrence.

Level of dependence: If Roy did not have alcohol through the morning and day, he would experience tremor in his hands and body, excessive perspiration, nausea and a sense of apprehension and panic. The number of years over which he had experienced these symptoms, his morning drinking and his tolerance to large amounts of alcohol indicated that he was severely alcohol-dependent. This was confirmed by his SADQ-C score of 38. He was also showing signs of psychological dependence, including loss of control or inability to abstain, failed attempts to cut-down or stop, and a persistent desire to drink.

Family background and social support: Roy's partner, Tracey, also drank heavily although not to the extent that he did. Tracey occasionally objected to Roy's very excessive drinking, saying that she did not like to see him getting drunk. In the past few years, Roy had also developed an additional problem. He had become impotent as a consequence of his excessive alcohol consumption. Tracey wished to start a family and, while Roy was not against that idea, he had lost interest in sexual activity.

Vocational and financial background: Memory problems and lapses were causing Roy difficulties at work. He had recently been reprimanded on several occasions by his boss because he had failed to carry out routine tasks that were part of his duties. He thought that the escalation in his drinking had occurred approximately 10 years ago, when he realised that he was falling behind his peers at work in terms of promotion.

Alcohol-related health problems: Roy's increasing problems at home as well as at work prompted a visit to his family doctor. Roy's doctor noticed physical signs which immediately raised her concerns that Roy was drinking excessively. She noticed his dilated facial capillaries, bloodshot eyes, and a coating on his tongue. Roy also complained of diarrhoea and sleeping difficulties. These, taken together with Roy's complaints of memory problems and impotence, were interpreted by the doctor as evidence of excessive alcohol consumption. She gave Roy a medical examination and had some routine liver enzyme levels analysed. While Roy's liver was not enlarged, there were elevated levels of a number of liver enzymes, confirming the doctor's hunch that Roy was drinking excessively. On a follow-up visit, she discussed these issues with Roy and organised a referral to a drug and alcohol team.

Psychiatric disturbance: As well as having a drinking problem, Roy was also experiencing depression. In response to his feelings of failure resulting from his lack of promotion at work, Roy gradually became unhappy and lost self-esteem. Increasingly, he found that he was feeling sad and depressed on more days than not. This depression was not particularly severe but it was constant and had been present for approximately 8 years by the time that he spoke with his family doctor. Associated with his loss of self-esteem was a sense of hopelessness about the future. He also had difficulties with a lack of concentration, a symptom typically associated with depression but which, in Roy's case, was mainly due to heavy alcohol consumption. The drug and alcohol team (which included a psychiatrist) determined that Roy met the criteria for a diagnosis of severe alcohol dependence. He also met the criteria for a psychiatric diagnosis of dysthymia, a chronic but not severe depressive disorder.

Stage of change: Roy's concerns about the effects of his drinking on his work and family life increased his motivation to try to change his drinking patterns. At the time that he was assessed by the drug and alcohol team, he was at a stage of preparation for change. His therapist used motivational interviewing procedures to help Roy to describe his own concerns about his excessive drinking and to identify the benefits he thought he would gain from changing this behaviour.

Goal-setting

Roy and his therapist discussed the implications of his severe alcohol dependence, memory problems and abnormal liver function tests, and agreed that moderated drinking was not appropriate. They chose abstinence as the most appropriate treatment goal. Given that Roy had experienced marked withdrawal symptoms on those occasions when he went without alcohol, options for detoxification were discussed.

Since he had a good relationship with his family doctor, Roy could have been detoxified at home with supervision and the assistance of Tracey. However, Roy preferred the option of a residential detoxification facility where he could be monitored while withdrawing from alcohol.

Strategies for action

Detoxification: Roy received inpatient detoxification with sedative medication from the benzodiazepine group. While staying at the detoxification facility, he was introduced to AA. Roy had never been interested in religion and found that the ideas about surrendering power and the spiritual nature of the organisation led him to be uninterested in continuing with AA. He all but refused to participate in the meetings. He was discharged five days after admission, having successfully detoxified from alcohol.

Antabuse: Roy and his therapist discussed the use of Antabuse as a way of assisting him to return to work and cope with the desire to drink in the initial period after his detoxification. Antabuse was appropriate for Roy because he:

- Wished to abstain from alcohol consumption
- Accepted that there was a need for an external control on his drinking
- Displayed no medical or psychosocial reasons against the use of Antabuse
- Was prepared to be supervised in the daily dosing of medication

Roy's partner, Tracey, was prepared to supervise the dosing of the Antabuse. She was pleased that Roy had decided to attempt to change his drinking habits because she had been concerned for some time about his excessive alcohol consumption. She also saw this as a good opportunity for her to curb her own drinking. She was initially wary about being involved in the Antabuse supervision because she had learnt through long experience that she could not control Roy's drinking. However, after discussion with Roy's therapist and their family doctor, she agreed simply to observe Roy taking the Antabuse each day. The therapist stressed that Tracey had no responsibility for policing Roy's medication.

Skills training: After consultation with his therapist, Roy agreed that in addition to taking Antabuse, he would also benefit from learning skills to assist him to maintain abstinence in the long term. These skills were presented with an empathic counselling style, which conveyed a positive regard for Roy and an enthusiasm for the possibility that he would be able to make lasting changes to his lifestyle. In total, this outpatient intervention involved 12 sessions.

Roy was trained in drink-refusal skills because many of his friends drank and it seemed unlikely that he would completely abandon his social network. He role-played and practised saying 'no' to offers of alcohol or pressure from others to drink.

Roy participated in relapse-prevention training aimed at maintaining his abstinence. In particular, the therapist helped him to develop strategies to address high-risk situations such as disappointments and stress at work, and social situations that involved alcohol. Even after Roy had made a commitment to abstinence, the therapist continued to reinforce and help Roy to clarify his reasons for deciding to change.

Referral for dysthymia: Roy was referred to the psychiatrist on the team for therapy specifically aimed at dealing with his chronic depression. Referral in this case was considered necessary because Roy's dysthymia was not purely due to his drinking. Although it lifted somewhat and his self-esteem improved as a result of his initial achievement of abstinence, continuing symptoms of dysthymia were considered to be sufficiently severe to warrant specific counselling. The psychiatric intervention was supportive and involved cognitive-restructuring procedures. Anti-depressant medication was not considered necessary.

Aftercare: Roy was successful in achieving and maintaining abstinence for a period of six months while he was receiving Antabuse. Thereafter, he maintained further abstinence for six or seven months. During that time, his relationship with Tracey improved markedly as did his self-esteem and general mood. He was successfully treated for his chronic dysthymia. Although he remained somewhat disappointed in himself because of his failure to progress in his occupation, he was able to put this in perspective. He was generally happier in his work and home life, and found that he could perform his work duties more efficiently.

Roy lapsed on two occasions, the first of which was approximately 12 months after the initial detoxification. The second of these episodes resulted from Roy's decision that he had earned a drink to reward himself for his period of abstinence! He continued to drink heavily for a three-week period before Tracey contacted his therapist. Eventually Roy returned briefly to treatment, encouraged by the supportive and non-judgemental attitude of his therapist. Further motivational interviewing and relapse-prevention training helped Roy to renew his commitment to abstain from alcohol.

Case 2: Mild Alcohol Dependence: The Case of the Unassertive Problem Drinker
Assessment

Background information: Kate was 32 years old. She had married Richard at 23 and had three children in the next four years. She had been working as a bank teller for several years after having her third child. Kate sought help after calling a telephone information service which referred her to a drug and alcohol agency.

Pattern and context of drinking: Kate had been drinking regularly since she was approximately 22 years old. Prior to that, she would only drink occasionally at parties and on special occasions. At age 22, Kate met Richard and they enjoyed going to restaurants and nightclubs. Approximately once or twice a week, Kate consumed between a half and a full bottle of wine. She did not often become drunk although she sometimes felt 'merry'.

After the birth of her third child, Kate's drinking gradually increased and she and Richard shared alcohol at most meals. Kate began having a glass of wine while she was cooking the dinner, before Richard arrived home. With time, she began to consume up to three or four glasses of wine regularly in the late afternoons. Occasionally, when feeling particularly stressed about the difficulties in her marital relationship, she would continue drinking with dinner and into the evening. On these occasions, she would consume up to 10 standard drinks. By the time she sought help, she was drinking this amount approximately three or four times a week.

Another situation in which Kate drank heavily was when she went out with friends. She had an active social life with co-workers and friends from her school days. On these social occasions, she typically drank at least a bottle of wine.

Level of dependence: Kate had developed some tolerance to the effects of alcohol but this was not particularly marked. She could easily go without drinking for a number of days without experiencing shaking, sweating or other withdrawal symptoms. She had tried to cut down on several occasions but found it particularly difficult when she was faced with stressful family situations or when socialising with moderate to heavy drinkers. Her SADQ-C score was 8, indicating a low level of alcohol dependence.

Family background and social support: Family difficulties that particularly exacerbated Kate's drinking related to her husband, Richard, and her mother-in-law, Patricia. Richard, whose job frequently required him to work late hours, tended to neglect home duties, leaving them to Kate, despite her own full-time job responsibilities. She was expected to arrive home early to care for the children, prepare the meals and clean the house. Kate found it difficult to talk to Richard about the stresses that she was experiencing because of the obligations she felt both at work and at home. These stresses were complicated by Patricia's regular visits during which she tended to make snide remarks about Kate's drinking and about the children's behaviour. Patricia would imply that the children were not being sufficiently looked after or disciplined. Although Kate did not agree with her mother-in-law's view, she found it difficult to say so. Instead, she would drink more than usual after Patricia left in the late afternoon and before Richard arrived home. On these occasions, she would often drink three or four glasses of wine in quick succession in an attempt to cope with her frustration and pent-up anger.

Alcohol-related health problems: A medical examination showed that Kate had no alcohol-related physical problems. She had no psychiatric or marked psychological problems evident in her thinking or behaviour. She was, however, experiencing considerable difficulties because of a lack of assertiveness and an inability to communicate her needs and feelings to her husband and mother-in-law.

Stage of change: Kate appeared unsure about whether she had a problem and whether she needed to change her level of drinking. Because of her ambivalence, Kate's therapist employed a motivational interviewing approach. They talked about the good things and the less good things about her drinking, and the concerns that Kate had about her drinking and its effects on her family and children.

Goal-setting

As a result of the motivational interviewing, Kate decided that she wanted to change but was not interested in the goal of abstinence because she did not believe that she was an 'alcoholic'. She also said that there were social situations where she would like to be able to drink alcohol. She added that she enjoyed drinking but recognised that excessive drinking was causing problems. In light of her preference for moderation and her low alcohol dependence, Kate and her therapist opted for the goal of moderated drinking.

Strategies for action

Behavioural self-management: Kate and her therapist agreed to an initial two-week period of abstinence from alcohol which would allow her to focus on improving various aspects of her life. After this period of abstinence, Kate and her therapist set an upper limit on her drinking of two standard drinks per day with a maximum of four standard drinks. She was provided with a self-help manual and day diary sheets. Kate learned how to monitor her alcohol consumption, to set limits on her drinking, and to practise strategies that helped her to slow down her drinking and keep within her set limit.

Other skills training: Kate role-played and practised using drink-refusal skills to deal with social pressure to drink excessively, especially when in the company of heavy-drinking friends.

Kate was taught how to use 'I-statements' to express her feelings openly and honestly to her husband, Richard. She began to feel more confident about making her needs known but found that she and Richard continued to disagree about household responsibilities.

Kate was also given assertiveness training to help her to deal more effectively with her mother-in-law's criticism. She role-played appropriate ways of telling Patricia that she did not like the comments about her children and that she disagreed with Patricia's views on discipline. Kate found this difficult initially and needed to practise. With time, she was able to assert herself in a way that prompted Patricia to stop saying things that caused her to become angry and frustrated.

Both during the period of abstinence and throughout the behavioural self-management training, Kate learnt to identify high-risk situations and devise strategies to cope with them based on the skills she was learning.

Referral for marital therapy: Marital difficulties continued because although Kate's husband was sympathetic about some of her needs, he still felt that the housework was her responsibility and could not see the potential impact of the difficulties in their relationship on Kate's drinking. There was not enough cooperation between Kate and Richard to involve him in a couples therapy approach to changing the drinking. Instead, Kate's therapist encouraged them to seek specialist marital counselling.

Aftercare: Kate succeeded in moderating her drinking for approximately three months until a particularly upsetting visit from her mother-in-law. On that occasion, she did not use assertiveness skills but decided to drink excessively and consumed approximately 10 glasses of wine. After she had contacted her therapist, it was decided that regular, monthly aftercare sessions would be useful. If difficult situations arose, Kate telephoned her therapist to discuss them. Gradually the need for such regular contact decreased as Kate became more confident about identifying and coping with high-risk situations. Four years later, Kate had maintained her moderated drinking. She drank only on social occasions or with Richard at dinner and generally maintained her two standard drinks limit. On some occasions, she exceeded this limit but rarely drank beyond four standard drinks.

Case 3: Opiate Dependence: The Case of the Shy Heroin User

Assessment

Background information: John was a 24-year-old heroin user and occasional dealer. He came to the attention of health authorities after he overdosed on benzodiazepines and alcohol during a period when he could not obtain heroin. He was taken to the emergency section of a major hospital by friends after he had been unconscious for a number of hours. He was observed in hospital overnight and a drug and alcohol therapist attended his bedside. John agreed to a further assessment session.

Pattern and context of drug use: From the age of 12, John had used cannabis and alcohol. After leaving home at the age of 14 and travelling to the city, he began drinking regularly and smoking cannabis quite frequently. He also became involved in petty criminal activities including forgery and shop-lifting. By the time he was 16 he had developed a regular heroin habit. He was not dependent at that time but was using three or four times a week, depending on how much money he had. Increasingly he spent time working as a male prostitute to support his developing heroin dependence. By the time he was 18, however, he had ceased this work and he became a courier for a drug dealer. The dealer provided John with heroin, as did some of John's customers as part payment of the delivery. Gradually, with time, he built up a habit of using approximately 1 gram of heroin a day. Usually he would inject before breakfast, around lunch time, in the early evening and late in the evening. By the time he was in his mid-twenties he was using approximately 3 or 4 grams of heroin a day.

Level of dependence: John was quite tolerant to the effects of this amount of heroin. If he missed out on injecting for some reason he would soon develop opiate-withdrawal symptoms. Even if he had not missed out on injecting, upon wakening before he injected he would find that his body ached and felt stiff, he would experience stomach cramps, notice his heart pounding, have hot flushes, feel miserable and depressed, would be tense and panicky and would have a strong craving to use opiates. He would typically inject within half an hour of waking up. These symptoms indicated that John was severely opiate-dependent.

Family background and social support: John's mother and father were both heavy drinkers and there had been frequent conflict in the family home. John was subject to frequent physical beatings from his father, who was always verbally abusive to him and to his mother. John ran away in his teenage years on four occasions before leaving home at the age of 14. When he left home he travelled to the city and lived in derelict housing with other adolescents slightly older than himself. At the time of assessment, John had been living in a *de facto* relationship with Jenny for the past six months. They shared rental accommodation with other heroin users in an inner city suburb.

Vocational and financial background: John had never had a full-time stable job and was currently receiving unemployment benefits. He had left school at the age of 14 years and not completed any certificate. Prior to that time he was often truant from school. He had left home soon after he finished with school. Apart from dealing, John had not recently been involved in other criminal activities and had no outstanding warrants or charges.

Drug-related health problems: At the time of his admission to hospital, John was malnourished. Blood tests showed that he was both Hepatitis B and C positive. John did not share needles with his friends or flatmates but did share with his partner, who generally used after him. He did not use condoms with Jenny but used them with occasional casual partners.

Psychiatric disturbance: John had been unhappy since he was quite young. He was also quite shy and reticent in social situations and tended to avoid them whenever he could, especially when he was 'straight'. When he did mix in a group he would try to use alcohol or more typically opiates to assist him to feel comfortable. If he did have to interact socially he would frequently feel tense and panicky, his heart would race and he would sweat, blush and feel very self-conscious. He was extremely concerned that people could see his anxiety and he worried about what they would think of him. These symptoms indicated that John was socially phobic.

Stage of change: John had been frightened by his recent overdose and was therefore prepared to contemplate changing his drug use. He was tired of the drug-using lifestyle but was not confident of his ability to resist the temptation to use. John's therapist used motivational interviewing strategies to help him to explore this ambivalence and John decided that he was prepared to attempt to change his drug-use behaviour.

Goal-setting

John and his therapist discussed his options. The alternative of a drug-free intervention, either on an outpatient basis or in a residential therapeutic community, did not appeal to John. He recognised that his high tolerance and dependence on opiates made ongoing injecting likely, which would continue to expose him and others to the risk of infections and diseases. Therefore he agreed, albeit initially somewhat reluctantly, to try a methadone maintenance programme.

Strategies for action

Methadone maintenance: Within four weeks, John had been stabilised and was taking 80 mg of methadone per day. At that time his social fears and phobias became more pronounced and he self-medicated with alcohol and benzodiazepines. He drank so much alcohol on one occasion that he was readmitted to hospital for emergency care.

Referral for treatment of social phobia: After a period of two months of daily attendance at the methadone maintenance clinic, a counsellor decided that John required some psychiatric referral because of his social fear. He was referred to a psychiatrist who began treating him for social phobia. However, John did not attend a number of appointments and eventually dropped out of treatment.

Skills training: Over the next two years, methadone maintenance staff repeatedly detected that John was continuing to use illicit drugs on a regular basis. They referred him to a drug and alcohol therapist for further assistance. Problem-solving skills were considered essential to provide John with ways of coping with daily problems and challenges to his commitment to abstain from illicit drugs.

John's therapist helped to him to develop strategies for coping with social pressure to continue using drugs. Problem-solving and drug-refusal skills were embedded in a relapse-prevention approach where the need for lifestyle changes was emphasised. Gradually, John developed enough confidence to move out of his shared accommodation and was successful in obtaining work.

Aftercare: With the change in environment, John developed a new relationship with a non-using partner. Having stabilised his lifestyle, John was again referred for treatment of his social phobia, this time with more successful results. He tried to withdraw from methadone completely on two occasions with the agreement of his prescribing doctor and dispensing staff. He reduced his methadone dose to 10 mg on each occasion. However, he could not cease completely, and remained on methadone after a 5-year period. John received regular counselling from the methadone maintenance programme staff.

Case 4: Polydrug Use with Associated Psychological Disorders: The Case of the Sedated Sexual Abuse Survivor

Assessment

Background information: Debbie was 23 years old. She had had two previous treatment presentations and had been detoxified once before. After a recent overdose, which was almost fatal, Debbie returned to a residential drug and alcohol treatment agency to seek help.

Pattern and context of drinking: Since the age of 15, Debbie had been using a variety of drugs including benzodiazepines, alcohol and, occasionally, heroin. She favoured benzodiazepines when she could get them. If she was unable to get benzodiazepine prescriptions from her frequent visits to various doctors, she would purchase them on the street. She had overdosed on seven separate occasions. Two of these overdoses resulted in serious medical emergencies in which she almost died from respiratory depression. At the time that she was assessed Debbie was using benzodiazepines, alcohol and anti-depressants, and she occasionally injected heroin. Her *OTI* results indicated that she was using an average of 25 tablets a day.

Level of dependence: Debbie was moderately dependent on sedative medications. She had a tolerance to the effects of benzodiazepines and had experienced some withdrawal symptoms on those occasions when she had gone without these medications for a prolonged period.

Family background and social support: Debbie had had an unhappy family life. Her family was regularly attended by welfare agency staff because of the neglect her mother showed towards Debbie and her siblings. She had never known her father, and her mother was often absent. Over the years, Debbie's mother had had a number of different male partners, some of whom lived with the family for periods of time. At the time of this presentation to treatment, Debbie was sharing accommodation with a female acquaintance but felt quite lonely and isolated.

Vocational and financial background: Debbie had been unemployed since leaving school at the age of 15. She had no job skills. She was receiving social security benefits.

Drug-related health problems: Debbie was malnourished and had poor physical health. Blood tests showed that she was Hepatitis B positive. Her frequent overdoses indicated that continued drug use posed a serious threat to Debbie's life. Debbie was referred for neuropsychological assessment to assess whether the overdoses had resulted in cognitive dysfunction. The neuropsychological report did not indicate any significant cognitive impairment.

Psychiatric disturbance: Debbie was anxious and depressed and had very low self-esteem. This, coupled with her family background and her multiple suicide attempts, alerted the therapist to the possibility that she might have been abused in the past. Using an empathic approach, the therapist asked about unwanted sexual contact and physical abuse. Debbie disclosed that from the age of 11 until she left home at 15 years, she had been physically and sexually abused by two of her mother's partners. The therapist believed that these episodes had markedly contributed to Debbie's depression and drug use.

Stage of change: Debbie felt quite desperate and was ready to take action to change her drug use. Unfortunately, her repeated experiences of relapse had led her to believe that she lacked the 'willpower' to successfully maintain change. The therapist therefore focused on ways of building Debbie's confidence in her own ability to make and sustain the change.

Goal-setting

Debbie and her therapist discussed her previous attempts at quitting drug use. Their discussion highlighted some helpful aspects of past treatments and identified periods when she had successfully abstained from using pills. The therapist reframed past 'failures' as indicating Debbie's need to learn additional skills to help her to confront challenges to abstinence.

Strategies for action

Detoxification: Debbie and her therapist agreed that medicated detoxification was necessary to protect her from the risk of fits or seizures, resulting from her dependence on benzodiazepines.

Referral for child sexual abuse counselling: As a result of the supportive reaction of the therapist to Debbie's disclosure, she was prepared to accept her therapist's referral for concurrent counselling to address issues related to the abuse. Her therapist felt that concurrent counselling was necessary because abstinence from drugs might have triggered flashbacks related to the abuse, which in turn might precipitate relapse.

Inpatient group programmes: Debbie and her therapist agreed that cognitive strategies would be particularly useful because Debbie tended to use drugs in a solitary fashion as a means of coping with negative thoughts and feelings. A group teaching cognitive restructuring and relapse-prevention skills was provided as part of the inpatient programme. Debbie also agreed to participate in a relaxation training group during her period of inpatient therapy. The group taught progressive muscle and meditative procedures and required a commitment to regular practice. For Debbie, relapse-prevention training underscored her new awareness that preventing relapse required skills and planning as well as a strong resolve to abstain.

As part of the inpatient programme, Debbie was introduced to NA. She found the social support and encouragement invaluable and continued to attend meetings after leaving the residential programme.

Aftercare: The residential programme had a firm commitment to assist clients in coping with the stress of returning to their home environment. In Debbie's case, the agency arranged temporary accommodation at a half-way house run by the drug and alcohol team. She stayed in this half-way house for two months during which she was assisted in obtaining entry into a job-training programme. Debbie relapsed to drug use repeatedly over the next two years. However, she stayed in touch with both the aftercare programme of the drug and alcohol agency and NA, and she therefore received further help through these difficult periods.

RESOURCES LIST

The resources below provide examples of how the strategies described in this book have been combined in treatment programmes offered to clients with abstinence or moderation goals.

Chaney, E.F. (1989). Social skills training. In R.K. Hester & W.R. Miller (Eds), *Handbook of Alcoholism Treatment Approaches: Effective Alternatives* (pp. 206–221). New York: Pergamon.
—Provides a detailed skills-training programme based on relapse-prevention principles.
McCrady, B.S., Dean, L., Dubreuill, E. & Swanson, S. (1985). The problem drinkers' project: A programmatic application of social-learning-based treatment. In G.A. Marlatt & J. Gordon (Eds), *Relapse Prevention: Maintenance Strategies in the Treatment of Addictive Behaviors* (pp. 417–471). New York: Guilford Press.
—Details a skills-training, cognitive-behavioural programme for clients with an abstinence goal.
Monti, P.M., Abrams, D.B., Kadden, R.M. & Cooney, N.L (1989). *Treating Alcohol Dependence: A Coping Skills Training Guide* New York: Guilford Press.
—A session-by-session skills-based programme.
Sanchez-Craig, M. (1984). *Therapist's Manual for Secondary Prevention of Alcohol Problems: Procedures for Teaching Moderate Drinking and Abstinence.* Toronto: Addiction Research Foundation.
—This therapist's manual details treatment guidelines for clients with moderation and abstinence goals and can be obtained from the Addiction Research Foundation Bookstore, 33 Russell St, Toronto, Ontario, M58 2S1, Canada.
Wanigaratne, S., Wallace, W., Pullin, J., Keaney, F. & Farmern R. (1990). *Relapse Prevention for Addictive Behaviours: A Manual for Therapists.* Oxford: Blackwell Scientific Publications.
—Provides a comprehensive session-by-session description of a treatment programme based on relapse-prevention principles.

A FINAL NOTE: EARLY INTERVENTION

INTRODUCTION

In this book, we have focused on methods for the treatment of problem drinkers and drug users with mild to severe levels of dependence. There is another form of intervention which has become a focus of attention recently, and which we believe is important to your work. This area is referred to as Early Intervention. It involves screening, detecting and intervening with excessive consumers *before* problems or dependence develop. Early intervention is essentially an outreach activity conducted in primary health care settings. It offers a brief, structured form of advice, typically at the point and time of detection. We believe that this form of intervention deserves special attention as it provides a promising future direction for reducing the harms associated with drug and alcohol use.

Early intervention also overlaps with another form of treatment, called Brief Intervention (see pp. 128–9), because early treatments tend to be brief in duration relative to interventions that may be offered to clients later in a drug-use career. Early and brief interventions are well researched and developed for excessive alcohol consumers; as yet little work has been done with other drug types. However, there is no reason why early and brief forms of intervention should not be extended to other drug classes (e.g. opiates, psychostimulants), especially in those countries or settings which have embraced a harm-reduction approach to drug use.

Early and brief interventions will largely remain the responsibility of the primary health care system, leaving specialist agencies free to address the needs of clients with more severe problems. Nevertheless, the specialist therapist should be able to inform those working in primary health care settings about methods for intervening with excessive drinkers (and drug users). Thus, the aim of this chapter is to equip you with basic information for the development of early and brief interventions within primary health care and other health and welfare settings.

As noted above, most early and brief interventions have been developed for use with excessive alcohol consumers. The following chapter therefore focuses on an approach for use with these clients.

Recommended Use

Early interventions are being increasingly recognised as an important and appropriate part of the overall approach to dealing with excessive drinking in countries including Australia and the United Kingdom. The public health principle behind the activity is that by encouraging the large numbers of excessive drinkers in the community to cut down their drinking to within recommended health limits, there will be an overall reduction in alcohol-related morbidity, mortality and associated social and economic costs for the general community.

These interventions are likely to be most effective with drinkers without severe dependence and/or entrenched alcohol-related problems: the less severely affected clients will be more likely to alter drinking patterns in response to clear advice from a credible health professional. Screening, however, will also detect clients with more severe alcohol problems. These clients should also be offered the brief advice and if they do not respond to it, should be referred to a specialist drug and alcohol agency for assistance.

The procedures employed in early intervention programmes can delivered in a short time, ranging from 5 to 30 minutes duration. Typically these are 'one-off' interventions, although a follow-up session is also strongly recommended to ensure that behaviour change has occurred.

GOALS

- To screen individuals for excessive alcohol use in primary and other health care settings
- To detect individuals with excessive levels of alcohol consumption
- To offer clear advice to reduce consumption of alcohol to safe and responsible levels

KEY CONCEPTS

'Excessive' Drinking

Excessive drinking refers to consumption that exceeds the guidelines for safe or responsible drinking recommended by national health authorities. These limits are described on p. 122.

METHOD

Settings for Early Interventions

Early interventions should be conducted in settings where: (a) the number of excessive drinkers is likely to be highest; and (b) where the impact of detection and advice to cut down will have the greatest effect. These settings (in order of importance) include:

- *General and specialist medical practices:* Because of their role in primary health care and their high rate of contact and credibility with the general public, general and specialist medical practitioners are ideally positioned to detect patients with drug and alcohol problems and offer them advice on safe levels of consumption.
- *General hospitals:* In general hospitals, there should be procedures for screening for excessive alcohol and other drug consumption among inpatients and outpatients, and procedures for appropriate intervention. At the very least, any general hospital that has dedicated drug and alcohol health workers on site should have routine formal detection procedures put in place. These detection procedures should be followed by early intervention and referral as necessary. This may include a letter to the referring doctor giving feedback regarding the level of excessive consumption and advising the need for follow-up of the patient.
- *The workplace:* Detection of excessive consumption should be a part of any routine health evaluation in the workplace. Such screening and early intervention will increase the health and safety of workers, and limit hazards and accidents occurring in the workplace.
- *Welfare and general counselling services:* Although these are not an obvious setting for detection activities, screening in welfare and counselling services offers the opportunity of referral for intervention, and potentially a better outcome for the clients of these services. It is likely in a significant proportion of cases that excessive alcohol or other drug consumption has contributed to the presenting problem.

Detecting Excessive Drinkers

If you or your colleagues work in one of the settings described above, then you need to be prepared to actively screen clients in order to detect those who might benefit from an early intervention. There are a number of screening methods, including simply asking your client about her drinking, using questionnaires, or medical examinations for clinical signs and biological markers of excessive drinking (see Mattick & Jarvis, 1993). Of these methods, direct questioning of your client or the use of standard questionnaires are the most efficient and cost-effective approaches.

We recommend that you use the Alcohol Use Disorders Identification Test (AUDIT) developed for a recent World Health Organisation early intervention project (Saunders, Aasland, Babor, de la Fuente & Grant, 1993) or the Canterbury Alcohol Screening Test (CAST) (Elvy & Wells, 1984) for screening clients in primary health care settings. A copy of the AUDIT is presented at the end of this chapter for your convenience.

To score the AUDIT, for each of the first eight questions, the answer will receive a score from 0 to 4. For the last two questions: 'No' scores 0, 'Yes, but not in the last year' scores 2, and 'Yes, during the last year' scores 4. The scores for each question are then totalled, with a score over 10 indicating hazardous or harmful drinking patterns, suggesting the need to intervene briefly to provide advice regarding safe alcohol consumption patterns.

How to Intervene

As noted earlier, the procedures used in early intervention programmes have generally been delivered in a short time, usually of 5–30 minutes duration. There is no research evidence to support the view that longer procedures will bring about a greater reduction in consumption than brief procedures (Mattick & Jarvis, 1993; Heather, 1989). Indeed, the art of an early intervention is to keep communication with the client direct and simple. At a minimum, after identifying that your client is drinking excessively, you or your colleagues should:

- Offer clear and firm advice to cut down
- Fully describe the appropriate level of safe and responsible consumption (see recommended health guidelines p. 122)
- Arrange a follow-up visit, wherever possible, to determine whether any behaviour change has occurred. If it has not then a further referral should be made for more intervention

In settings where you have more time to provide assistance, you or your colleagues should:

- Further assess the extent of the problem and the readiness of your client to change her drinking (see Chapter 2, *Assessment*)
- Offer personalised feedback of the negative health effects of the excessive alcohol consumption (see p. 46–8)
- Set out methods of limit-setting and general behavioural self-management skills (see Chapter 11)
- Either provide your client with a self-help manual or pamphlet or, if your resources are limited, give your client a list of books available locally with clear advice to purchase and read the material
- Arrange a follow-up visit to assess the impact of your intervention and to offer encouragement or referral where necessary

Trouble-shooting

If your client fails to respond to the screening procedure and advice, this indicates that she may have more severe problems requiring a referral for specialist assistance. Alternatively, you should also consider the possibility that your client is still at a 'pre-contemplation' stage for change (see p. 24) and, despite an awareness of the possible negative consequences of her drinking, is content with her current level of consumption.

RESOURCES LIST
Brief Self-help Manuals

Heather, N., Richmond, R., Webster, I., Wodak, A., Hardie, M. & Polkinghorne, H. (1989). *A Guide to Healthier Drinking: A Self-help Manual*. Sydney: Clarendon Printing. —This brief and colourful manual is available from the Brief Intervention Unit at the University of New South Wales, Sydney, NSW 2052, Australia.

Robertson, I. & Heather, N. (1985). *So, You Want to Cut Down Your Drinking?* Edinburgh: Scottish Health Education Group. —Adapted for local readers, this attractive publication is free for those in Scotland but sample copies are available from Scottish Health Education Group, Woodburn House, Canaan Lane, Edinburgh EH10 4SG, UK.

Other Resources

Elvy, G.A. & Wells, J.E. (1984). The Canterbury Alcoholism Screening Test (CAST): A detection instrument for use with hospital patients. *New Zealand Medical Journal*, **97**, 111–115. —Provides a screening instrument for use in primary health care settings.

Heather, N. (1989). Brief intervention strategies. In R.K. Hester & W.R. Miller (Eds), *Handbook of Alcoholism Treatment Approaches: Effective Alternatives* (pp. 93–116). New York: Pergamon Press.
—This chapter provides information on the research base underpinning the use of early and brief intervention methods with excessive drinkers, as well as detailing methods of intervention.
Mattick, R.P. & Jarvis, T.J. (1993). *An Outline for the Management of Alcohol Problems: Quality Assurance in the Treatment of Drug Dependence Project*, National Campaign Against Drug Abuse monograph series No. 20. Canberra, Australia: Australian Government Publishing Service.
—This monograph sets out the evidence and methods for the use of brief/early intervention, and places these activities within the public health approach.
Pols, R. G. & Hawks, D. V. (1992). *Is There a Safe Level of Daily Consumption of Alcohol for Men and Women?* Canberra: Australian Government Publishing Service.
—This monograph sets out the evidence for safe/responsible levels of alcohol consumption, as well as daily consumption amounts. It is highly recommended, especially for those settings where such information has not been distributed. It is available from the Drugs of Dependence Branch, Australian Department of Human Services and Health, GPO Box 9848, Canberra, ACT, 2601, Australia.
Rollnick, S., Heather, N. & Bell, A. (1992). Negotiating behaviours change in medical settings: The development of brief motivational interviewing. *Journal of Mental Health*, **1**, 25–37.
—This excellent article demonstrates the application of a motivational interviewing approach to brief/early intervention.
Saunders, J. B., Aasland, O. G., Babor, T. F., de la Fuente, J. R. & Grant, M. (1993). Development of the Alcohol Use Disorders Identification test (AUDIT). WHO collaborative project on early detection of persons with harmful alcohol consumption II: *Addiction*, **88**, 791–804.
—Validated brief screening instrument for use within primary health care settings.

AUDIT
Please circle the answer that is correct for you

Name: _____   **Date:** ___/___/___

1. How often do you have a drink containing alcohol?

   NEVER   MONTHLY OR   2–4 TIMES A   2–3 TIMES A   4 OR MORE
               LESS   MONTH   WEEK   TIMES A WEEK

2. How many drinks containing alcohol do you have on a typical day when you are drinking?

   1 OR 2   3 OR 4   5 OR 6   7–9   10 OR MORE

3. How often do you have six or more drinks on one occasion?

   NEVER   LESS THAN   MONTHLY   WEEKLY   DAILY OR
               MONTHLY   ALMOST DAILY

4. How often during the last year have you found it difficult to get the thought of alcohol out of your mind?

   NEVER   LESS THAN   MONTHLY   WEEKLY   DAILY OR
               MONTHLY   ALMOST DAILY

5. How often during the last year have you found that you were not able to stop drinking once you had started?

   NEVER   LESS THAN   MONTHLY   WEEKLY   DAILY OR
               MONTHLY   ALMOST DAILY

6. How often during the last year have you been unable to remember what happened the night before because you had been drinking?

   NEVER   LESS THAN   MONTHLY   WEEKLY   DAILY OR
               MONTHLY   ALMOST DAILY

7. How often during the last year have you needed a first drink in the morning to get yourself going after a heavy drinking session?

   NEVER   LESS THAN   MONTHLY   WEEKLY   DAILY OR
               MONTHLY   ALMOST DAILY

continued

AUDIT *(continued)*

8. How often during the last year have you had a feeling of guilt or remorse after drinking?

   NEVER   LESS THAN   MONTHLY   WEEKLY   DAILY OR
                  MONTHLY   ALMOST DAILY

9. Have you or someone else been injured as a result of your drinking?

   NO   YES, BUT NOT   YES, DURING
               IN THE LAST   THE LAST YEAR
               YEAR

10. Has a relative or friend or a doctor or other health worker, been concerned about your drinking or suggested you cut down?

   NO   YES, BUT NOT   YES, DURING
               IN THE LAST   THE LAST YEAR
               YEAR

Note. Reprinted with permission from Saunders and colleagues (1993).

INDEX

Wiley Titles of Related Interest

ADDICTIVE BEHAVIOUR
Cue Exposure Theory and Practice

Edited by D. Colin Drummond, Stephen T. Tiffany, Steven Glautier *and* Bob Remington

Offers a critical review of exposure and the practice of behavioural therapy in the context of the psychological treatment of addiction.

0-471-94454-8   288pp   1995

YOUNG OFFENDERS AND ALCHOL-RELATED CRIME
A Practitioner's Guidebook

Mary McMurran *and* Clive R. Hollin

Offers a framework for the development of a cognitive-behavioural programme with young offenders. The programme deals with the different stages of intervention from screening for problems through to encouraging positive changes in lifestyle.

0-471-93839-4   208pp   1993

EXCESSIVE APPETITES
A Psychological View of Addictions

Jim Orford

" ... a valuable addition to the literature ... it presents a lucid and highly informative account of the major issues in the addictions. It can be highly recommended."

British Journal of Addiction

0-471-93613-8   378pp   1992

SAFE PASSAGE
Recovery for Adult Children of Alcoholics

Stephanie Brown

This book is about the children of alcoholics and what they, as adults, must do to cure themselves of the effects of growing up with alcoholic parents. The author shows how group therapy and self-examination can help them discover and face the truth about themselves.

0-471-53221-5   288pp   1991